P9-DID-024

"Staff Sergeant Harris has made a choice not embraced by veterans of wars past to talk and talk and talk about what he's experienced—a soldier turned messenger. He leaves crowds standing at attention, as he honors his friends who have fallen."

—**August Skamenca**, reporter, *CBS News*

"After eight deployments in the War on Terror, I can speak to the challenges of the modern battlefield. Like Shilo, I know the combat of recovery from catastrophic wounds. I know the grief of losing comrades in arms despite your best efforts to protect them. And like Shilo, I know something about medals. Service to our country is what we do, who we are. In *Steel Will*, we see what happens to an ordinary man in extraordinary circumstances. We see what happens when an ordinary man rises above a bleak prognosis, when an ordinary family surrounds their hero with love and hopefulness, and when an extraordinary, miracle-working God places his hands on the one he loves."

—**SFC Leroy Petry**, United States Army Medal of Honor recipient

"This book should be required reading for every American, especially our youth. Shilo Harris is a true patriot and an American hero. This book embodies the essential spirit of America by reminding us that being a hero isn't always judged by your accomplishments. It is often judged by your sacrifice so others can have their accomplishments under a blanket of freedom."

—**Ric Savage**, former professional wrestler, television host

"SSG Shilo Harris, in his writing, has exposed his soul like no other author. His life is open and raw, revealing his unwavering faith, his clear understanding of the risks of war, and its heartbreaking impact on all those who are touched by it. He questions whether his actions really made a difference, but his faith and God's omnipresence within allow him a sense of peace and well-being. Shilo was a soldier and remains a soldier, injured and recovered, with an enduring commitment to serve as best he can even though the battlefield has been altered. *Steel Will* is a book that will emotionally rip you apart but will have you cheering at the end. A definite read!"

—**Fred Gregory**, Air Force Vietnam vet, astronaut, NASA Deputy Administrator

"This book is an honor to read! Shilo's heroism and life story are truly an inspiration to all. Shilo makes me proud to be an American. I highly recommend this book to all who value freedom!"

—**Eric Turner**, rock guitarist, founding member of Warrant

"I've seen and done a lot of things in my life. US Army. Ranger. Special Forces. Golden Knights. A midair parachuting collision at 150 mph killed my partner instantly and severed both my legs. I thought my story was tough. But reading *Steel Will* put me in the fire, in the coma, and on the rocky road to recovery. When the last page was turned, I felt honored to know the man of *Steel Will*, Shilo Harris."

—**SFC US Army (Ret) Dana Bowman**, HALO for Freedom
Warrior Foundation

"SSG Shilo Harris, and hundreds of thousands of soldiers like him, put themselves in harm's way and in God's hands for the cause of freedom. For these warriors, uncommon valor is the benchmark. To be sure, Shilo's story is dramatic. But the focus of *Steel Will* is clearly a call to action to support America's troops, their families, caregivers, and our nation. God bless our military and God bless America."

—**COL Don "Doc" Ballard**, US Army (Ret), US Navy Corpsman,
USMC DOC, Medal of Honor recipient 1968

"As a combat veteran and fellow wounded warrior, Shilo Harris's account of his life, combat, military career, and horrific wounds is one of hope, inspiration, and the overcoming spirit I have built my life around. It is a journey into a soldier's life abruptly plunged into the depths of human misery and despair, but through love and faith, he finds the 'steel will' to push against all odds and set the example for his family, his fellow warriors, and everyone around him. I would recommend this book to anyone looking for a great story and motivation to overcome the adversity we all face in life."

—**Jason Redman**, US Navy SEAL (Ret), author of *The Trident:
The Forging and Reforging of a Navy SEAL Leader*

STEEL WILL

MY JOURNEY THROUGH HELL TO BECOME THE MAN I WAS MEANT TO BE

Shilo Harris

WITH ROBIN OVERBY COX

BakerBooks

a division of Baker Publishing Group
Grand Rapids, Michigan

LONGWOOD PUBLIC LIBRARY

© 2014 by Shilo Harris

Published by Baker Books
a division of Baker Publishing Group
P.O. Box 6287, Grand Rapids, MI 49516-6287
www.bakerbooks.com

Printed in the United States of America

All rights reserved. No part of this publication may be reproduced, stored in a retrieval system, or transmitted in any form or by any means—for example, electronic, photocopy, recording—without the prior written permission of the publisher. The only exception is brief quotations in printed reviews.

Library of Congress Cataloging-in-Publication Data is on file at the Library of Congress, Washington, DC.

ISBN 978-0-8010-1655-4

Scripture quotations are from the Holy Bible, New International Version®. NIV®. Copyright © 1973, 1978, 1984, 2011 by Biblica, Inc.™ Used by permission of Zondervan. All rights reserved worldwide. www.zondervan.com.

To protect the privacy of those who have shared their stories with the author, some details and names have been changed.

14 15 16 17 18 19 20   7 6 5 4 3 2 1

In keeping with biblical principles of creation stewardship, Baker Publishing Group advocates the responsible use of our natural resources. As a member of the Green Press Initiative, our company uses recycled paper when possible. The text paper of this book is composed in part of post-consumer waste.

For the caring and daring soldiers of the 1st Squadron,
89th Cavalry Regiment, 10th Mountain Division

CONTENTS

Contents

FOREWORD

I first met Shilo while changing places at a talk radio program in Brownwood, Texas. He had just finished up a segment of the show and I was the next person to be interviewed. This chance encounter has led to a relationship that has blessed my life.

His story is very compelling. His unflinching, stark honesty about his life experiences, good and bad, makes the tale even more impactful.

During my nine-plus years serving on the House Armed Services Committee, I have encountered many men and women who have volunteered to protect America and her interests from the worst of humankind. I have marveled at the strength of our warrior families to endure multiple deployments and the related hardships.

I thought I had an understanding of the price they and their families were paying for that service. After reading Shilo's and Kathreyn's story, I am embarrassed to discover how little I really know. My praise of their sacrifices was always heartfelt and sincere, but after the glimpses into reality Shilo has provided us, I grieve at how little I have actually done to make their roads just a little bit less difficult.

Shilo is clearly a man of tremendous faith. Reading his story blessed my life, and I know it will touch the life of anyone who reads it.

K. Michael Conaway
US House of Representatives
Texas, District 11

ACKNOWLEDGMENTS

You know who you are. Too numerous to name. Our lives would be incomplete without you. We are grateful beyond words.

INTRODUCTION

Iron and carbon are sifted out of dirt, heated upward of 400–500 degrees Fahrenheit, and then held at this unbearable temperature until the nanotubes diffuse to form a new crystal structure. As it cools, the mixture essentially heals, and becomes converted over time to a substance we know as steel. Ancient peoples in India, three hundred years before Christ, produced steel. By the ninth and tenth centuries, this metallic fusion became charcoal. Modern economies smelt iron ore in a blast furnace to make steel. Munitions experts around the world have long used tempered steel to make weapons of war. And I have come to know, too well, what tempered steel does to a man, a woman, a family.

I am a man who has lived through hell. It is hard to share this experience. The carnage. The devastation. The loss. But I will do it. Because I will always know the smell of C-4, the echo of end-of-life screams, the whiteout of the blast, the grease of blood on fragments of limbs, the metallic taste of ash on a bit-through tongue. I will always know the horrors of war.

So I will tell you what an explosion does to you on the outside. And I will tell you what an explosion does to you on the inside. I will describe panic like a tsunami in your blood vessels. I will utter the painful realities of post-traumatic stress. And I will demonstrate what it means to live fearlessly, with a clear understanding of the Grace that can redeem mayhem.

For a long time I struggled with how to share this story of love, and loss, and love again. I must start at the worst part, when steel, embedded in my bones, changed me from the man I was into the man I was meant to be.

13

GLOSSARY

ADVON advanced echelon unit typically deployed or redeployed as one of three groups; advance party or ADVON, main body, and rear unit, or REARVON.

AIT advanced individual training; generally NCO or drill sergeants provide specialized training in a soldier's MOS (military occupational specialty).

AK-47 machine gun.

AO area of operations; geographical location of military mission.

BAMC Brooke Army Medical Center; component command over SAMMC (San Antonio Military Medical Center) and other US Army medical treatment centers in the San Antonio, TX, area.

BFV Bradley fighting vehicle.

C-4 plastic explosives with claylike consistency.

C-17 cargo aircraft; sometimes outfitted for medical transport; often used for transport of deceased.

CCATT critical care air transport team; used to transport and care for critically ill or wounded in a highly portable intensive care unit.

CEA cultured epithelial autograft; extensive permanent burn coverage using application of donor skin graft sheets.

DU depleted uranium; byproduct of enriched uranium; armor-piercing round for the 25mm cannon on a BFV.

EFP explosive formed penetrator; a bomb.

EMT emergency medical technician.

EOD explosive ordnance detachment; bomb disposal team.

FOB forward operating base; military unit deployed ahead of main echelon establishes a semipermanent or temporary base for mission readiness.

FRG family readiness group; military support group for spouses, used primarily during deployments to share information/support for military families.

GSR gunshot residue kit; portable test kit used to confirm presence of gunpowder and to assist in rapidly focusing on key suspects.

HEAT high explosive antitank warhead; specialized ammo.

HME homemade explosive device; unconventional warfare, a roadside bomb.

HUMVEE high mobility multipurpose wheeled vehicle.

ICU intensive care unit.

IED improvised explosive device; a homemade but severely dangerous bomb.

ISR Institute for Surgical Research; Department of Defense's primary facility for treating combat burn casualties.

M-4 carbine assault rifle issued to military.

M-9 semiautomatic pistol issued to military.

MC-130 special missions aircraft.

MOS military occupational specialty; nine-character code used to identify a special job or role in the military.

MRE meal-ready-to-eat; a self-contained field ration.

NCO noncommissioned officer; rank associated with E-4 (enlisted rank, fourth tier) and up, including E-5 or SGT, E-6 or Staff SGT, E-7 or Master SGT, E-8 or Sergeant Major, E-9 or Command Sergeant Major.

NVG night vision goggles; allows images to be produced in near darkness; also called NOD or night optical device.

O-1 to O-10 rank designation for officers; starting with O-1 or 2nd Lieutenant, O-2 or 1st Lieutenant, O-3 or Captain, O-4 or Major, O-5 or Lieutenant Colonel, O-6 or Colonel, O-7 or Brigadier General, O-8 or Major General, and O-9, O-10, and O-11, generally referred to as 3-star, 4-star, or 5-star general.

PTSD post-traumatic stress disorder; a severe anxiety disorder that develops typically after exposure to psychological trauma.

PX post exchange; similar to small department or convenience store; may be used only by those with military privileges.

RPG rocket-propelled grenade; shoulder-fired antitank weapon firing rockets equipped with explosive warheads stabilized in flight with fins.

R&R rest and relaxation; rest and recuperation; a respite of usually fifteen days, excluding travel time, given to soldiers in combat deployment.

SAMMC San Antonio Military Medical Center.

STSD secondary traumatic stress disorder; compassion fatigue; gradual lessening of compassionate response after working extensively with trauma or trauma victims.

T-RATS semiperishable foods in compact packaging.

VBIED vehicle-borne IED; weapon of mass destruction; weapon of choice for terrorists around the world to create mass tragedy/accident events using vehicles, buses, boats, or ships.

WARRIOR ETHOS code of ethics followed by American soldiers: I will always place the mission first; I will never accept defeat; I will never quit; I will never leave a fallen comrade.

WWP Wounded Warrior Project; private fund-raising organization to provide health and welfare relief to wounded veterans and their families.

XO officer who is second in command; reports to the CO or commanding officer.

1

METALLICA

It was just a normal day. The calendar by my bunk was turned to February 2007, and I scratched a big black square across the 18th. I finished fastening the canvas straps on my ammo pouch and peered out the small window near the foot of the bed. The sun rose red above the Iraqi sand; one day closer to finishing the mission we were sent to complete. I was nearly at the halfway point in this deployment and plans were falling into place for R&R with my wife and kids. I lifted their photo from the shelf and hid the memory of brown eyes by my heart; I could not look at it for long. The weathered paper rested in my pocket against my armored vest. Time to lock and load.

"First in, last out" was our motto. I was a Cavalry Scout in B Troop, 1st Squadron, 89th Cavalry, 10th Mountain Division out of Fort Drum, New York. We were stationed south of Baghdad, near a farming community called Yusifiyah. Our mission was to run reconnaissance to gain information on the enemy and to ensure roads were safe for travel by military and civilians. We gathered intelligence from human sources and communications traffic in the region. We were a frontline squad; utilized day and night to collect data to support coalition forces and either arrest or destroy the enemy. I had to observe and call up everything I saw, not only to those fighting on the ground but also to those back in the command center. We were trained to gain and maintain contact with the enemy.

But as the hours ticked by on the 19th, I noticed a few things that weren't typical, that make you uncomfortable when you're out in sector. A new lieutenant was in charge of our mission, our radios weren't working right, and a civilian had called in an IED (improvised explosive device) for investigation.

The road our convoy had to travel looked like a minefield. Huge craters the size of VWs interrupted the asphalt every twenty to fifty meters. Nicknamed "Metallica," this gravelly trail was so dangerous that walking on it was safer than driving on it. The road cut through the Triangle of Death, a trio of small Iraqi cities south of Baghdad that had become a hotbed for the insurgency. It was treacherous terrain despite the palm trees, the wheat grass, the sight of the emerald Euphrates River in the distance. The heat left a haze that hovered over the scene; sweat dripped off my forehead and slicked the headset attached to my helmet. I took a swig from my water bottle, my lips already salty and dry from the dirt.

We usually did a foot patrol, but this particular day we didn't have that luxury. There wasn't time. Our orders were to locate the IED and secure it for the explosive ordnance disposal (EOD) team. Our Humvee was the third in a convoy of four. There were five of us: my driver, gunner, two dismount soldiers including the medic, and myself. We were a team but we hadn't been together for long. I was called up to lead this squad after tragedy took the life of a young soldier early in their deployment. The team took the loss hard; the trauma resulted in the loss of two more soldiers to post-traumatic stress disorder (PTSD). The remaining crew was brave, highly skilled, and ready to perform any mission handed to them. At the same time, they were kids. It wasn't hard to imagine them on the gridiron or at their high school prom just a few months earlier. Like me, they were volunteers. We all knew we had a job to do, and we were committed to it. It had not taken me long to figure out that I would never serve with better men. In a very short time period, we'd become brothers. Sharing the same living quarters, meals, stories, and combat scenarios created a strong bond between us. Warriors, we would literally kill for each other.

◆ ◆ ◆

On patrol, we moved at a slow pace, keeping a safe distance from the vehicle in front of us and scanning the roads for bombs, traps, anything out of the ordinary. An IED is generally not a complex device—it's a homemade bomb. It needs a switch, a fuse, and a charge for deep penetration of armor, and can cause death and destruction through its detonation, concussive blast, shrapnel, and fire. IEDs were usually made using artillery or mortar shells, with varying amounts of explosive materials added. Sometimes we found IEDs embedded in walls behind propaganda posters; the deception was made obvious by the trailing trigger wires. Sometimes they'd be concealed in the cement of a concrete curb. It wasn't unusual to find an IED buried in an animal carcass along the roadside. Sometimes they were hidden under rotting garbage or beneath abandoned cars. Traveling under bridges or overpasses, we watched overhead for grenades or explosives, which were commonly dropped on our convoys. The enemy could watch from a distance, then detonate the trap as we drove by. By simply burying the explosives in the dirt, the enemy could implant a bigger bomb that was not readily detected without intelligence. Underground, these explosives were easily daisy-chained together so one initiator could destroy an entire line of vehicles or interrupt and destroy a convoy. Wherever it was hidden, an IED could be ignited with something as innocuous as a cell phone.

In this particular instance, our intelligence sources were skimpy on details and our commander shared what he could. We were all quiet as we surveyed the area, armed and ready. My driver slowed to idle speed as our vehicles rumbled past open countryside; it was deserted. On one side ran an irrigation ditch; thick, murky green water pooled and snaked through marsh grasses. On the other side was open farmland sprinkled with bombed out buildings, some remains still intact. We kept watch, following the lead vehicles. The thick tires of our truck kicked up a cloud of dust even though our speed was minimal. Our gunner stood in the back of the Humvee, weapon trained and watchful of anything unusual. We were on high alert, quiet, listening to static from the lead vehicle.

The holes in the road from previous IEDs were so huge that we had to drive on the edge of the roadway to make our way around them. My driver moved carefully around a wide crater in the dirt, our tire tracks matching the ones that had gone before us.

Then all hell broke loose.

◆ ◆ ◆

We hit an IED buried in the road right behind the driver's seat. An inferno exploded in the sky and blew thousands of pieces of shrapnel through the air. Everything in the truck erupted. Later reports indicated you could see the black mushroom cloud for miles. Multiple explosions set off in the vehicle, blowing a debris field across several acres.

My Kevlar helmet was torn from my head in the initial blast, and my ears were ripped from their sockets. I collapsed in the vehicle, unconscious and on fire.

Engulfed in flames, the vehicle was destroyed. When I came to, I saw some of the squad trying to reach me. I began to thrash around in the front seat, struggling to escape. We carried an AT-4 missile launcher loaded with 84mm high explosive antitank warheads in the back of the Humvee, and it exploded in the heat, creating a tornado of fire around me. I had to get my body armor off because it was on fire and melting into my legs. The ammunition in the storage pouch around my waist continued to explode, but I thought it was enemy fire and I struggled to locate my weapon to return fire. The blast had crushed bones, torn off limbs, burned flesh, incinerated clothing, and reduced everything to chaos.

As I was looking around trying to take in the carnage, I quickly realized I was in trouble. My men were gone. As I called for a radio report I looked at the cable and it had melted off the hand mike. I was disoriented, and seconds seemed to stretch out for days. I strained to make sense of what was happening around me. Everything was burning. I continued to hear what I thought was gunfire but was really all the ammo we carried in the back of the Humvee that continued to ignite and cook off around me. It rung my bell pretty good—and I felt unbearably hot. My movements were erratic and I couldn't think clearly. I couldn't locate my men, but I knew I had to get out of the truck.

The door on a Humvee weighs about three hundred pounds, and I fought to get it open. I tried kicking myself out of the vehicle, but the pressure of the blast had caused the ground beneath us to implode. I had to get out of that death trap . . . I had to reach the rest of my squad to tell them to be alert. Adrenaline pumping, I shoved the door of the Humvee against the gravel and finally got the door open. One of the crewmembers from the truck in front of us came to rescue me. Completely exposed and disoriented, I tried to direct security and recovery procedures. I was trying to tell him, "Pull over, get our men out!" He pushed me away from the fire, trying to get me to come with him so he could start combat lifesaving procedures.

He shielded me with his body, bullets zinging by as ammo continued to explode in its casing, cooking off in the Humvee beside us.

My men supported me between them, pulling me further away from the carnage. My collarbone had snapped in half. Blood dripped down the sides of my face, oozing out of my mouth, nose, eyes, and openings where my ears had been. I looked down and saw that the sleeve on my right arm had melted into my skin like plastic. My body was smoking. I'd seen soldiers on fire before. I knew it was bad.

But I had to figure out where my soldiers were. I heard radio traffic. "We have contact IED and small-arms fire. Need medevac and air support."

I looked over at my mangled left hand, thinking, *Man, I better get a day off for this.*

My body continued to burn but I had one focus . . . my soldiers. The acting platoon sergeant came and stood over me, straddling me as I lay on the ground. He looked me over and our eyes met. In my mind, I couldn't imagine how injured I was. We were friends; I was counting on him to take care of my men. But I saw in his eyes something I didn't understand until it registered—fear. I had no idea that what he was looking at was a soldier who had been burnt and damaged beyond recognition.

● ● ●

Lying on the ground, I could hear the helicopter coming in. I could feel the rotor wash of the chopper as it prepared to land; the dust blew through our site. The crew chief got out of the chopper and the medics helped load me in. The crew chief told me, "Hang on, we're going to get you out of here. You're going to be okay." I looked down at my left hand, the skin hanging off the bone with pieces of my fire retardant gloves dangling from the bloody tissue. I fought to stay conscious.

I told the crew chief, "I know. I'm fine. But where are my soldiers?" I had no idea I had severed both ears and most of my nose; the skin on my face was charred off; I'd lost some fingers, broken my back, and fractured my collar bone. I was still burning, and over one-third of my skin was gone. The medevac took off for the 28th Combat Support Hospital (CSH) in the Green Zone in Baghdad, trying to stabilize me in flight as the burning continued. The rotor blades of the Blackhawk screamed overhead as I watched the smoking remains of our convoy disappear from view.

I came in and out of consciousness during the flight, aware of my surroundings but afraid we would not make it. As soon as we landed in the Green Zone, the nurses and staff at the CSH went to work cutting my clothes off and working on my injuries. I was frantic, yelling at them, "I'm going to ask you one more time, do you know where my soldiers are?"

As the trauma team prepared to insert an IV into a remnant of my arm to induce coma, one blood-soaked doctor told me: "You'll find out in a couple months."

2

GOING HOME

The storefronts along the roadway that cuts through Coleman have changed, but the west Texas wind that burns through town has stayed the same. Neat rows of old homes stand watch on quiet streets, while haphazard ranchettes, trailers, and clapboard houses change hands on a regular basis. When you stroll through town, you can find the locals parked outside the café, leaning on their trucks at the gas station, shooting the breeze outside the police station, picking up a cold cola at Owl Drugs. If you keep heading east through town, you'll come across a good spot to get a tire changed or your car detailed, and while you're at it, you can pick up some shiners, a pint of grub worms, or a few lures, all at Harris's Bait and Tackle. You might see a kid in blue jeans and a dirty T-shirt bent over a tire, trying to get the lug nuts to loosen up. Nearly thirty years ago, that kid was me.

● ● ●

A dusty pickup was up on the tire jack. Grass poked out from the undercarriage, signs that someone had been off the road more than a few times. I removed the flat and studied the long gash where the rubber meets the rim, ready to make my diagnosis. I rolled the tire over to where my dad was standing and showed him the damage. "Needs a new tire," he told the driver.

"Do what you gotta do," the guy told him. "Just don't tell Janie where I've been."

I rolled the tire to the back of the store, found another one that matched in size, and rolled the new tire back out to the truck. My dad ducked his head toward the jack and told me, "Go ahead, Shilo, get it changed," and continued to talk to our customer.

The two men leaned on the bed of the truck and watched me work as the talk turned to fishing, weather, and local gossip. I wrestled with lifting the tire back into the wheel well, tightened up the lug nuts, replaced the hubcap, and lowered the jack.

"Good as new," I told them.

My dad motioned to the bed of the truck. "Get rid of all that crap."

I knew better than to ask questions. I climbed into the back of the truck and pulled out a dozen empty beer cans, shotgun shells, three empty Copenhagen cans, a couple of empty Jim Beam bottles, and a pair of pink bikini bottoms.

"Gimme those," the guy said, grinning at my dad as he tucked them in the pocket of his jeans.

My dad asked him, "What'd you catch?"

"Something pretty," he answered, and opened up the dented cooler in the bed of the truck. He pulled out a bigmouth bass and handed it to me. I ran my finger through the gullet and lifted it up in the air to feel how heavy it was. The scent of the lake made my nose itch to go fishing.

"Nice one," I told him. He nicked my ball cap with the tail of the fish and set it back in his cooler.

"That's how a man does it." He pointed to his truck. "Now don't go counting those beer bottles you're pulling out of the bed," he warned me, and turned back to my dad. "My 'check liver light' came on while I was driving over here."

The two men laughed and tapped their bottles, one against the other, before they both took a swig. "Want one?" he asked me.

"No, sir," I said, watching my dad as he swallowed the rest of his beer and threw the bottle in the trash can.

The town of Coleman made its living off of the outdoors; locals as well as folks from out of town chose our low hills interrupted by lakes, live oaks, and mesquite brush to hunt, fish, and live off the land. We'd moved here from McCamey, my hometown, when my dad opened up this business. His idea of a workday started before sunup and ended after dark.

"Ring him up," my dad said. "Forty bucks for the new tire, and Shilo, don't forget the beer."

"Yes, sir," I answered, and entered the sale into the cash register. I swept the front of the store, emptied the trash, mopped the restroom, and re-stocked the candy counter while my dad traded war stories with the guy in the red truck. A steady stream of customers came in for another hour or so to pick up bait or lures before my dad hung the closed sign in the window. He started counting the cash in the drawer, stuffing most of it in the pocket of his jeans.

"Gimme another beer," he told me, and grabbed his keys to lock the front door. "Time to go."

It was well past dark, and I knew the day wasn't nearly done. We'd make the usual rounds before heading home, stopping at one guy's house, then another, and finally the Stabbin' Cabin for one last beer.

●●●

"Dad, can we go home now?" I asked him, putting the eight ball in the corner pocket.

"What for?" he answered, setting his beer bottle on the edge of the pool table.

"It's nearly midnight."

"One more," he told me, handing me the keys to his old white crew cab truck. "Go start her up and I'll be right there."

I climbed in the truck, put the keys in the ignition, pushed down on the gas, and let it idle without shifting into gear. I waited in the dark for two hours. I knew better than to go in and ask him again if we could go. From where I sat in the truck, I could hear the raucous laughter and commotion of the pool hall. I'd been here before, and I knew it sometimes ended badly. My stomach was in knots as I hoped against hope that he'd walk out that door. Finally I watched him come down the steps and walk to the truck. I switched on the headlights. "Scoot over," he told me, and climbed in.

He revved the engine, making it roar to life, and pulled forward out of the parking lot. He turned the truck around and kicked up a wide spray of rocks as we hit the shoulder and pulled onto the main highway. I hung on for dear life, the smell of beer, whiskey, and cigarettes clinging to my dad's shirt while I pushed my face out the window to smell the night air instead. The wind stung my cheeks as our speed increased. I shivered, keeping my fears to myself.

There wasn't a lot of traffic that time of night in Coleman. No taillights to follow heading out to Hoard's Creek, just what little moonlight reflected off the pastures and farmland we crossed. Our high beams caught the eyes of a longhorn standing near a barbed wire fence, his head barely turning as we flew past. We wove, and my dad dodged a dead armadillo on the road's shoulder, the front wheels wobbling as he overcorrected.

The house was dark when we finally pulled into our driveway. I opened the screen door and turned the knob as quietly as I could to avoid a scene between my mother and dad. It was no use. The dog announced our arrival, and my mom snapped on the kitchen light, wrapping her robe tightly around her middle. "Your dinner is on the table," she told me, and gave my dad a look that told me all I needed to know. I wolfed down my baloney sandwich, grabbed my math book out of my backpack, and headed for my room. The page full of algebraic equations didn't take me too long to solve.

I arose from the floor where I was working and crossed the hall to peek into my little sister's room. She was sound asleep. A wedge of moonlight filtered in from the window and I could see her arms wrapped around her magic bunny. Her long hair covered part of her little face. I whispered, "Night, Solitaire," and closed her door. I walked into the bathroom, scrubbed the oil and grease off my hands with a washrag next to the sink, and brushed my teeth. I rinsed out my rag, hung it up to dry, and folded my towel evenly before putting it back in the center of the rod. I stared at myself in the mirror, dark hazel eyes looking back at me.

The clock on my nightstand said 2:30. Four hours before I'd need to get up and start over again. I jumped a little when the yelling started. By the time I climbed into bed it had reached a fever pitch and I could hear glass shattering against the living room wall. His screams, her replies. His rage, her tears. I closed my eyes as hard as I could and tucked my pillow tight around my ears so I could not hear what I knew would come next.

I was eleven.

3

BRIEFLY A CHILD

The rut. The scrape. The ripple. The run. I'd always been drawn to hunting and fishing because of that elemental feeling of control. When you've got a fishing line taut with the promise of a great big bass, or a buck with eight or ten points in your scope, your adrenaline starts to flow. The hook's yours to sink. The trigger's yours to pull. My grandfather knew that sometimes what I needed was a place to breathe. Some people have an easy button; my dad had a nuclear button. If things were hot, my grandpa would give me a call, and we'd truck out to the lake to camp, fish, and calm things down.

"War changes a man, Shilo," he told me one night. We were camping on Lake Coleman and had just finished off a pile of catfish. He raked the fish bones into the fire, and I watched them melt into liquid, change into ash.

"Yes, sir," I said, staring into the flames.

"You know your dad loves you, right?"

"Yes, sir."

The night fell on us like a dark blanket. A hundred years earlier cowboys had settled at the same site, moving longhorn cattle from Coleman up to Dodge. My grandpa poked his stick back into the campfire, holding the oak limb in place until the tip glowed a deep orange. He used it to make tally marks in the sand for each fish we'd caught that evening. "I can't believe you caught one bigger than mine," he chuckled, "and on chicken liver at that." I grinned at him. A breeze came around and stirred the dry leaves. I scooted closer to the fire.

We both listened as a chorus of coyotes barked in the distance. From where we sat on the rocks by the lake, they sounded like puppies but we knew better. A pack of coyotes making that much noise had to be on the trail of dinner—yelps like that made the night sound lonely. I knew something about that feeling. There wasn't a lot to do in Coleman. Hunting and fishing gave both of us what we needed more than anything else.

◆◆◆

My grandpa was a retired military man. After losing my grandmother, he had a big hole in his heart and time on his hands, and fishing and hunting was the best he knew to do. If he didn't call me to go fishing, I'd call him. Before or after a fishing trip, he loved to make pancakes and always made plenty. We could finish off a huge stack between the two of us.

He used to warn me, "You be you. You don't have to impress anyone. Just God."

I watched the way he treated people, whether it was the waitress in the café or the kid who needed a mentor. Most of the time, he was like fine sandpaper, smoothing out my rough edges and trying to build the man in me. But he could be tough as nails, just like my dad. This was my heritage, to be strong. Something in me understood that there were character traits in both my father and grandfather that I needed to emulate, and others that needed to be overcome.

Sometimes my granddad rubbed me raw. Once he picked me up in Coleman to go fishing out at the lake. It was a long drive, and halfway there he fell asleep at the wheel. I steered us the rest of the way while he slept. When we got close to the lake, I tapped his shoulder so he'd wake up and guide us to the fishing spot. He rubbed his eyes, grabbed the wheel, and parked in a gravel lot near the water's edge. We gathered up our poles, and he warned me to be quiet as we approached the water.

My granddad had some nearly superstitious rules about fishing, and I was about to come to an understanding about one of them. I raced ahead of him, excited to get down to the water. When I reached the lake, I set my poles down, and one of them fell in, slapping the water and making ripples move from the shore. When my granddad saw what had happened, he told me, "That's it, we're done."

I turned and looked at him, and saw fierce anger in his eyes. I asked, "What do you mean?"

"I told you not to disturb the fish. We're done, get in the truck."

We walked back to the vehicle and left.

I was silent and disappointed, but I had learned just how angry and compulsive he could be. We spent the rest of the day visiting family in the area, but the day was ruined. He had shown me what could happen when you didn't listen to his instructions. The lessons he'd learned as a boy, the lessons he'd sown into my father's life, and the lessons I learned from him firsthand were diminished sometimes by rage, anger, and misunderstanding. It was the way it was. We didn't dwell on what we did wrong to one another or hold any grudges. There was a lot of forgiveness all the way around, but none of that was spoken aloud. Men didn't speak of such things, and we kept our emotions tucked inside.

● ● ●

I watched the fire and rubbed the belly of my dog, Catahoula, who was worn out from racing through the woods while we fished. "Glad I didn't drop a pole this time?" I asked my grandfather. He gave me his slow grin, nodded his head, and silently watched the fire.

When you sit beside a fire and tell jokes and trade stories, there's nothing better. "Tell me about the war," was my frequent request, and my grandfather would take me with him across the ocean, onto the beach, with his platoon, engaging the enemy in a firefight.

"A man's gotta make his peace with God every day, Shilo."

"Yes, sir."

"Don't ever forget that."

"No, sir."

The bushes stirred beside us. "Hold on," he told me, handing me my shotgun. "Think it's a bull ape?"

"I bet it is," I whispered, and tiptoed toward the row of mesquite bushes.

He reminded me, "Remember I told you about those apes that escaped out of the circus over in Burkett? Folks say those bull apes are still wreaking havoc around these parts."

"Be careful," he told me as I ran toward the thicket. I loved racing through the hills after a wild hog or lying in wait for a stag to come feed from the corn we'd left for him. I wasn't too sure what to expect from a primate. I followed the sounds of the bull ape for about half a mile; his grunting and squealing left a trail of noise about twenty yards ahead of me, but I was gaining on him.

"Get him, Cat!" I called to my dog. Catahoula was trying to herd him back to me but I soon called her off, not sure what a bull ape would do to her since I'd never actually seen one before. I was almost close enough to get a shot before the moon disappeared behind a cloud and I lost my way.

I waited a few minutes, crouched beside a tree stump, trying to catch my breath, waiting to see if the ape might finally make an appearance. I hung on to the dog's collar, telling her to wait. No sound came from the bushes, and I wasn't about to head into the fray just in case he was not alone. It wasn't unusual to find rattlesnakes curled on a rock in the night air, or rabid foxes, or more wild hogs than you could handle. I grew impatient and headed back to the lake the same way I'd come.

"That's enough, girl," I told Catahoula. "We didn't really want that ape anyway."

By the time I got back to camp, my grandpa had spread out his sleeping bag and was dozing about ten feet from the fire. "You git one?" he asked.

"Nah, it ran off," I answered, and watched a grin spread across his face.

"Hit the sack—it's near midnight," he murmured as I approached, and I spread out my bag close to his.

"Night, grandpa."

"Night, son."

Lying on my back, I took in the stars overhead. The cicadas picked up their song and grew louder, stirring me awake instead of asleep. I thought about my grandpa and the years he went to war. He was always there when I needed him. I thought about my dad and the years he went to war. Grandpa explained it once this way: "Vietnam changed your dad. Back then they didn't put a name to it. Now the VA calls it PTSD, post-traumatic stress disorder. That's what's bothering your dad, and I don't have any idea how to help him."

I listened again to the coyotes; it seemed like anything that might threaten us had moved away for the night and I yawned, turning over in my sleeping bag to lie on my side and watch the fire. The thick logs we'd added earlier were burning low, and the charred wood crackled as it broke. I didn't have to hold my breath; I slept, safe and sound.

###

Come daylight we gathered up our sleeping bags, left the campsite like we'd never been there, and headed back to town, stopping by the coffee shop. "Hey, A. B.," the waitress called out to my grandpa, "what y'all been doing?"

My grandfather set his arm over my shoulders and said, "Just fishing with my grandson. You shoulda' seen the bass he caught last night!"

His eyes gave me something. "Let's get you home, Shilo," he said as he waved goodbye to his friends and we headed for the door. My hands and face felt grimy from lying by the fire all night, and I was looking forward to taking a long, hot shower.

When we pulled up to the house, my dad came out the door and hollered my name. "Shilo, get over here!"

"Yes, sir?" I answered.

My dad was always trying to toughen me up, physically as well as mentally. He had a sly look on his face as he steered me to the backyard. "Time for commando training."

Behind our house he'd been working on a pretty elaborate obstacle course, and had built a stage with a climbing tower and a system of ropes that went from one tree to the telephone pole and back. It was the envy of all my friends. "Start climbing," he told me. My grandpa looked at me and winked, hardly lifting his palm to wave goodbye. I pushed up my shirtsleeves and went to work.

The early morning sun hit my shoulders as I sweated my way up the rope for the tenth time. The muscles in my arms felt like they were going to burst wide open and my legs shook from trying to gain my footing on the pole to leverage my way up.

"Do it again," he hollered. "Higher," my dad yelled. "Higher!"

I gave it all I had and hit my fist against the top bar. "Finally," he called, "now shimmy across that pole to the tower and climb down."

Splinters dug into my palms as I balanced on a pine bar about twelve feet off the ground and clung to the pole that led to the tower. I didn't want to fall. I was determined to do what my dad wanted me to do. If he wanted me to be tough, I'd be tough. There wasn't much below me but grass, yet I had a feeling I was high enough in the air that it wouldn't be a soft landing. I bit my lip as I traveled across, tasting the salt of my own blood as I reached for the tower. "All right, soldier, now climb down. Quickly!"

When I got to the bottom of the tower, my dad hit my palms with his own, oil-stained from years of working rigs near Odessa. "Think you're strong enough?" he asked me.

"Yes, sir," I answered.

"We'll see about that," he muttered, and walked toward the back door. "Be ready to do it again tomorrow."

I brushed my hands off on my jeans and turned toward him, wiping the sweat off my forehead using my sleeve. I caught him looking at me. He winked and gave me a grin. That look gave me everything I needed. I knew what I needed to know: he was proud of me.

I walked slowly back to the house, finding my mom at the kitchen stove. She touched my arm and pulled me to her, hugging me close. "You're getting tall as me," she whispered, and handed me a plate of scrambled eggs and toast.

"Thanks, Mom," I told her. Our eyes met. There was a knowing between us. Something neither one of us could say out loud. Something about my dad's hardness and her softness. Something about being expected to be a man when you're just a kid.

4

OLD BOYS,
YOUNG MEN

When most folks think of Friday nights in Texas, they think of football and hometown heroes. Friday night lights for me were the light bulbs overhead at the store, when my folks worked long hours to keep the business afloat. But our lives were quickly unraveling, as other lights appeared in our lives . . . patrol cars cruised past the shop, investigating my father's involvement with illegal drugs. My dad began to disappear for long periods of time, and his reputation for working hard and playing hard began to change. So did mine.

There were fifty-three people in my senior class, and I got along with just about every one of them. No one accused me of being a scholar, but I was smart enough to know that it didn't take a lot of effort to do well. If anything, my teachers saw me squander a bit of what they perceived as raw talent. Mrs. Herma Jean Johnson was my favorite, and she was proud of my work, as long as it was not a last-ditch effort. She'd tell me, "You could be the class valedictorian if you weren't so busy being the class clown!" She coached me in public speaking and prepared me to compete with brains rather than brawn. But I loved making people laugh, and you could count on me to find the humor in anything around me.

●●●

Being a cut-up wasn't always a good thing. I remember the time I skipped school with a few friends. It had snowed the night before, which spelled only one thing for my group and me: mudding. There were about five of us driving and our girlfriends were playing hooky right along with us. We all had trucks set up for play. My buddy, Macaroni, and I both had '79 Ford F-150s with four-wheel drive, mud tires, and the usual heavy-duty engine. The ground was still frozen from the night before, and as the sun began to thaw the earth, it created the perfect surface for mud dogging. We drove out to Memory Lake and went off-roading, spinning out of control in the ice and sludge. We talked a guy into buying us some beer and booze, and continued to hit our favorite mudding spots. It was so cold we finally decided to shoot some pool at one of my dad's hangouts, the Stabbin' Cabin.

We all slogged into the bar, taking over the pool tables. The owner hollered at us, "If the law shows up, you guys run out the back door!" While I was racking a set, a bunch of guys we'd had trouble with in town showed up. They outnumbered us two to one. We didn't want a run-in, but we weren't turning our backs on these guys. We kept our pool sticks handy and tried to continue our game. One of the guys asked my girlfriend to dance, and I made it clear that wasn't going to happen. Suddenly the guy ran at me with a knife. To protect myself, I whacked him with the cue stick. It was on.

It was like someone threw a grenade in there, and the whole place erupted in a brawl. My girlfriend threw pool balls at the crowd, trying to fight back. No sooner did I finish fighting one guy before another one climbed on. There was blood everywhere. I heard the bartender scream, "Shilo, COPS!"

We ran for the back door, my friends tumbling into the bed of my truck and my girlfriend jumping in the cab. I threw it in gear, slammed on the gas, and tried to get away. I hit a car, reversed, and gassed it until I pushed another car out of my way. I finally plowed my way through the cars around me and pulled onto the roadway. As we sped down the road, my girlfriend was frantic.

"Shilo, are you okay?"

Breathless, I looked down at my shirt and realized it was torn. I was worried about ruining it. "Man, I love this shirt." Then I noticed blood had saturated my other sleeve. I pulled it over my head as I raced down the road and found knife wounds all over my arms and across my chest.

What started as harmless fun had turned into a nightmare that I was lucky to have survived. And what was left of my childhood was gone. I realized I wasn't the only one struggling to stay out of trouble. There was a reason those guys were after me in the Stabbin' Cabin. My dad had started using and selling methamphetamines. The guys who attacked us did so because my father was taking business away from the local dealers, and they believed I was his partner. I was straddling two worlds, one that made sense and another that was swiftly spinning out of control.

● ● ●

I became keenly aware that my father was dealing with demons that were putting our whole family in jeopardy. I struggled to be like him, as well as trying to be very different. One day he caught me using dope and wrung me out. "Shilo, you leave this crap alone. Don't go anywhere near it!"

His words didn't match his actions. If being a man meant being like my dad, then my choices were going to mirror his.

But living with the consequences of my decisions was about to hit me square in the face. I soon discovered there were two words that no teenage boy wants to hear: "I'm pregnant." My high school sweetheart told me that what we'd done together resulted in a child that she planned to bring into the world, with or without me.

I wanted to man up and had two words for her: "Marry me." Her parents had two words for me: "Hell, no."

We were too young, too unsteady—two children who'd made a baby. She named our son Joshua and I have always been proud to be his father, though he deserved a man who was ready for him in ways that I was not. I was told to steer clear of him, and I tried to abide.

When I finished high school, my mom called me into her room one Sunday morning and said, "That's it. I'm done." She didn't have to tell me more. She was finally calling it quits on a marriage that was marred by years of heartache. She'd kept her vows for as long as she could. She'd coped by focusing all of her time and attention on working at the store and watching over us kids. I coped by trying to keep my popularity in check, by being the class clown, the Boy Scout, the loyal son. Solitaire coped by hanging on to me. And that worked for us, for a long time. Like most families in a volatile home, we kept the hard parts a secret, living in denial and clinging to the false hope that things would get better. They didn't. My father was convicted of drug possession and sale, and was shipped off to prison. Our family was officially torn apart.

● ● ●

If we'd been part of a church family, maybe we would have had the support we needed. But we were alone in dealing with my dad, and asking others for help just wasn't a habit that we shared as a family. Faith was not a part of my childhood. There was very little mention of God. When my parents argued about religion, it was my dad's belief that God was there, but he had no use for organized religion. He didn't trust the church and didn't seek to be part of it in any way. For my dad, submitting to God would have required surrendering the things that helped him cope with his undiagnosed PTSD . . . the booze, the drugs, the lifestyle.

Surrender would have given him his life back, but he didn't know that. My folks didn't have a living faith that mattered to them, and neither did I.

My mom warned me, "Shilo, get out of here. Get out of here while you still can."

I went down to see the Army recruiter. Diploma in hand, I pitched my case. "I want to enlist, make me a soldier," I told him.

"Well, the Army's looking for a few good men, let's see what we can do." He signed me up for a battery of tests, vocational and physical. Then he told me words I'd waited my whole life to hear: "You're in."

I was ecstatic. I ran right out to see my friends, to let them know I was finally getting out of Coleman. We celebrated out at Memory Lake, toasting the future with cold beer and big plans. The excitement was cut short just a few hours later. I got pulled over by the Texas Highway Patrol on my way home. The officer was a friend of mine, and I tried to talk him out of giving me the Breathalyzer test. "I'm going to join the military. I've got this plan all worked out," I explained.

"I'm not sure you're telling me the truth," he said, and ran the test. My uncle was the judge, and he put me on probation and told me how stupid I was. The military recruiter wouldn't touch me after that. What I did wasn't right, and it changed the trajectory of my life.

5

LOST AND FOUND

Shilo! You hear that?" my father asked. "That's what it takes! Believe! Achieve! Succeed! Your best weapon is a well-developed mind!"

After I ruined my chance to join the military, I had my father's mantra in my head. Despite his incarceration, my father's lessons stuck with me. I was going to put all that motivational salestalk to good use. I moved to Abilene and applied for a job at a local department store. I wanted something that didn't involve tire dirt and dust. I figured I'd start out in the men's department and work my way up the food chain. As luck would have it, they hired me in the china and crystal section.

I was a natural salesman. All of those Zig Ziglar and Harry Lorayne tapes my dad made me listen to hadn't fallen on deaf ears. I had a lot of bravado for someone who really didn't have a clue what was going to come next. On my first day at work, a lady wanted a closer look at a four-hundred-dollar vase. She told me it was exactly what she was looking for. "Yes, ma'am," I told her, "this one's a beauty." I reached up to the top shelf and flipped the heavy lead crystal in the air, the Waterford vase landing like a football in my open palms. She nearly started bawling, and said, "I'll take it."

I told her, "Lemme go in the back and get one in a box for you."

"No, no . . . I want that one before you break it."

I sold everything that wasn't nailed down, using my gridiron moves on lead crystal and porcelain wedding dishes. I was no bull in a china shop, and prided myself on doing good work regardless of what department I worked in.

But I realized I wasn't earning enough to get me where I wanted to go and contemplated a position in the oil fields. Despite the decisions my father made that took him down some bad roads, I still valued his opinion, and I drove to the prison in Huntsville to talk it over with him.

"Don't do it, son," he said. "You'll be an old man in six months."

He'd had plenty of his own ups and downs in the oil business, enough to know what he was talking about. But I'd had enough of china and crystal. I wanted to do a man's work for a man's pay. I got a job with an oil company based in Abilene, but to get to the oil fields we had to drive a couple hundred miles. In west Texas that's a short trip, but those were some long days.

We were called roughnecks for a reason. If you're a roughneck, you're slinging pipe. Our job was to set up an oil derrick a couple hundred meters tall in order to drill down a few kilometers to hit a target that wasn't much bigger than a kitchen table. We dug the main hole, then set the pipe in place to start drilling. We used triple pipe, so we could push ninety-foot sections of pipe into the earth at one time. You carry and load the pipe as a team. I worked seven days a week, ten to twelve hours a day, for weeks on end.

As we drilled, rock cuttings and mud would float up and out of the hole while we tried to reach the oil trap. The deeper we went, the more pipe and casing we had to add. Once the pipes were in place, five thousand feet into the earth, we had to continue to irrigate the drill site with water and creosote. All the mud that came out of the hole had to be trucked away.

The process was rarely smooth or safe. Once pipe broke underground, we'd work nonstop to fish out everything that was broken until we got it right. Then the process started all over again. Hands, arms, and legs were at risk around the heavy equipment, and the crude oil would eat at our skin. The hydrogen sulfide gas that came out of the ground was dangerous.

We'd work a site for two or three weeks, then move on. There was no such thing as a weekend or holiday when you were drilling. It was back-breaking work.

I spent a lot of time on the road, driving to oil fields in rough parts of the state. Whenever I met anyone who worked in that area of Texas, I'd tell them, "You grew up hard." You work, drive, sleep, work, drive, sleep.

It wasn't unusual to work three or four shifts back to back. Sometimes I volunteered for it, just for the money, but by the third shift I would be exhausted.

One thing a young man won't do is tell you he's lonely. He just acts out. I did it through drinking and carousing in places known for trouble or troublemakers. Working as hard as we did on the oil fields left me with plenty of cash in my pocket but sometimes little common sense. I fell for a girl who made that loneliness disappear for a while, and we had two beautiful boys together.

You might say I was all hat and no cattle. I had plenty of bravado, plenty of stories, plenty of good intentions, but my life wasn't adding up to much. As long as I had a few bucks and a few Buds, I thought I was good to go. I don't think I need to tell you I was a selfish man. With three children to support, I was no prize, but I sure acted like I was. A man puts up a pretty big front when he's in that much pain.

◈ ◈ ◈

That all changed when I met Kathreyn. Big brown eyes full of compassion. Wisdom beyond her years. A sparkle and spirit that drew me in. We knew each other in high school, but we were raised on different sides of the tracks—the Baptist church was on her side and the beer joint was on mine. Her family had a farm outside of Coleman, and they were a hard-working bunch. One hot summer night we were at the same party, and there was a cold beer sitting on the table so I took it. Kathreyn approached from around the corner and asked, "What are you doing?"

"We're going to the lake, you wanna go?"

"No, but that's my beer."

I pointed at my truck and told her, "Well, get in because it's going with me."

"No, you can have it."

So I climbed in the truck without either one of them. I had tried my Don Juan on her, but it didn't work. She said, "If you want to date me, you'll be at the Baptist church on Sunday morning."

I declined. There were five Baptist churches in town and I wasn't going to try every one looking for her. The only time I'd been to church was with my grandpa, and he and I had quickly turned that into a forty-five-minute nap. But it wasn't long before I decided I was going to do whatever it took to get to know Kathreyn. She told me I was a diamond in the rough, and something deep inside me decided to believe her.

Any rancher in Texas will tell you that a stallion is just a colt with unruly intentions, and being raised on a ranch, Kathreyn saw past that part of me. We met day after day and talked and laughed; she got me. She had a really strong work ethic that included getting up early to go to work, and being ready to do the same thing the next day and the day after that. Part of me wanted to warn her against the kind of guy I was. I tried to tell her I was a hard man to love. But I wanted her to love the man I knew I could be.

The first time she took me to church, I listened to her pastor talking to a packed little congregation, and the message he delivered was aimed right at me. He told me about a man named Jesus; a man whose Father loved me, a Savior who purchased me, hung on the cross, paid the debt, and set me free. It was a lot to take in, but there was an audience of one in particular who was watching me, to see if what was said had any meaning to me—Kathreyn's father. I knew I wanted to put a ring on her finger as soon as he'd let me.

As it turned out, he wouldn't. He'd seen guys like me before. Coleman was his hometown. He knew our family's history, my father's run-ins with the law, his drug trafficking and prison term, his divorce from my mother, my carousing around town. Kathreyn's pleas for him to trust me fell on deaf ears.

I drove to the ranch one afternoon to ask for Kathreyn's hand in marriage. She wasn't with me, and I felt it would go best if her dad and I talked man to man. I found him in the yard, working under the hood of his tractor, and when he saw me pull up, he started walking toward the house. I asked him if we could talk, and he stormed into the house, leaving the back door standing ajar as I followed him in.

Kathreyn had lost her mother when she was eighteen, and her father had been left with a gaping hole in his life. I was about to tell him that I wanted to take his daughter with me, and I knew that was going to leave another gaping hole. I sat down with him and told him I was in love with his daughter and wanted to marry her. He would not agree. He would not let me have her. I could tell his heart was breaking, and so was mine.

As I drove away from the man who'd raised this young lady from infancy, I thought about what it took to release her to a man like me. I had never met a woman like Kathreyn before, someone who believed in me with her whole heart. But I had no idea of how to convince her father that I could be trusted. We went ahead with our marriage plans, despite his disapproval. We felt so lucky to have found each other; we even won our cake topper as a door prize at a wedding show. Kathreyn chose a gorgeous bridal gown, but it was way over our budget. Her grandmother sewed one just like it, her wedding gift to both of us. As the big day approached we were both excited but nervous, scared to death that Kathreyn's girlhood dream of having her father walk her down the aisle would come crashing down.

On our wedding day he showed me what it takes to be a father: he showed up to walk his little girl down the aisle. I had envisioned her father grabbing me like Daffy Duck and snapping me in half like a twig, but he didn't kill me. And he not only let me live, he put his daughter's hand in mine. Tears streamed down our faces—relief for me, and joy for Kathreyn. She had always been Daddy's girl.

6

NINE ELEVEN

We started our married life in Brownwood. Kathreyn earned her degree from Tarleton State University in Stephenville, and she landed a job at the Federal Land Bank. I worked part-time at JCPenney and full-time for Don King Land Surveying. I was gradually working my way up the ladder and became a team leader. My first day on the job as team leader we drove out to a huge spread. Three or four hundred acres needed to be surveyed and I needed to prove I could handle it. We reached the site and set up our equipment on one of the vectors, but I could not get our GPS to work. I kept after it for a couple of hours and finally realized I had to go back to the office to tell Don that something was wrong. I was so disappointed. I knew I was doing everything I could do to get it set up, but I was failing miserably.

I humbly walked into the office to tell Don what had happened, and I looked at the television in his office. "What's going on?"

"Shhh . . . shh . . ." he said, and we both watched as what looked like a twin tower in New York City exploded and came crashing to the ground.

"Is this a movie?" I asked him.

Messages scrolled across the bottom of the television, indicating our country was under attack. While we were watching, another plane crashed. I felt helpless. I was so angry. Our eyes were glued to the television for the next several hours.

Kathreyn and I met for pizza at the mall later that day and talked it over. There were several large televisions in the restaurant, and we watched the day's events replay on all sides. "I've gotta enlist," I told her. She looked at the images on the television and back at my face.

"I know," she told me.

We picked ourselves up and walked through the mall and into the recruiter's office, where I grabbed some literature. Over the next couple of months, I researched the possibility of enlistment. I had some items on my record that were going to get in my way. I was twenty-seven years old, without any college credits, and I was still undecided about my career in life. My work history illustrated that fact: oil fields, department stores, land surveys. Even at twenty-seven, I hadn't figured out what I wanted to be when I grew up.

The Air Force recruiter didn't waste his time on me. As soon as he saw that I had no college experience, he moved on. When I walked out of his office, I ran into the Army recruiter, leaning against the wall outside. He looked straight at me like he had something to say, and I asked, "Are you waiting for me?"

"Yep," he answered. "Step into my office."

He tried to entice me with his pitch about dirt bikes and Dirty Harry. I stopped him midsentence. "Look, I'm twenty-seven years old and I know what I'm stepping into. I want to put my family behind a gate and take the fight to the enemy."

He nodded, knowing I was serious. I continued, "They attacked our home. Sign me up."

He looked over my past record and told me it was going to take some work. "If you want this, you're going to have to earn it."

I agreed. He gave me a lot of running around to do, getting various pieces of paper rounded up. He told me to study for the ASVAB (Armed Services Vocational Aptitude Battery) test. The higher your scores on the ASVAB, the more options you have as an enlistee. He took me out on a few trips with other recruits so I could explore different military occupations.

Kathreyn and I continued our conversation about the future and what it meant to enlist. We had begun our life together, and I knew I'd never make another decision without her. It had come time to sign on the dotted line. I asked her, "Babe, what do you think?" I knew it would cost her something to make that commitment. At a minimum, it would mean leaving all her family and friends in Coleman.

She looked at me with those dark brown eyes, took in the resolve and determination she saw in mine, and declared, "I'm with you."

● ● ●

I told the recruiter, "I don't want my past to haunt me anymore. I'm ready. Let's do it."

"I'll see what we can do," he told me.

He called a lieutenant who wanted to put me through a final interview. He grilled me over my paperwork and then peppered me with tough questions about my expectations. I told him about my father's service, as well as my grandfather's. I had a pretty clear understanding of what I was signing up for. The men I admired had served admirably and had known combat. I wanted to protect my country, just like they had.

He asked, "Why does the Army need you?"

I answered, "I'm ready to serve. The assault on our homeland has really affected me. I want to keep my family safe."

The officer said, "I think you're intelligent, I think you have a lot to offer, so I'm going to take a chance on you. Don't mess this up."

This time there was no celebration with my hometown buds. There was a quiet conversation with Kathreyn, confirming what we knew. "You know what's going to happen, don't you?"

She nodded.

"Afghanistan," I told her.

7

TOUR OF DUTY

I knew I was made for this. My dad had trained me to be a soldier from day one. I just didn't realize how well trained I was until I shipped off to basic training a week after our first wedding anniversary. I did so well at the obstacle courses one day that one of the drill sergeants asked me, "Private Harris, are you on drugs?"

I was kind of shocked. "What do you mean?"

"Man, you act like you ain't never been with a woman before!"

It did make me feel good to know I was in good shape. I had done enough smoking and drinking before basic training that I should have been challenged by the course. But here I was, the fourth oldest recruit in basic, and I had some of the highest scores in both physical and technical performance.

After basic, I attended advanced individual training, and over Father's Day weekend, I got a card from Kathreyn. "You're going to be a dad," she told me. I was ecstatic. There was no Father's Day gift I could have loved more than this happy news.

A few weeks later, Kathreyn came to see me on family weekend. She arranged with the hotel to borrow a VCR to hook up to the television in our hotel room. She showed me a video of her first sonogram, and we both cried happy tears. We didn't know if it was a girl or boy, but it didn't matter. We were ready to start our family together.

Sixteen weeks later I was on orders for Schweinfurt, Germany, with the 1st Infantry Division, 1st Squadron/4th Cavalry Regiment. The Army sent me back to Brownwood to do some hometown recruiting while I waited for my flight to Germany. We worked on getting Kathreyn's passport application completed so she could join me. We knew with her pregnancy we were cutting it close.

The Army sends service members overseas in advance, to make sure housing arrangements are in place before your family members are allowed to join you. Gone were the days of, "If the Army wanted you to have a family, they'd have issued you one." I felt excited as I prepared to leave my home state for an overseas destination. The flight was long, and it took hours to get through customs and processing at the airport in Frankfurt. I arrived at our post, got my barracks assignment, and reported for duty at my new unit. I'd like to say I got a warm welcome, but when you're almost thirty years old and are only a private first class, there are big invisible question marks hanging over your head. Either you've been in the Army a while and have been busted in rank, or you've been a civilian and couldn't cut it, so you joined the military. There was another guy like me who'd enlisted right after 9/11, and we stuck together. We knew it wouldn't take long to prove ourselves.

● ● ●

For the first few weeks, I lived in the barracks while I waited for our quarters assignment so I could send for my bride. Kathreyn called me after I got in country to tell me more good news: "It's a girl!" After that, I literally ran from one office to the next, trying to get all the paperwork ready to get Kathreyn overseas. She was seven months pregnant; if I didn't hurry and get her to Germany, she'd be in the "no fly" window. Then it dawned on me. I was rushing to move her to Germany so that I could leave her alone with a new baby and a new life while I went to war. I felt extremely selfish. I called her.

"Babe, why don't you have the baby at home, close to your dad and family? Once you get here, I'm going to leave and I don't want to do that to you."

Kat did what I knew she would do. She chose me. "I'm not having this baby without you. Now get me to Germany."

I found a German doctor and hospital, and we received our assignment to post quarters. Upon her arrival, Kathreyn immediately began acclimating to a new country and a new way of life. She met her new OB-GYN, and we toured the hospital. Nothing made sense to us in German, but we recognized the labor and delivery area. This was the *krankenhaus* where we'd have our baby and start our family. In the coming weeks, Kat made our little apartment look like home. We got the crib set up, put baby clothes and blankets in place, and I got to know my new unit. Kathreyn and I enjoyed our snowy new surroundings. These two west Texas kids had never seen it so cold or wet.

It was Thanksgiving, and we had a lot of soldiers in my unit who had no family nearby, so we opened our shoebox apartment to about fifteen single soldiers to share a meal. We all crowded in the kitchen to watch Kathreyn work her magic, until she finally kicked us all out so she could finish cooking. We had people sitting on the floor, on the couch, at the table, anywhere there was a space. I fixed a plate for our new baby, excited knowing that our little one would soon arrive.

The next morning I drove Kat to the hospital, where we started the process of induction. Hours went by. Contractions were getting harder and closer. Finally the doctor came in and took a peek. "Things look okay. I'll check back in an hour or so."

No sooner had he left than the midwife came in, saying, "*Schnell, schnell! Kommen!*" Interpretation? "Fast, fast, the baby's coming!"

I said, "Oh no, I'll go get the doctor!"

The midwife sharply said, "*Nein*, the baby is come and you help!"

In the back of my mind I was thinking, *Heck, no, I'm not even remotely qualified for this!*

But no time for debate—soon, there she was, my beautiful daughter. After cleaning her up, the midwife wrapped our baby girl in a blanket and tried to hand her to me, but I was so weak in the knees I was afraid to hold her. I did not want to drop her. I was amazed that I could cradle her tiny body in the palms of my hands. After three boys, I did not know whether I had what it takes to raise a girl. I was so proud of Kathreyn, and together we chose the name Elizabeth Diann, after Kathreyn's mom.

Soon I was able to take my girls home, and Kat settled into a routine of nursing, housekeeping, and sleeping while I went to work. A new baby in the house was exhausting, but we were extremely content.

◆ ◆ ◆

My unit received its first deployment orders, which surprisingly had us slated to go to Kosovo instead of Afghanistan or Iraq. Like everyone else in my unit, I felt some disappointment in receiving orders for a peacekeeping mission instead of combat. Most of us were anxious to be part of Operation Iraqi Freedom. But having a new baby changed my point of view. Going to war meant I might never see Lizzie grow up. I was okay with Kosovo. Every time I looked into little Lizzie's eyes, my own eyes would tear up. I did not want to leave her.

Kathreyn began to attend her deployment briefings and family readiness group meetings, all in preparation for the day we'd have to say goodbye. We spent our holidays exploring the little village of Schweinfurt. The German people have mastered Christmas. The marketplace covered with snow, the hot spiced wine and gingerbread, the tiny lights illuminating shop windows . . . it was all bittersweet to me with our deployment on the horizon. We did our Christmas shopping at the Post Exchange (PX), focusing what little money we had on Lizzie instead of each other.

In January our unit was heavily involved with tactical training. For most of the men in my unit, we were hoping our orders for Kosovo would not materialize. Reports coming out of Iraq pointed to the need for more troops on the ground, and we were trained and ready. If we didn't go to Kosovo, there was hope that we'd be shipped off to Iraq instead. We were given plenty of family time and tried to enjoy it despite the uncertainty. One evening, I walked through the door with some happy news: "We're not going."

"What do you mean you're not going?" Kathreyn asked.

"To Kosovo. Our deployment's been cancelled."

"You're kidding!" she cried, throwing her arms around me.

"We'll get orders for someplace else, but for now we're staying put."

We were sent on several details to Kaiserslautern, Germany, to prepare other units to deploy to Iraq, and performing that duty was like rubbing salt in the wound. We didn't want to load other soldiers onto aircraft to go to war. We wanted to board those planes ourselves.

I warned Kathreyn, "There are a lot of rumors going around about where we're going to go. Don't believe everything you hear. As soon as we get new orders, you'll be the first to know."

We spent the next couple of months enjoying our tour in Germany. Our unit continued its combat training, with gunnery exercises in Grafenwoehr as well as lots of field exercises around Schweinfurt. Then I came home one night with a new set of deployment orders.

"Turkey," I told Kathreyn.

"Excuse me?" she asked.

"We're going to Turkey."

She threw her arms around me again. To her, Turkey meant no combat, no war. I had to explain to her, "We'll probably get deployed to Iraq out of Turkey." Her face fell. She didn't want me to go anywhere, but our unit started rotation briefings, and we prepared to ship troops, beans, and bullets to Turkey. But it wasn't more than a few days later when those orders were cancelled as well.

Not knowing when and if we would be deployed was stressful. I'm not saying it was as stressful as actually being deployed, but we weren't allowed to go more than twenty minutes from home just in case we were called up again at the last minute. Twenty minutes will barely get you downtown, so we stayed close to home.

Then one day I carried orders through the door once again.

"Iraq," I told her. "Iraq."

Kathreyn's face fell. It was not what she wanted to hear, but it was what we had been expecting. You couldn't walk by the *Stars and Stripes* newsstand or surf the internet without seeing reports of fighting in the streets of Baghdad, emails from family members, photographs of what was happening to Saddam Hussein. Every soldier in my unit wanted the chance to engage the enemy, and the sooner the better.

The first thing I told her was, "I don't want you focused on the news when I'm over there. We only get one TV channel, the Armed Forces Network (AFN), and don't believe what you read online. Just wait for me to call."

She asked me, "Every time I hear about Iraq, how am I supposed to know where you are?"

"I'll keep you posted through email and phone calls as often as I can. Just don't worry. I'm going to be fine."

Our unit was given block leave, and Kathreyn and I decided to fly home to Texas to show off our little family. It would be my last chance to see my parents and family before going to war, and that purpose for the trip remained unspoken. We talked about having Kat remain stateside, but she wouldn't hear of it.

"I want to be in Schweinfurt, near rear detachment. That's the only way I'm going to find out what's really going on." She'd become friends with other spouses in our family readiness group, and they'd all agreed to stick together while we were deployed. "They're my family, now," she told me.

When we returned to Germany, I tried to fill her with reassurances, while the briefings I received at work gave me a different picture of what was in front of us. Violence had increased throughout Iraq, and there was no telling when I'd actually be able to reach her with any news, good or bad.

The entire community showed up to send us off from the post gymnasium. We had only a few minutes before we'd load onto our buses and head for the airfield. I held my wife tightly, Lizzie wedged between us in a little cocoon. I pressed my hand against her tiny palm. Kathreyn had made a little fabric book for her called *Who Loves Baby?*, and I pointed to one of many pictures of me in the album.

"Daddy," I told her. "Daddy loves baby." Kathreyn and I looked at each other, overwhelmed with emotion. There were no words; we'd said them all.

In typical Army wife fashion, Kat sent me off with kisses and prayers.

8

SOLDIER BOY

There might have been some folks who disagreed with our mission or role in the Middle East, but there was solidarity amongst soldiers. We knew what was in front of us. No matter what the media said back in the States, we were never confused. We traveled by bus to Nurnburg, and loaded up on a commercial flight bound for Kuwait. There wasn't a lot of noise on the trip to the airport. As I looked behind me at the sea of soldiers offloading from the bus, I felt proud to be part of this unit. We were the cavalry, and we were ready to get to work. A cav squadron is divided into subgroups called troops, and I had been with my current troop for only a few months. Our troop was further divided into platoons, and my platoon commander didn't care for me. He thought I was just a dumb, older guy. In my mind I was thinking, *Get me to the battlefield.* I had a lot to prove.

The Army breaks down its personnel hierarchy into four basic categories, officers (O-1 to O-11), warrant officers (W-1 to W-5), enlisted noncommissioned officers (NCO, E-4 to E-9), and enlisted (E-1 to E-4). Officers serve based on presidential appointment and can resign their commissions at any time with stipulations; enlisted service members join the Army based on their agreement to serve for a specific period of time and are not free to leave the military until their current enlistment contract has been satisfied.

If you're an enlisted soldier, the day you start basic training, you're an E-1. If you want to be promoted up the ladder, you do so through training, performance, and/or schooling. I was an E-4, and there were a lot of young kids who had the same rank as me who'd joined the military right out of high school. But my Bradley Fighting Vehicle (BFV) commander was career military, an NCO or E-6, and he assumed I was someone who had joined the military as a last resort. There was a stereotype about guys my age that didn't have any rank. "What'd you do to screw up, Harris?" he asked me.

"Nothing, Sergeant. Just joined to serve after 9/11."

He wasn't hearing it, and loaded me down with all of his gear. As I passed through the airplane scales, I realized I'd become my commander's grunt. With my weight of 170 and the gear I was humping, I was at nearly five hundred pounds total while he was traveling hands-free.

The plane was huge, with twin turbines, able to carry all we had. We dumped our gear in cargo storage and settled into our seats, prepared for departure. I was mentally winding down and ready to take a nap. I talked to the lieutenant sitting next to me for a few minutes; we agreed it was smart to catch some sleep.

The jet took off, ascending at a sixty-degree angle into the sky. As I looked out the window for one more glance at friendly soil, the right engine exploded. My first thought was, *Oh my God, I'm going to die and we're not even going to make it to Iraq.* The plane remained at its ascending angle but began to sink toward the ground. I had my eyes shut, trying not to imagine the chaos of crashing before our mission had even begun. The pilot leveled us off and got the jet safely on the ground. There was a fair amount of cussing and praying that washed over the crowd of soldiers around me. I'd venture to say there were a few of us who needed to change our underwear as well.

After we caught our breath, nerves jangled, we loaded our gear back onto buses and headed for Kaiserslautern, where we'd attempt to leave again, this time on another commercial flight that we prayed was in better shape. It was a long flight; we were pretty subdued after the first failed attempt. Most of us slept, knowing the next year would give us ample sleepless nights. In the darkened sky over Asia, I felt the plane rise in altitude before the loadmaster announced our descent onto the airstrip at Kuwait. I looked at the soldiers around me and tried to memorize their faces, hoping we'd all sit and drink a beer together when our mission was done.

Our first thirty days in training were dedicated to getting us acclimated to the heat. If you've never lived in the desert before, it can take some adjustment. Sand and grit got into everything I owned, and the air turned red as the temperatures rose. Our home for the next month would be a tent set up for six dozen soldiers pitched next to seven hundred other tents with six dozen soldiers apiece. There were thousands of us waiting for deployment into Iraq. We took turns getting bussed to Camp Buehring for training, our vehicles making their way through a blackout of sand and wind. When the sandstorms died down, there was nothing to see but miles and miles of desert terrain interrupted by the movement of nomadic Bedouin tribes herding their goats, camels, or sheep across the sand. It was desolate. Named for LTC Charles H. Buehring, one of the highest ranking US casualties of war at the time of his death in October 2003, the camp was set up to take care of preparing us for combat.

● ● ●

At Camp Buehring we were issued more protective gear, particularly our Kevlar body armor. We were told we'd need it. The Kevlar reminded me a little bit of the gladiator movies I'd watched over the years. We had our own version of sword and shield. Unlike its ancient counterpart, our shield was worn as a vest, a complex ceramic compound backed with polyethylene and shaped into armor plates. The synthetic fibers of the Kevlar vest are five times as strong as steel, and if you stretched the layers of fabric from end to end, they'd equal twenty-one yards of lightweight, pliable, antiballistic material.

Kevlar's the stuff used to replace steel belts in racing tires. It's sturdy and pliable. Bullets aren't deflected off Kevlar; they become embedded in this "spider web" of material and most of the time cause minimal body trauma. With additional ceramic plates in the front, back, and sides for greater protection, the armored vest added about twenty pounds. The ceramic plates are made from a compound of boron oxide with a backing of polyethylene, the same material you find in plastic shopping bags. This combination is extremely hard and heavy.

We were told the vest had considerably upped the survivability rate of the Iraq war, and that was good news. Parts of your body unprotected by the vest were a different story. One of the trainers told me, "Watch your shoulders. First shot through your unit patch goes straight to the heart."

You never had the impression that you were armored to the point of being impenetrable.

We carried a couple of "swords," including an M-4 compact rifle with a shortened barrel, scope, and telescoping butt stock that didn't take long to heat up. I called her "Sweety" and she became a trusted friend. We were also issued an M-9 9mm Beretta semiautomatic pistol that weighed a couple of pounds.

Our battle dress camouflage was a maze of desert-colored patterns that would make us blend in with the sand and dirt of rural and urban areas, as well as the varied types of vegetation we'd find in Iraq. We were given helmets with Kevlar technology as well as night vision goggles, giving new meaning to the term "big-headed." With commo attached, we were wired for duty. Our boots were standard issue, lightweight yet as sturdy as possible. One thing we learned we'd need to reorder pretty often was cotton socks. The heat made sweat pour out of your feet, and there was nothing worse than mucking around in that pond of bacteria and fungi you created in the bottom of your boots.

Our trainers were set on getting us ready for war, which included work on identifying and dealing with the threat that was taking lives every day: IEDs. Once our initial six weeks of training was completed, the rest would happen on the job. We returned to our tent city to prepare for transport into combat. There was a good bit of down time as we waited, time to think about where we were headed. We got "three hots a day" in the chow hall and took turns waiting in line to use the internet café. There was a large PX with plenty of creature comforts, except the ones you wanted most—your family.

9

TIME TRAVEL

On March 2, 2004, I crossed the border into a country that was once described as the jewel of Persia. Leaving Kuwait and traveling into Iraq was like stepping back in time hundreds of years. You left behind the modern skyline and entered a demilitarized zone void of anything new, modern, clean, or light. Dirt roads led nowhere; bombed-out buildings were home to no one but stray dogs and stray civilians; children were homeless and living off the garbage they found around their villages and towns. There was no mistaking the stench. I saw poverty unlike any I'd ever experienced in my life. We were in a war zone.

I knew exactly why we were here. These people needed help. All you had to do was cross into Iraq, west to east, to see that Saddam Hussein's oppression was rampant, the enemy was evil, and the Iraqi people deserved freedom.

● ● ●

Our unit was based at Tikrit, Samarra, and Baqubah. As Cavalry Scouts, we would make our way from one forward operating base (FOB) to another. The first FOB we called home was in Ad Dawr, near where Saddam Hussein had been captured. We were housed at an abandoned military installation. It had a water supply system in place and a few bunkers and concrete buildings converted into troop quarters. We weren't the first unit to be housed at FOB Wilson, but there was a lot of area to explore that seemed to have been left untouched.

We stored our gear in a big warehouse, occupying one area with cots, gear, and so forth. We spent our first few days working on our Bradley vehicles, clearing roads in the area, and running traffic control points. When we weren't on a mission, we spent some of our down time exploring the bunkers, warehouse, and living areas of FOB Wilson. The warehouse itself was cavernous, with an inner chamber walled off with glass. A couple of my buddies and I went in to explore, finding an office area full of gas masks and suits. We all wondered what the previous occupants had done in this space.

I remember thinking, *Geez, if this area is full of gas masks, what are we doing sleeping right next to this place?*

As we continued to explore our "home," I had the feeling that this was not a typical Iraqi military installation. Outside the warehouse, there was a set of bunkers near our vehicle maintenance area, and we decided to go inside, tactical flashlights out. The first bunker was full of tubs of chemicals, huge open drums of purple powder. We found scales, more gas masks, and chemical supplies. At the top of the bunker, bolted into the wall above our heads, was a small metal door large enough for us to crawl through. We went through the crawl space and entered another bunker that resembled a bomb shelter. It had a big hole in the roof. Inside the bomb shelter were metal spring frame bunks, no mattresses. Each bed had a pattern of indentation that resembled the shape of a human body. The room was filthy, and I had the sense that something bad had happened in this room. It looked like bodies had melted into the bunks, melted into the frames, and had been cleaned out.

We crawled through another hatch that led to a smaller compartment, but changed our minds as it narrowed and backed out of the hole.

"I don't know about you, man, but I'm not sure I want to go in there."

We didn't know if we were exposing ourselves to chemicals or radiation and decided to explore that area another time. It was kind of creepy. We returned to the first bunker, and the young specialist who was with me was running his hands through the tubs of purple powder. "Stop," I told him. "You don't know what that crap is."

In this first bunker there was a desk, and I began to rummage through the drawers. I found papers written in Arabic, French, and English, and also a bottle of pills with a warning label in three languages, "Take two when exposed to radiation or contaminants."

I stuck the bottle of pills in my pocket, thinking I just might need them based on what we'd seen so far. I also wanted to show them to my commander.

We found a door that led to another bunker that was full of radio equipment, handheld military-grade radios, and communication materials. Everything was covered with dust and debris, but it was clear that the equipment had been used at some point. We walked down to the last bunker and found a pile of missile warheads, undeployed chemical rockets. I was starting to get a very sobering picture of what we were dealing with. We'd located a bunker with a testing chamber, a bunker full of chemicals, a bunker full of commo equipment, and a bunker full of missile warheads. This had clearly been a compound used for making and dispensing weapons of chemical warfare.

I took the information we'd found and brought it to the captain. He was fascinated with what we'd found and started his own investigation. Within twenty-four hours, the unit area was filled with people whom I can only assume were CIA. About a dozen agents dressed in civilian clothes and armed with weapons, cameras, and equipment came on scene. They cordoned off the area with tape, confiscated our camera data cards, and took my pills.

My captain told me, "This is way above your pay grade," and told us to stay out of the way. Within a few days, we were moved to another FOB to resume the mission we'd been sent to accomplish.

10

BAND OF BROTHERS

ome sweet home became the inside of the Bradley. The Bradley is an Infantry armored fighting vehicle and is set up to transport soldiers while providing cover fire to suppress the enemy. It can hold a crew of three—the commander, gunner, and driver—as well as six soldiers. There's a 25mm chain-gun cannon, a tank-destroying missile launcher, and a machine gun on board. I was a dismount/gunner/driver, which means I rode or stood in the back of the vehicle, with a weapon trained on the area around us. From that position, I could swivel my body and machine gun to reach the enemy, but I was exposed a good bit as well. We traveled extensively, and I was ready for my first taste of combat. Soaking up every bit of training as a new recruit, I was ready to prove myself. Our cavalry regiment was the tip of the spear; it was our job to find the insurgents and attack.

As we traveled the roads around the FOB, our ammo and weapons constantly filled with grit. We'd spend half the night with brushes of various sorts, using even our toothbrushes to scrub out the sand that accumulated in our weapons. We stored our gear on the exterior of the vehicle, trying to make use of the interior for sleeping or staying out of the heat, but it was crowded, noisy, and hot. The weight and motion of the tracked vehicle made baby powder out of the soil and dirt, and it was hard to get rid of the grit.

Green rice fields were interrupted by random dirt trails, flanked with date palms and more detritus from the bombings and explosions of preceding combatants who'd worked this same region. The vegetation was sturdy and hopeful; olive trees grew from clods of dirt mixed with explosive debris. We inspected homes and huts built centuries ago, stones wedged together in intricate detail through primitive means, while we stood guard in twenty-first-century battle gear. Bread ovens sat in the farmyards, constructed from bricks made of goat dung mixed with clay from the riverbeds. I felt like a stranger in a strange land.

After leaving FOB Wilson, we moved to another location and took possession of some old bunkers on an airbase about fifty kilometers from Samarra—FOB McKenzie. For housing, the military had moved in some portables, and three of us were assigned to one hooch. Our temporary lodging was desolate, deserted, and right out in the open. There was very little protection from the elements or the enemy. We didn't have anywhere to store our gear, so we started running missions around the base, trying to reconnoiter any spare wood or furniture we could find to upgrade our living quarters.

It's amazing what can be built with old pallets and ammo crates. Using our "Yankee ingenuity," we built bunk beds. We could sleep on top and store all our gear below. We wanted room for chairs and a place to hang out, so we found some huge nails and pounded them into the wall of our hooch so we could hang up most of our stuff. The walls of the hooch were so thin the nails came out the other side, so from the exterior our temporary home resembled a huge porcupine. Though it didn't rain often, when it did the rain would pour through those nail holes. The first sergeant got so mad he made us remove the nails and repair the holes. We would leave most of our personal belongings at FOB McKenzie, then deploy on missions that could last two to three weeks at a time.

Our primary job was to run traffic control points (TCP), as well as clear primary transportation routes and conduct terrain analysis. Our troop was the reserve unit for the division or brigade, and we were used as a flex platoon. As our unit moved, we'd have to catch up with them. US Forces were moving north, focusing tactical operations on Tikrit and Kirkuk. As tactical operations moved north, thousands of vehicles tried to flee from Samarra. We protected the outer cordon of Samarra, capturing people, ammo, and supplies, anything or anyone that was suspect. At night we'd set up over-watch positions, conducting surveillance of high-risk IED areas.

As we captured insurgents or anyone with suspicious cargo or connections, we took statements and then moved them to detainee areas. Plastic zip ties worked as lightweight, low-tech handcuffs on the battlefield.

● ● ●

When I was acting as dismount, I walked through the dirt next to the roadways, searching for trip wires or any foreign objects that might warn of explosives. It was not a high-tech job. It required astute observation, as we didn't have many gadgets or gizmos to do what we'd been trained to do. As the war went on, more sophisticated methods would be developed to detect explosives, but the foot soldier was basically the cornerstone of our detection system at this point in the war. Our radar was between our eyes and ears.

Some rocks looked a little less than random along the road, and I would kneel carefully in the sand, picking apart some gravel next to my boot. Bombs were hidden in and around anything—dead or alive.

Once we discovered bombs in place, we'd send for the explosive ordnance disposal (EOD) team to disarm or detonate or do it ourselves. We'd secure the area, but if the EOD team was delayed, we'd try to destroy the IED by firing at it from several hundred yards away. The EOD was usually comprised of bomb technicians who suited up in bomb suits and operated a remote-controlled minesweeper. If there was no conflicting mission, we'd assist the EOD by providing cover. After the bomb had been disarmed or detonated, that piece of road could be considered safe for a short window of time, hopefully long enough to travel through.

When we found a hot zone, each soldier in the patrol climbed out of the BFV to expand the search, weapons drawn and ready. When explosions were heard, we would hunker down. Huge blasts could rip open roads, leaving craters from the size of a refrigerator to a Mack truck. Our squad would hide in the undergrowth, trying to locate the insurgents who'd set the traps. If you spotted a civilian running from the site, you fired in his direction to help discern his innocence. You knew if he was running away, he was probably guilty. If he returned fire, it was on.

During this deployment, I learned a little Arabic and tossed in some sign language, which gave me a way to communicate with the locals. We had to rely on our handbooks, but it was not hard to adapt to the language as you were asking the same sets of questions over and over. Based on the intelligence shared with us, the insurgency was gearing up for increased activity, calling the threat "Bloody Easter." Things were going downhill at Fallujah fast.

●●●

We were feeling excited to be in the action; everyone was mission ready. We were broken up into hunter-killer teams made up of two Bradleys and one tank, and the five-ton trucks convoying our equipment and supplies were deployed separately. Our gear would be carried to Fallujah, and we'd meet up with it later.

En route to the waiting conflict, the wheel hub on the company XO's tank shattered, and we were stuck waiting on parts. As we sat in the pitch black, using our night vision goggles, we soon spotted several blackout lights headed our way. All of a sudden we had Humvees with mounted artillery all around us. The truck commander yelled, "What the hell are you doing in our AO (area of operation)?"

The XO told him we were waiting on parts, and the two started talking. Apparently this was a light Infantry unit, tracked vehicles with Humvees, and they were getting shot at and hurt. They asked our unit for help. The XO called back to the commander to get permission to assist. It sounded like this was going to be a real fight for us, but I felt like I'd been run over. My allergies were kicking my butt. While we waited for the tank parts to arrive, I found the team medic and got some relief. I'd been nauseated all afternoon, and my head was stuffed so full I could hardly breathe. I told the medic, "Gimme whatever you've got. I can't afford to be sick." I took three or four antihistamines and returned to the Bradley. It was time to roll.

As our team traveled into Baqubah, we could see the firestorm ahead, and discovered it was coming from an insurgent position set up in the local hospital. Protocol dictated that we were not to fire on soft targets like community centers, clinics, or hospitals, but the Infantry unit had taken a severe beating. They'd already lost a company grade officer in a mortar attack, as well as several members of their unit.

The fight continued to worsen the deeper we traveled into the village. Between the two Bradleys and the repaired tank, we were able to answer with heavier firepower than the light artillery. It was spray and pray combat—we hoped to run off the innocent and immobilize the guilty. Rocket-propelled grenades volleyed back and forth, and we targeted various sections of the city as we increased speed. As a soldier, you knew this was the kind of battle where it was probably time to say goodbye to your arms or legs, if not your life, yet that's what you'd prepared to do. Our attitudes were a mixture of fear and excitement; the adrenaline was pumping.

I yelled at my buddy, "If we get hit with one of those, we're done! This is bad juu-juu!" and we continued to volley shots with the enemy. When we heard bullets going past us, we started firing the 25mm Bushmaster at the enemy, popping out of the hatch to lob a grenade, sinking down in the turret to traverse, and popping up again. Our explosives left the local buildings in shambles, gutting walls and whoever was hiding behind them. A lot of what I saw through the back periscope on the BFV indicated enemy fire continued to rain down from the nearby hospital. You couldn't leave the hatch up on the Bradley because the turret had to traverse, so we were popping up and down out of the vehicle.

After a few rounds, the gun jammed. The gunner moved the gun barrel so we could pop up the back hatch of the Bradley to provide rear support while he and the Bradley commander worked on the jam. My insides were churning, but there was no way to deal with it. I just kept firing. We fired .203 ammo rounds toward rooftops and the hospital to keep the enemy suppressed until the Bradley could reengage using the thermal sights and HEAT (high explosive antitank) rounds.

After a few short moments we were up and running again in the turret. We dropped back down in the Bradley and continued offensive fire. As the hours went by, the return fire diminished and we felt pretty sure we'd killed some bad guys and run many more of them off. Through the quiet, we kept a keen eye on our surroundings, using the time to regroup and catch our breath.

We remained on high alert throughout the next couple of days, patrolling for IEDs and any significant movements in sector. The enemy had settled down a good bit. During a brief period of quiet, we were taking a breather when I heard a loud pop and saw some dust blow off the side of our armor. I looked up at the roofline and watched as an insurgent aimed at me with his AK-47.

Everybody was yelling, "Take him out!" He had his eyes right on me, and started taking off when I began to lock and load the 40 mil .203 grenade launcher. I put it on the rooftop. I don't know if I got him but he was quiet after that.

We continued to patrol the area for IEDs, finding one along a row of concrete curbing beside the road. You could see how one section of cement had been removed and replaced with a fake curb, the outline of the artillery round exposed in the concrete. We tried to shoot it with a 25mm armor-piercing round, but it just bounced off the cement. The Bradley vehicle has a 25mm cannon that can take various types of ammo, so we ordered a few rounds of depleted uranium to destroy the IED. It's not something that gets used a lot. When our commander found out we ordered DU rounds, he cussed us out.

We used a HEAT round instead.

By day four, we looked like a rangy group of gypsies. Some of us had nearly full beards and we looked pretty bad. We hadn't bathed, hadn't shaved, hadn't washed, hadn't eaten anything but MREs. I was fighting a bad case of dysentery and was losing it at both ends on a fairly frequent basis. Even if we wanted to clean up, all our gear had been forwarded to Fallujah with the first convoy before we got diverted.

We had quite a bit of ammo left over, so instead of turning it in, we started shooting each other. We were shooting crowd suppressors (Nerf rounds) into each other's Kevlar vests to see if we could knock one another down. The .203 has a 40mm grenade launcher mounted on the bottom of the M-4, and the Nerf rounds we used resembled a small beanbag. I got shot with a beanbag that nearly knocked me out. I fired back at my buddy using more Nerf rounds. You didn't cut up with ammo when anyone was looking, and we sure as heck didn't know the colonel was coming around the corner. His first words were, "Have you lost your freaking minds?"

He started in on the senior NCOs and then tore into us. We stood at attention and took our licks when the XO came out from behind his tank to defend us. The young lieutenant went to bat for us, explaining that we were doing them a favor by diverting to his AO to assist. We all stood quiet, waiting for that to sink in with the commander.

"Well then, I guess I'm here to say thank you," he said. He took a closer look at us. "You guys look like hell. You're disgusting." He aimed his icy stare over at his captain.

"Why do these guys look like crap?" While we waited on an answer, I shoved my ammo in my pocket.

The XO explained that our gear had been en route to Fallujah when the firefight began. The colonel gave the XO hell for not getting us what we needed to clean up. We were told to get ready to move out and were given some housing, showers, and USO shaving kits to clean up. I took turns throwing up in the ditch while we got briefed on where we were going next. They finally sent me back to the FOB for an IV when I nearly passed out. I'd survived my first actual combat experience, and despite the sickness I was ready and willing to go at it again.

11

MISSION READY

Finished with the support mission, we were diverted from Fallujah to resume traffic control outside Samarra. The city was locked down. No traffic was allowed unless civilians could prove the necessity. One day a cab driver with a chip on his shoulder came through our checkpoint. We normally didn't have any trouble with him, but he got belligerent and nasty, and he was not agreeable to search and seizure. The senior NCO asked him, "Why are you trying to get smart with us? We're trying to protect your family."

He continued to rant and rave, so we pulled his car over for a thorough inspection. We found an armor-piercing round in his trunk, which was enough evidence to zip him up and send him to detainment. We began to tear his cab apart from end to end, looking for more evidence. He refused to give us any information about his collusion, and the more he protested, the more we tore up his vehicle. If he was helping the insurgents, we were going to use that against him.

He told us, "I drive cab, I drive cab," but cab drivers typically don't carry armor-piercing ammo. Through an interpreter, he confessed that he'd been threatened with assassination if he didn't carry weapons or ammo, and he was given a lot of money to transport enemy contraband in and out of Samarra. We put him in the back of the Humvee and dressed him in a helmet and camo shirt to disguise him as one of us so we could find his compound. He told us where the enemy was located, and we conducted surveillance for three days. The air cavalry sent Kiowa helicopters to conduct surveillance on the compound and forwarded the information to the commander.

We loaded up the Humvees and headed out to the middle of nowhere. We didn't want to give the villagers or enemy any reaction time, and swarmed the compound. We rolled up to the grouping of five or six buildings and raided the place with very little resistance. We broke up into teams and searched several buildings simultaneously. "Clear!" you could hear, as one building after another was checked. We spoke to the dirt farmers in the compound, and they swore to Allah that they were not doing anything wrong. There was a trench running down the center of the compound where it appeared the locals threw all their trash. There was no such thing as sanitation and the whole area reeked of raw sewage.

Our unit worked its way through the group of farmhouses and sheds, spreading out in an arc and closing the circle. One by one, we searched the outbuildings but found nothing more than tools and hardware. We blocked the rear door on a house with one team, and the other circled around to the front door, crawling beneath the windows and then rising as we reached the corner of the house. I kept my eyes trained on the windows overhead as well as on the second floor, expecting enemy fire. We crept alongside each other, weapons rising as we reached the front door.

I could hear my buddy's breath in short, jagged snorts from his nose and nudged him. "Settle down, we're good."

Helmets low on our head, body armor covering our hearts, we were about to see if our protection was enough. The platoon sergeant looked at each of us to see if we were ready, then prepared to fire as he burst through the door. We followed him, a huge surge of adrenaline kicking in as we entered the front room. You could see dishes of food on the table, steam coming from a full teacup, so we knew the house had been occupied. The sergeant burst into the next room, weapon drawn, and found no one. "Clear," he called out.

We started to search the perimeter, knowing that based on the information we were given by the cab driver, there had to be weapons or ammo in the area. Everyone was detained; the men were zip-tied and separated from the women and children. Some of the women began to cry and wail, and we continued to conduct our inspection. An older woman wrapped her abaya around the children next to her, her black robe providing little protection from what could happen next. Again, the men swore to Allah that they were simple dirt farmers. As we questioned them, their answers implicated no one and everyone. There wasn't a soldier there who believed they were innocent.

Standing in that compound, my buddy and I looked out across the farm, and both of us commented simultaneously that one field looked too well groomed, out of character, suspicious. Right out in the middle of the neatly plowed field was a small island of debris, roots, rocks, and branches. We nearly ran to the center of the field, we were so sure we'd found what we were looking for.

When we reached the debris pile, we found a huge hole in the ground. A ladder descended about twelve feet underground. The underground bunker was well constructed, like a storm cellar you'd find at a farmhouse, with wall and roof supports to keep it from caving in. Entering the hole, we found a huge cache of explosives and ammo, estimated at over two thousand pounds. There were American weapons in the hole: grenades, ammo, and machine guns, as well as old Russian AK-47s and ammo. We found Soviet Stinger missiles and hundreds of rounds of munitions that these simple dirt farmers shouldn't have had.

One of the important lessons we learned from that search was that if the women were crying, it was probably a life-or-death situation. From that point on, if we went into a house on a search and someone started boo-hooing, something was wrong and someone was guilty. We didn't have any women assigned to our unit to assist with interrogating or searching Iraqi women or children. It was a cultural taboo to put those women through the process we used with the men. Later that year, a National Guard unit would join us to assist with interrogating females. We'd learned that in spite of the Iraqis' claim to hide and shelter their women, they would treat them like crap and would strap them with C-4 to turn them into suicide bombers when necessary. We needed our own females to protect them as well as us. But in the meantime, we had gleaned some wisdom from this raid. Tears spelled trouble.

After we found the weapons cache, we loaded up the prisoners. We were still in tactical mode, highly alert, but felt the danger was primarily averted.

● ● ●

We felt sure we'd found the bulk of the weapons and ammo cache, but the commander wanted us to do a final sweep of the area for any remaining ammo or weapons. My buddy and I walked around one small house, and hearing some noise, wanted to investigate. We'd already rounded up all the people in the compound, or so we thought. I carried Sweety up, ready to gun and run.

As I turned the corner, I came nose to nose with an Iraqi. I aimed Sweety right at him, ready to fire into his cheekbone, and I almost shot him. But I could tell something wasn't right. He couldn't have been more than a teenager, but he was severely retarded. His face was disfigured and grotesque. As he charged me, my finger rested on the trigger, but I didn't fire. He had no weapon. He was tethered to a stump in the ground, with a rope around his leg. As I looked closer, I found the rope had been embedded in his leg for so long that the skin had mushroomed up around it. He was covered in piss and feces and stank like hell. He had whip marks and wounds on his body. I could only assume he'd been beaten and tortured by his own family. It made me sick to my stomach.

I ran back to where our NCO was standing in front of the detainees. "Sir, did you see what they're doing? There's a human being back there tied up like a dog. He's covered with crap. They should be shot for treating someone like that."

I was enraged. I looked at one of the men we'd pulled from that house. "What are you doing? Don't you realize this is a human being? Where is your decency? Are you even human?" I looked at the commander, expecting him to take corrective action. I wanted him to hold someone accountable for the inhumane treatment of this young man. I was fuming and furious.

He told me, "Simmer down, don't get involved. We're not the civil police. You're not social services. Stay in your lane."

He could tell I was frustrated, and asked me, "Where are you going to take him? There's nowhere else to go."

I looked down at my uniform and thought about the man I was and the warrior ethos within . . . *I will always place the mission first.* There was no way any of us would treat another human being the way that young man was being treated. But there was a question in my gut, something that was becoming unanswerable in war: What can the human heart handle? I remembered what my dad had told me about war, about the hell of it. He was right.

We knew that same compound would be a hot zone again; it would get added to the inventory of houses we'd cleared and buildings we'd need to clear again. No one in our squad had been injured or killed, making it an ugly but good day in Iraq. As we headed back to our FOB, I thought about the soldiers next to me. We were a close-knit group. Life at war with my fellow soldiers was everything I'd hoped it would be, even if hell was all around us.

12

ARMY STRONG

We slept, ate, and did everything together in close proximity, a kinship rapidly developing between us. Mealtime and mail time were important parts of the day. We ate a lot of MREs or mystery meat. Salmon in a pouch, pound cake in foil, meatloaf in congealed gravy—the whole point of an MRE was to give you a bunch of calories in a limited amount of time. I didn't mind the rations. We invented a new casserole by mixing peanut butter with liquid cheese and pouring it over spaghetti. It sounds nasty, but if you had a bottle of Tabasco, it was almost edible. Hot sauce was golden. If you had a bottle, you could barter for just about anything.

Water was golden as well. With temperatures that could go up and over 140 degrees and seventy pounds of armor and ammo weighing us down, water was vital for survival. Sometimes we'd get T-rations (T-rats) shipped to the unit, big premade trays of food that were heated up and served in our unit area. One night they served us snow crab legs and it was all I could do to try seafood when it was over a hundred degrees in the shade, but I was so sick of MREs it was worth the risk. The guys I broke bread with were like brothers. We fought with each other, teased one another, and would fall on our swords for each other if the situation required it.

We had a bunch of soldiers assigned to our unit from the country of Georgia. They looked like a cross between mercenaries and gypsies. They were kind of ragamuffins, and when we had extra socks, underwear, toiletries, or whatever, we'd pass them along to these guys. They loved their weapons, and were always walking around with a pile of rocket launchers on their backs, similar to how you'd see an archer carry a quiver of arrows.

When I was getting over a bout of dysentery, one of our Georgian soldiers decided to try one of his home remedies on me. We'd been pulling guard duty, and I was sick. He asked me using sign language, "You hungry?" He made a motion with his fingers, like he was putting food in his mouth. I nodded, but rubbed my stomach with a painful look on my face. He stood watch while I puked in the ditch. I was leaning over, hands on my knees, when I heard a loud pop. We were not supposed to be firing our weapons, and I jolted up. He'd just shot a black bird.

"What the heck are you doing?"

He plucked all the feathers off, then rammed a sharp stick through the hole the bullet had left. He started a small fire in the ditch next to us, and squatted in the dirt, roasting that dead bird over the fire. When it was fully done, he presented me with my meal; it was the first time I actually ate crow.

If we were pulled off the road on a short halt, we would send money to a street vendor for a kabob or a loaf of flatbread. We weren't supposed to do it, but sometimes you wanted something, anything but an MRE. Most of the meat you saw hanging in the local markets was pretty raw and rangy looking, and it was hard to believe that this was what the locals ate on a daily basis. The goats in the marketplace weren't there to graze; they'd be slaughtered on demand and skinned on the spot, the fly-infested raw meat hanging on a hook until it was grilled or steamed. No, thanks.

One day we stopped by a farmhouse and the man of the house offered to cook us a chicken. He grabbed the bird out of the yard, hacked its head off, and came back forty-five minutes later with a fully roasted meal. It was delicious. After that, when we were desperately hungry for home-cooked food, we'd snare a chicken and get a local to do the same thing again.

I reached Kathreyn after two weeks of back-to-back missions. She asked, "How've you been?"

"Good," I told her. I always said that, regardless of how many land mines we'd found, how many soldiers were gone, how much destruction I'd witnessed. How do you start those sentences, those conversations? I shared what I could.

"Got the pictures, can't believe how everyone's grown," I said. "Hey, I really need some new sunglasses. Can we swing it?"

I was very specific: Oakley's, antiballistic lenses, carbon fiber frames, totally cool. I overlooked the price tag of three hundred dollars, telling her they were exactly what I needed. When mail arrived with those Oakley's, I was ecstatic. No more dollar-store sunglasses for me. No more GI-issue shades. These were the real deal. I called her as soon as I could. "You don't know how badly I needed those!"

"Your dad said next time get them at Dollar General."

I laughed. "I don't think they sell Oakley's," I said, and told her I'd send a photo soon.

Continuous patrols throughout the combat theater continued for months on end, with casualties mounting by the day. We were making progress against the enemy in our sector, but it was slow going and the end was not in sight. I ticked off the days on my calendar. R&R couldn't come quickly enough. Kathreyn shared news with me about home. "Lizzie ate her first banana . . ."

At mail call one day I received a letter from my two boys back in Texas. Albert had lost his first tooth, and Nicolas had made his first peewee league touchdown. News from home was welcome but it messed with my emotions. It was hard to be a warrior and a dad simultaneously. I sat by myself for an hour, celebrating and commiserating at the same time. It was hard to miss those firsts.

Soldiers live for windows. The length of time you're in country can seem daunting, but if you looked at the timeline you were on, with the opportunities for R&R or end-of-tour, it made the days bearable. You knew your family was doing the same thing. There were so many things you just expected your spouse to handle in your absence.

● ● ●

After six months of deployment, we returned to a quiet homecoming at Schweinfurt. The rear detachment commander told us, "No snow skiing. You're going back in two weeks."

When Kat and Lizzie picked me up at the unit headquarters, I heard the best thing I'd heard in months, "Dadda." Lizzie recognized me, and she could say my name.

"Man, I can't believe she remembers me."

Kat held up the little book that had been in Lizzie's hand when I left. "I filled this with your pictures, and she reads it every night." I squeezed both my girls in my arms, and we headed home.

Kat asked a lot of questions while I was on leave, but I didn't want to talk a lot about the war. For one thing, I didn't want to scare her, but there were things she'd heard on the news that I had to clear up for her. She asked me, "I know not to believe a lot of what the news says, but how bad was it?"

In my mind, I wanted to tell her, "It's bad."

I looked at my bride. She'd given up everything to follow me to Germany, only to be left alone in a foreign country while I lived a brutal life. How do you tell your wife about your fellow soldier losing a leg, or another warrior fighting a losing battle with PTSD? I knew she would relive those stories in her mind, long after I was back in harm's way, and I just didn't want to make it harder than it was. She said the stories she got in the local military paper and the ones she heard online or from friends back in the States didn't match. A lot of what was reported was lost in translation, and yet, depending on the news agency doing the reporting, the coverage could become clear as day or as muddled as mud.

She asked me about injuries, and I tried to tell her what I wanted her to hear, versus the truth. I didn't want her worrying about explosions day in and day out.

"Kat, just because you see something on the news from Iraq doesn't mean it's happening in my sector. Even if it's five miles away from me, it might not have anything to do with my unit. It's a huge country." I tried to hug it out with her. "Don't worry, baby. I'm home."

Yet in my mind our homecoming was bittersweet. The real heroes had already gone home, their simple wooden coffins draped with the flag of our country. As great as it was to be home, there was something unsettling about being away from my unit. The job was unfinished, and when it was time to say goodbye to my family once again, I was ready. Lizzie held my neck, and Kathreyn had to pry her little fingers away when it was time to say goodbye. "We're halfway," I told them. "We're almost done."

13

GOING BACK

Back in theater, we resumed duties with traffic control. I was the gunner on our first day back; our normal gunner was back in the States on R&R. One day, on a run from the traffic control point, our Bradley ran over a road that had been troubled with IEDs. We were careful, but the road was pocked with holes. Suddenly a blast erupted in front of us, rocking the BFV backward in the dirt. The IED was hardwired; someone had hit a trigger and they hit it too soon. There were enough explosives to rock our vehicle.

I was watching the road through my periscope, and when the blast hit, I saw rocks, fragments, dirt, and then blue sky before we rocked back to earth again. I tried to radio the driver to get off the road and out of the vehicle, but my commo cable had detached in the blast. Staff Sergeant Perez, the Bradley commander, was in the turret, and the explosion had covered him with debris. I started kicking the turret, trying to get the driver to get off the road so I could figure out what was wrong with SSG Perez. I was thinking, *His face is going to be hamburger meat*, and wasn't ready for that, but I kept calling, "Staff Sergeant Perez, Sergeant Perez!" I checked the two dismounts to see if they were okay, and started trying to wake up SSG Perez.

He'd been knocked unconscious, and when he came to he started saying, "I'm screwed up, I'm screwed up," and wouldn't pull his hands down from his face. I expected to see the worst.

I called him by his first name, "Carlos, Carlos, come on, you gotta take your hands down so I can figure out what happened to you."

When he pulled his hands down, I was relieved to see his face. It was covered with burn marks and tar, and his glasses were covered with debris that had melted in the blast, but I told him, "Dude, you're good. You're okay. You've just got tar stuck to your face." He was burned but he was okay.

He said, "I'm messed up."

I tried to reassure him, "No, you're good. You're shook up but you're good. You're okay, you just got tar stuck to your face and your glasses are covered with crap."

He shook it off and we got busy checking the other soldiers on the vehicle. The desert heat had made an enemy of the pounds of protective gear we wore, but it was all worth it when it came to avoiding injury. It had been a close call, but we handled it together, as a team.

I took an informal role as team counselor. SSG Perez and I became really close after that IED blast, and he finally trusted me on the squad. He was a leader and mentor to me, and I watched how he operated. Even though I was a lot older than many of my fellow soldiers of same rank, we were peers and they felt safe talking to me. We'd go over Dear John letters, news from home, and whatever was bothering us on any given day. We all needed each other that way.

A few soldiers came to talk to me after we'd been in an engagement. Combat turns a teenager into a man in a matter of hours. When a kid has a near-death experience on the battlefield, you can watch his face change over the course of the day. There are tears, prayers, relief, unbelief, and by the time he's processed what happened to him, he's not a kid anymore.

One of my soldiers had a girlfriend and a wife, which isn't the way you're supposed to do things, but he needed some help nonetheless. He told me, "I told my wife I want a divorce, but I can't stand not being there for my kids."

"That's important; those kids need you," I told him.

"But I'm in love with this Arabic girl in Germany. She's got me twisted in knots. Her parents don't want her to have anything to do with me."

"That's understandable," I explained. "Look at where we are."

There was no convincing him to stick it out with his wife. He was determined to end things and try to make it work with the girlfriend. I felt sorry for his wife and kids, trying to make things work stateside, clueless to what he was doing with his Laura of Arabia. He had twenty minutes on the phone each day, and he took turns calling either his girlfriend or his wife.

I had a hard time getting in line to use the phone. Twenty minutes just wasn't enough time. Some days I'd look at the line for the computer stations, and then look at the lines for the phones, and choose the shortest one. I could usually whip out a few emails faster than I could make a phone call, and hearing Kathreyn's voice was hard. I didn't like to say the words, "Good-bye."

● ● ●

Near the end of our deployment, I was selected for ADVON, the advance team that returned home to prepare the barracks and take care of any issues related to the team's homecoming. I had a new baby when we left for Iraq, so they sent me home two weeks before everyone else to give me some extra time with Elizabeth. Getting picked for ADVON is kind of a double-edged sword. On the one hand you want to be with your family, but on the other hand you don't want anyone in your unit resenting you for leaving early. I really didn't want to leave my unit, but they needed a mature adult to take care of our return details, and they didn't want to send a barhop to do the job. I shipped out to Kuwait, was issued a clean uniform, and boarded a civilian aircraft to return to Germany. From the airport, we were bussed back to Schweinfurt, and the few of us in the advance party were reunited with our families.

Lizzie and Kathreyn were there to meet us, along with other members of the family readiness group, who wanted each and every soldier to get a warm welcome whether they had family there or not. The bulk of the unit would be returning in a couple more weeks, and in the meantime, I got inundated with phone calls and conversations about loved ones who were still overseas. Everyone wanted to hear how her spouse was doing.

I was an E-4 at that point, preparing for promotion to E-5 just two and a half years after enlisting. Kathreyn was really proud of me. The rear detachment commander told me I had enough points for promotion and had passed the selection board for E-5. I was hopeful the chain of command had approved my move up the ladder. I picked up a copy of the newspaper, the *Army Times*, and found my name on the E-5 promotion list. I called Kathreyn. "I made it! E-5!"

"Sergeant Harris, I am so proud of you!" she told me.

The rear detachment put together a quick promotion ceremony and pinned my new rank on before the unit returned from Iraq. Being on ADVON meant you weren't home to celebrate, you were there to prepare for the unit's homecoming, and as NCO SGT Harris, I had a new set of duties to perform.

The hardest part of being on ADVON was hearing about what happened downrange when you were away from battle. I was happy to see my new daughter and to spend time with the family, but it never left my mind for a second that our unit was still in harm's way. A few days before the unit returned, I got a call from one of the guys on rear detachment. He was being released from the Army, what we call "chaptered out," because he'd gotten in a lot of trouble before we were deployed. He told me, "Hey, we got the injury report and a list of KIA."

My heart sank.

He went on, "Kinzer's dead."

"Whoa whoa whoa," I answered. "What did you say?"

"Scott Kinzer, he got killed in action."

I was sitting at my house, on my couch, with my wife and my baby girl, hearing that one of my best friends had just been killed in an RPG attack in a raid on Dululyah, as part of Operation Sunrise. He'd been searching for residents harboring insurgents when he was killed. I was devastated, and I was so angry. I was so angry that I was sitting at home while he was in combat. If I could have gotten on a plane, returned to Iraq, and found retribution, I would have done it. I was furious at myself for not being there for him. The news just gutted me. Scott and I had been in the same platoon, and then he transferred to another troop. But we still kept in touch. Our friendship was significant to me. He was a real quiet guy and a great soldier. Everyone liked him. He was excited about getting married as soon as he got stateside. He was smart, older like me, and we hit it off early on.

I thought about a conversation we'd had before we got deployed. He opened up to me one night. "Hey, I really like you."

I laughed. "I'm not that kind of guy."

He said, "Screw you, I'm not gay."

"I know, man, I'm just kidding."

Scott told me, "I just admire who you are and I respect what you've gone through to get to this point."

"I feel the same way, man."

He asked me that night, "Can I call you my best friend?"

I told him, "I'm honored. Sure. You're one of the best people I know."

He said, "You're not like these other puppies," which was how he referred to a lot of the younger soldiers in the unit.

Hearing that he'd been killed just tore me up. An RPG is designed to kill a tank. I'd seen what it does to a human being. I knew he'd been killed instantly.

Kathreyn tried to comfort me. "You don't understand," I told her. "This guy was significant in my life, and in the life of every single person he met. Here I am on the couch, and I've got buddies over there getting shot."

I held my head in my hands. "He was such a good person. He had a full life ahead of him. Everyone loved him . . . he was soft-spoken, great-natured, super smart. It's just a terrible loss."

The unit created a memorial for him in front of the troop command center, and it honors the life and service of a great American, William Scott Kinzer. A memorial is a meaningful tribute but it just doesn't cover the loss. You don't get used to losing a fellow soldier or a friend. I was closer to my soldiers in just a few months than some of the people I'd known all my life back home.

When you lose a childhood friend, it's unexpected. But when you lose a brother in war, it's part of the job, part of what you signed up for, and there's no way to prepare for it even though you know it's going to happen. You've got to put that loss away, bury it down deep inside you someplace, because you still have a job to do. But every day I see their faces. And I think of every soldier we lost. Every day.

◆ ◆ ◆

ADVON received word that the troop had made it to Kuwait. They'd all be issued clean uniforms and then return to Germany. We staged the families in the gym for the homecoming. Because I was on ADVON, I was allowed to walk between the staging area and the area where the troops were setting up in formation to enter the gym. A soldier would ask me, "You see my wife, is she here?" and I'd go check.

"Yeah, man, she's here."

"Is my girlfriend out there?" another one would ask.

"Yeah, man, she's there."

"SGT Harris, you see my wife and kids?" another would say.

"They're here," I'd answer. I was like a Ping-Pong ball, bouncing back and forth between the troop formation and the family waiting area. Finally, the colors were posted and the troops entered the gym. The screams and applause were deafening. The 1st Infantry Division, 1st Squadron/4th Cavalry Regiment was home.

14

HOME IS WHERE
THE ARMY SENDS YOU

After I returned from my first deployment, Kathreyn, Lizzie, and I packed our suitcases, sent our household goods ahead as cargo, and headed for our new post. I'd been reassigned to another cavalry unit. There was no breathing room between assignments. As soon as we got to Fort Drum, New York, Kathreyn got a new job and so did I.

I never wanted an office job. Some guys opted for branches of service or a military occupational specialty (MOS) that would ensure they wouldn't deploy, or would work in the rear echelon, but I was a frontline kind of guy.

When I showed up at my unit, the 10th Mountain Division, my first stop was the command sergeant major's office. The NCO who saw the sergeant major with me that day had a different point of view than mine. While we were waiting for the sergeant major, he tried to tell me about his combat experience on the OPFOR (Opposition Force), but I couldn't take him seriously. The OPFOR is the unit the Army uses as a mock enemy to train forces for deployment, but this guy had never seen actual combat. I just wasn't convinced he'd truly addressed the enemy.

We were called into the office and stood at attention before Command Sergeant Major (CSM) Fred Morris, ready to do what we were told. CSM Morris told me, "SGT Harris, you've got combat experience, and I need that in my TOC (tactical operations center). I need you in my shop to help me train all these new soldiers."

As soon as he finished, the bells and whistles were clanging in my head. I really didn't want to be the coffee boy. In my mind, an E-5 in the TOC was going to spend his day as a gopher, and I wanted more combat experience.

When CSM Morris was done, I asked him if I might say something. He agreed to let me talk. I stood at attention, "Sergeant Major, I don't mean any disrespect, but I think my skills might be better used on the ground."

He said, "You'll work where I tell you to work."

"Yes, sir." You didn't argue with CSM Fred Morris.

I stayed at attention when the guy next to me spoke up. "Sergeant Major, may I say something?"

The sergeant major looked at both of us with disdain and gave the other soldier permission to speak.

"Sir, I'll take SGT Harris's position if you'll put me in the TOC and him on the front line."

The CSM answered, "You can go to hell. You'll work where I tell you to work."

We were done.

We went into tactical training mode once again, preparing for eventual redeployment to Iraq. New York provided new terrain for training and it was a relief to be out of the desert climate for a while.

Over the course of the year, Kathreyn and I had some much needed family time, and Lizzie and I got to know each other. She was my girl, always ready to play when I was off duty. We made friends with other families in our unit, and life was good. Kathreyn held down the fort while I left for more advanced training at Fort Knox, Kentucky, taking care of the family as well as working in the family readiness group (FRG) to support other military spouses.

My first son, Josh, was finally allowed to establish a relationship with me, and between deployments we'd been working on that as well. His mother agreed that he could join us in New York as I prepared to return to Iraq, and Kat had taken on the role of mothering both a toddler and a teenager. I'd joke and tell her the two weren't that different. She had a job working for the US Department of Agriculture and had enrolled Josh in the local high school. He'd acclimated to Army life pretty quickly and was doing a great job at school. I talked with my two other sons, Nicolas and Albert, as often as I was allowed, but there wasn't a lot of contact between us. When it came time to head back to Iraq, our FRG prepared a big send-off, and we had a rough time saying goodbye one more time. I held Kat close, squeezed Elizabeth as hard as I could, and told Josh to take care of the family for me.

15

ALI BABA IN BABYLON

We deployed to Iraq through Kuwait for training once again and spent a month preparing for the changes in the battlefield since our homecoming in 2005. I became platoon sergeant for the commander's personal security detachment (PSD). I was happy to be close to the tactical situation, but I learned that our squadron commander ate nails for breakfast and he didn't even use milk. He hit the ground running.

I was two pay grades beneath what the position required and I felt that dearth of knowledge and experience on a daily basis. The sergeant major tried to train me when he could, but we'd knock heads sometimes over what I didn't know. He'd educate me pretty quickly, landing with both feet on my butt, telling me what I did wrong. I'd let him cool off and then ask him if he'd let me tell him what really happened. Sometimes he'd let me explain. We had a great relationship. He was trying to help raise me up to the next level, to the level I needed to be at, but we were downrange and there was not much time for that. We were on solid missions, back-to-back once we hit the ground, and like a lot of other soldiers I got daily on-the-job training. The CSM told me an E-6 would be arriving shortly to replace me, and just to hang tight in my current position until my replacement arrived.

As part of the commander's PSD, it was our job to ensure route clearance ahead of the command vehicle. One day the commander wanted to turn around in a sector that I deemed unsafe. He cussed me out on the radio, telling me, "I'll turn around where I need to turn around," and the soldiers in my platoon heard the butt-whooping on the radio, just like I did. When we got back to the unit I was fuming. I asked to speak to the commander. I wanted to give him a piece of my mind, hopefully without being court-martialed. I was an E-5 trying to get the soldiers in my command to trust me, and being cussed out on the radio by the squadron commander wasn't going to get me to that goal. I walked into his office, and he said, "Can I help you, Sergeant?"

I stood at attention and answered, "Yes, sir. Sir, you neutered me in front of my soldiers. I'm an E-5 in an E-7 spot and you're putting me down in front of my soldiers, who I'm trying to teach to trust me."

He said, "Are you done?"

I said, "Yes, sir."

"Get the hell out of my office."

We got along fine after that, but a couple of weeks later, I was transferred to B Troop, first platoon, to replace another NCO who'd been sent to the PTSD clinic on one of the other bases near Baghdad International Airport. He'd witnessed the gruesome death of one of his soldiers and needed some time away from combat.

The CSM came to me and told me, "This isn't a punishment. It's a necessary move. I'm trying to operate a unit in a combat zone, and I need you to move to the line. You've done a good job."

The commander called me in and told me the same thing, and off I went to join B Troop. The troop was assigned to a quick reaction force (QRF) and did patrols for Liberty and Victory Bases. They were in recovery mode after the death of a teammate and were given light missions in order to give them time to recover, heal, and rebuild.

I got to know the guys in my truck pretty quickly. My roommate was Shawn Dunkin, from South Carolina. We were basically the same rank; I had a few months of seniority, so I was the truck commander and he was the senior dismount, but we quickly became best friends. Shawn was a consummate professional. He did everything right. He was a nut about computers, and between the two of us, we rigged up our hooch with enough gaming equipment to keep us preoccupied when we weren't in sector. Like me, Shawn was married, and we had a lot in common. We were hooked on James Bond and held "007" movie marathons when we had time off.

Between his leadership abilities and his goofy sense of humor, I knew we'd be friends for life.

Our team medic was Matt Bowe from Moon Township, Pennsylvania. Matt was an all-American kind of guy. He played a lot of football in high school, was close to his siblings, and loved to rap, making up edgy lyrics that were pretty popular. He was a trauma specialist; he wanted to be a doctor someday and was smart enough to achieve that goal. Matt was usually in the middle of formation when we were on patrol, but he could hold his own in any situation. He was the most competitive man I ever met. You could see his determination to be the best at whatever he was doing.

Adare Cleveland from Anchorage, Alaska, was our gunner. He loved being a soldier but planned to become a police officer as soon as this tour of duty was done. An outdoorsman, he filled us in with stories of the rugged beauty of Alaska and made us all want to visit. He told tales about his mom and sister when he got homesick, and we could all relate. He was extremely loyal and was always looking out for his teammates. You could count on Adare to say, "I've got your back."

Our dismount was Adam Devine, who was actually an Infantryman who'd been deployed with the Cav—and we never let him forget it. Adam had a huge heart for kids, and whenever we pulled over you could find him surrounded by a swarm of Iraqi youngsters. I asked him one time, "Why the candy?" He told me, "I don't want these kids to see us big Americans as goons with guns. Maybe we can change this next generation with a piece of candy." Adam lived with his eyes and heart wide open, and could see and feel the big picture.

●●●

We ran patrols in Humvees. Lighter than the Bradley, the Humvee was a little more agile with less armor. It had a flat underbelly, which absorbed the full force of explosive power from beneath. That meant whoever was sitting in the Humvee didn't stand much of a chance if the explosion originated beneath him. We were told Humvees with a v-shaped hull were being manufactured stateside. The modification would dissipate explosive forces in a v-pattern away from the interior of the vehicle, but we were using the flat-hulled armored variety instead. They'd also begun to include a shrapnel protection layer (SPA) in the interior of the Humvee, but we weren't equipped with the newer models yet. What choice did we have? Between the body armor on us, as well as the blast kit added to our vehicle, along with the tactical intelligence of our leadership team, we had as much protection as this battlefield could provide. The rest of our protection was between our own eyes and ears. We had to outsmart the enemy, which wasn't hard most of the time.

Running patrols in this sector wasn't predictable. We patrolled two distinct areas. Iraqi Family Village (IFV) was a breath of fresh air; when we showed up there it was like a Fourth of July parade. The people were happy to see us, respectful of our role, and friendly toward US soldiers. The kids would run alongside our Humvees, begging us for candy, money, anything on the vehicle, and the market vendors would try to hand us meat or bread. It wasn't hard to do a "knock and talk," checking with the locals to see what information they'd give us that would help identify problem areas as well as probable insurgents. Not surprisingly, they were incredibly tight-lipped, unable to trust each other due to centuries of turf tensions that had nothing to do with this war. We were alert, but we could relax a little. We observed the buildings, housing, and marketplace, but the threat level wasn't high. Shia and Sunni were enemies, day and night. The Shia in IFV were grateful for our protection, but they had waged war with the Sunnis in Al Farat for a lot longer than we'd been around.

If we were running traffic control points or had to stop civilians or vehicles for investigation or search, we used a pretty basic set of rules called EOF, or Escalation of Force. Shout, shove, show, shoot—we'd issue a verbal warning to halt, followed by some nonlethal persuasive physicality, and if that wasn't convincing, we'd lift our weapon to demonstrate our intent to use it, and finally, deliberately aimed shots could eliminate the threat. In IFV, that generally wasn't necessary. But it was a different story down the road.

A half mile away from IFV sat the village of Al Farat. It was hostile. Two villages, a stone's throw from one another, and they had completely different temperaments. One village loved us; the other hated us. At Al Farat we got shot at every day. We entered Al Farat in a more tactical posture. We were alert, and our mindset was more aggressive. You knew something was apt to happen. Our gunner would hunker down in the hole on the Humvee to make sure he didn't get sniped. We kept our weapons locked and loaded. We found IEDs on a frequent basis. Bad guys in Al Farat would pop up and fire some shots off a building without aiming for an actual target. It was more like a hope shot. They knew if they stayed on the rooftops too long they'd get tagged, detained, or killed. We had observation towers keeping watch over Al Farat, and marksmen could fire on the civilian compound with accuracy if necessary. If the volley of bullets was sufficient, we'd go into Al Farat to search and seize ammo, weapons, or bad guys.

As you entered Al Farat there was a walled compound set up just before you entered the larger sector of the city. There was a small mosque as you entered the village, and although it was used for religious purposes, we were certain it held a pretty basic arsenal of weapons and ammo. Every time we searched the village we'd come up empty, but we were fired on frequently enough to know there was a pretty big hidey-hole somewhere in the mosque. Because we were near a central supply route, the weapons in vogue could change and you'd be up against more than you bargained for. When the Sunnis weren't fighting us, they were fighting with the Shia. You kept your head on a swivel. Getting shot at every day gave us no peace of mind.

● ● ●

One day, soon after Saddam Hussein had been executed, we were tasked to do a census in Al Farat. We were given the mission to poll the local populace to find out how the people were feeling about Saddam's hanging. Did they feel threatened or relieved? Did they agree with the execution or not? What was the prevailing mood? It was part of the government strategy to win "hearts and minds" in the war, one village, one bullet, at a time.

We drove our convoy of four Humvees to the compound at Al Farat. There were basically two entrances into the compound, which was roughly the size of an American apartment complex. Both entrances were too narrow for our Humvees, so we ended up leaving our vehicles on the outer perimeter with the rest of the platoon while the eight of us on the survey team, seven dismounts and our lieutenant, entered the compound. As dismounts, we'd provide security, and it was the job of the lieutenant to conduct the census session with the locals. We expected to stay alert as the survey continued, but we weren't predicting any real combat.

The wall surrounding the compound had four sides, with three solid walls and one with a large hole where a car bomb had blown up a couple of days earlier. We'd been involved with the cleanup operation; a vehicle-borne IED (VBIED) left a dent in the perimeter. The suicide bomber was the only fatality. It had been a particularly gruesome day for all of us. We chased dogs away from the site of the explosion as they tried to consume what was left of the man's head.

There was very little room to maneuver as we walked through the compound, making it a little ominous to pass beneath a roofline or in front of a doorway. If hostility picked up in the compound, it was going to be a short census. In an urban setting, ambush is always a possibility, so we were diligent in investigating any movement or activity. It was not unusual to get fired on from one direction, only to deal with an attempted ambush from another side. There were a lot of blind spots, and once we arrived on scene, the enemy had various ways to reach the mosque to fire or hide their weapons.

As we approached the first building to start the survey, we received a report that an Iraqi civilian had been shot earlier in front of the mosque, and we went to check it out. The body was spread out on the ground and some locals told us the man had worked inside. We became more concerned about an ambush and IEDs in the area, so we had to quickly clarify the man's identity. We used our gunshot residue kit (GSR) on the dead man's fingertips to see if there were any explosive remains. The swab we used to wipe the man's fingers and hands read positive for explosives. It was obvious this was an enemy combatant, not a religious aide. But instead of investigating the death of the civilian, we were told to leave the investigation to the Iraqi police force itself and to continue our census inside the village compound. It was looking more and more likely that we would encounter shooters on rooftops, IEDs, and insurgents hiding in plain sight. This would not be a simple census exercise.

As we conducted our survey, we learned most people didn't care. Saddam Hussein had been gone for several years, and the fact that he was now dead didn't seem to concern them. We worked our way through the compound. When we came to one building, Shawn and I went inside with the lieutenant while the rest of the team stood outside the door. Adare pulled security with his squad automatic weapon (SAW), and Matt stood watch as the medic. While the lieutenant tried to interview the lady, Shawn and I took turns checking on the crew outside. We sat with this Iraqi lady in her kitchen, asking her the questions on our list. She offered us tea, and we talked over chipped teacups about the conflict in her village. A security badge lay on the table. The lieutenant asked her son's name and pointed out that the name she gave us did not match the name that was listed on the flimsy laminated badge on the table. She got very nervous. Shawn kept asking her, "Where did this badge come from?" and she became very defensive.

"We'll have to take the badge with us. We don't think it's official," the lieutenant explained. At that point we began to hear gunfire from close range, as it rang out in the walls outside the apartment. We raced outside to check on our team, and decided we needed to secure our route out of the compound before dark. Right next to me stood a seven-man team who'd been told to accept me as their NCO, and I was the new guy, replacing their former truck commander. I knew they were watching me, trying to figure out what kind of leader I would become. Would I be foolish and possibly get them all killed? Or would I be courageous and protect them in adversity? I needed them to know I was a soldier, their brother, there to protect them.

"Stick to the wall for cover," I told them. The shots died off.

I asked the lieutenant, "You call it in?" His hands were shaking so bad I took the radio and tried to coordinate with the rest of the platoon on the outer perimeter to let them know we were under fire and trying to return to our vehicles.

I told the team, "This is what we're going to do. Adare, cover the rear when we start to move. Shawn, take point. Bowe, you're with Adare, rear security." The gunfire had been coming from a two-story building diagonal from our location. I motioned to Shawn to move with me to the corner. I told him, "Go low," and I went high.

As soon as Shawn and I checked the direction of fire, the wall in front of both of our faces was hit with gunfire. "Holy . . . " I yelled, and we backed away from the corner. The whole team stood with their backs against the building as we quietly discussed what to do to leave the compound and return to our vehicles.

"Damn, that was close, huh?" I asked, trying to relieve a little tension.

I got on the radio with the platoon sergeant, who told me, "Just come to the truck, they're not shooting at you."

"The hell they're not," I told him. "Sergeant, we just got fired on, and we're returning fire." I was so pissed. I handed the radio to the lieutenant. "Let's get out of here," I told the team. I looked at the end of the building, and moved to the front of the line to move the squad toward the direction of the outer wall.

I motioned to the team to follow me, and we rushed to the western perimeter. We found some Iraqi civilians standing in an alleyway near the bombed out vehicle. We ran toward the alley, taking cover against the wall, and the civilians started calling, "No Ali Baba, no shoot. Walk with us. No problem."

I saw a makeshift gate ahead and told them to open it up. They refused, telling us, "No Ali Baba, no problem here." It was typical circle talk, finger-pointing designed to distract us from the mission at hand. There was no way I was going to trust their "no problem here" nonsense after the shots that had been fired. I looked at my troops. We all had our weapons drawn, the platoon sergeant had told us to work our way out, and that's what we were going to do—without being killed in the process. Our sharpshooter was with us, and he was on the lookout as we traversed the western perimeter. Adare was like a dog with a bone, super vigilant, keeping watch as we progressed.

We were going to have to move through the gate. When I say gate, I mean an old car door and a pile of debris used as an entry or exit point. As we tucked against the wall in the alley, gunfire hit the sides of the building, and the Iraqis ran for cover. I told the team to stand aside, to cover me out of the line of fire, and ran for the gate as hard as I could. I balled myself up and pushed through it. Matt held back until the last soldier, Shawn, was ready to cross. As soon as Shawn met us on that wall, we covered Matt and then moved to the next point. Shots continued to volley from one alley to the next. We entered the building from where the gunfire had originated.

I told the lieutenant, "Tell the platoon sergeant we're under fire!" Shawn and I kicked in the door and worked our way down the hall, clearing the building one room at a time. The heavy metal doors were stuck shut and difficult to open. We shoved down doors and continued to clear each room. The large metal door frames made from pieces of channel iron were hard to destroy, but once we got our hands in the door frame, we could wedge our rifles in the casing and clear the room pretty quickly.

We continued the process, checking each closet, entry, or exit point. We pointed the muzzle of our rifles through piles of trash, bedding, and clothing, opening bureaus and closets, looking for trouble. We finally got to the last room at the end of the hall. We still hadn't found the enemy, and I felt pretty sure they had to be hiding out here. I motioned the team to move against the wall, and pulled the metal back on the door frame so I could get it open. I lay down on the ground, pulled out my 9mm, and kicked the door open. I could see spent shell casings on the floor. I stood up, pushed the door open wide, and we charged into the room. It was empty. I rushed to the left of the window and looked outside. They'd fired on us from this room and must have escaped over the balcony and the exterior wall.

We rushed down the northern perimeter to reach the opening we needed to access our vehicles, keeping our eyes on the rooftops, the wall, and surrounding buildings. We made it out and joined the rest of the platoon, keeping our weapons trained on the perimeter wall. The adrenaline was flowing strong.

The platoon sergeant asked, "What the hell? Where were you?"

"We were under fire, they're in there!"

He said, "No way."

"Sergeant, we've been under fire for the past fifteen minutes!"

The rest of the team chimed in, filling him in on what had happened. After we debriefed, I knew that our brotherhood was on solid ground.

16

TRIANGLE OF DEATH

We transitioned our mission near a trio of farming communities exploited by the enemy in recent months, an area dubbed the "Triangle of Death." We called our team the Hellcats, and our mission was to run reconnaissance around Yusifiyah, gain information on the enemy, and ensure roads were safe for travel by military and civilians. The triangle was a volatile mixture of local nationals, insurgents whose goal was terrorizing the local nationals to intimidate them and keep them from participating in any government reforms, and counterinsurgents who worked covertly to try to clear the populace of troublemakers.

Iraqi national forces had taken on many duties associated with policing and protecting their villages, but the enemy was still very real. In the early days of the war, Saddam's munitions factories had been left unguarded, and much of the cache of explosives had been buried in the surrounding countryside. The area was on the supply route to Baghdad, so it wasn't unusual to find bad guys traversing our sector. It was our job to continue to discern their vulnerability and exploit it.

Insurgents as well as Saddam loyalists tried to terrorize the locals in what resembled gang wars. They would use the combat zone to become gangsters in their own country. Thugs would use any opportunity to become the big guy by killing people in front of other Iraqis, intimidating the local populace and making them vulnerable. Sometimes foreign Muslims came in from Pakistan and Iran to recruit young Iraqis to become thugs. They would pay them to become part of the insurgency. Giving them money, ammo, and IEDs, they could then use them to recruit other thugs.

In this war-torn country, poor as it was, flashing dollars at most guys was all the motivation needed. The Americans couldn't intimidate the locals in the same way. We wouldn't threaten to kill their families or destroy their livelihood. The young males in our midst had a cruel dilemma: the Americans will give me free gasoline, but the insurgents will rape my wife or kill my family. It was hard for us to compete under those circumstances. Their threats had teeth.

As we protected our sector through the battle-scarred and fire-charred farmland of what was once a place called the Fertile Crescent, I saw what might have been, and what was. I spotted date palm trees and groves of oranges, lemons, and limes. The Tigris and Euphrates Rivers meet near Yusifiyah, and if I really took in the landscape around me I'd be reminded of home—farmland for growing and harvesting, rivers for fishing and hunting. From the front seat of my Humvee, I could watch the farmers in their long black robes tilling soil once turned by Sumerians, ancestors who brought us the wheel and the plow. As our military vehicles trekked through the region once known as Babylon, its primitive beauty struck me.

We'd been trained to gain an understanding of the Iraqi people and the tribes for whom peace has long been a problem. The Iraqi Muslims split themselves into two main factions, majority Shia and minority Sunni, two sects that have tried to outlast and overpower one another for a lot longer than this war, decade, or century. Kurds and Christians battled for their place here as well.

As I peered through my field glasses, I saw villagers head for the mosque and I heard the muezzin sound the call to worship. The loudspeaker blared five times a day in Yusifiyah and in towns and villages all over Iraq. Muslims gathered for prayer while our troops protected their freedom to do so. A villager stopped in the dirt by the road, pulled out his prayer rug, and spread out his mat facing Mecca. He leaned into his prayer posture, shoulders down in front of his knees, and as he did so, I wondered if his prayers resembled mine in any way. *Can this war mercifully come to an end so we can get the heck home?* As American soldiers, we were in Iraq to protect this man's freedom to do simple things like pray. Sometimes I wondered if we were really making a difference. It was an odd juxtaposition of worlds, ideals, and beliefs.

While we searched for the enemy, we also tried to make friends with the local populace. In the process of creating bonds of trust with farmers, families, and businesses in the region, discernment was critical. We were a frontline squad; we were never so friendly that we lost sight of our mission. We moved from house to house to establish our presence and position in the village. Sometimes that involved slugging through dirty canals and muddy fields filled with cow manure. Sometimes it meant working our way through market stalls, on the lookout for explosives or IEDs.

Operating out of Camp Stryker, I loved my role as team leader of the Hellcats. We were not unlike the coalition forces, there to support and protect the innocent, but we had a lot of work to do to teach them how to do that for themselves. The men who volunteered for the coalition forces were easy enough to work with—they weren't that different from each one of us, trying to earn a living to support their families. We traveled with an interpreter who could communicate our mission to the local populace; our goal was to build, not destroy. More and more Iraqis were war-weary and ready to develop a democratic way of life. They didn't necessarily like all Americans, but they didn't like the foreign fighters either. We got along for the most part. We were trained to gain and maintain contact with the enemy, yet we were also trained to gain and maintain contact with the locals, and sometimes it was hard to tell them apart. Innocent Iraqi men, women, and children were collateral damage and that bothered all of us. Freedom has never been free.

There was no front line for battle. We couldn't draw a line in the sand, with the enemy on one side and our troops on the other. We cleared a road one day and had to clear it again the next. You couldn't pick out the enemy based on how they dressed or where they lived. We used cordon and knock patrols to set up a secure perimeter around a civilian sector and pounded on doors to gain access and intelligence. Information was power. We needed these people to tell us what we needed to know in order to clear and maintain each route through and around the community. Although farmland hampered the enemy's ability to hide, there were enough roads in and around the area of Yusifiyah to enable insurgents to blend into safe areas, hide weapons or munitions, attack, and then disappear. Changes in routine signaled danger.

At home, if I wanted to get a deer I'd follow his tracks: the scrapes of hooves on sandy trails, the scars of antlers rubbed against tree bark, the scent of animals in season. I used to watch the way a deer behaved when there was no threat of danger, and I knew how it would respond when scared or provoked. A deer's behavior is predictable. When vegetation is scarce, it changes its feeding spot and moves on to the next opportunity. Sometimes there's a big herd of youngsters, other times you're stalking the old guys. If you're the hunted, first and foremost you're going to want to find a way to escape. Some parts of deer hunting reminded me of what we were doing to the enemy.

If I were on foot patrol, I'd follow the tracks of the insurgents—conversations with neighbors, recent purchases at certain stores, and arrangements with others to meet or use local transportation. We watched how the locals acted when they didn't know they were being watched. Other times we followed them to see where they were going, who or what they were stalking. If everything the enemy needed was nearby, it was harder to pick up subtle changes in their routines, connections, and behaviors. We knew we were getting close by their movement, as well as their lack of movement. We had two mindsets, warrior and peacemaker, and were ready to offer both.

I carried an M-4 rifle, with an M-68 close combat optic attachment for night vision on my shoulder that had a thirty-round magazine, as well as an M-9 pistol in my holster with forty-five rounds at the ready. At my waist I carried a large knife and a police baton for crowd control. I carried anywhere from seven to twelve extra magazines of ammo as well. I guess you could say I was armed and dangerous. I got a reality check every time I put on my body armor or adjusted my weapons. Altogether, it added an extra fifty to seventy pounds of weight, and you liked to think you were protected. But we saw too many casualties to believe we were invincible.

On night patrols, we used our night vision goggles and thermal detection devices to detect traffic near the roadways. Our infrared lights illuminated the roadways we searched after dark, giving each neighborhood an eerie green cast. What the naked eye could not detect, we could spot using the technology we were issued. A handprint on the side of a tree, vehicle, or wall would leave trace heat that could be detected using thermal imagery. Once we read these signs, we knew where to find the enemy. There was nothing innocent about day, night, or the dirt under our boots or beneath our tracks.

●●●

Thoughts of home kept us going. One thing a soldier doesn't want to worry about when he's at war is his family. I had to trust that my family's needs were being met if I was going to concentrate on the safety of my unit. As I drove through the small villages and farms and thought about what Saddam Hussein's brutal regime had robbed from these hard-working people, I couldn't help but turn my thoughts toward home. I saw families destroyed in front of me every day, and it took its toll. I wanted to believe that what we were doing would someday mean these families would be safe once and for all, just like my own.

I thought about the contrasts between Kathreyn's life at Fort Drum and the women we saw in the marketplace in Yusifiyah. I didn't think my strong-willed wife would like it here very much. Women in Iraq have very different rights and privileges compared to their husbands. Marriage is considered a national duty, a contract between two families in the same kin group. Once married, the woman relinquishes whatever freedoms she has in order to come under her husband's authority. While Kathreyn freely worshiped at our post chapel, Iraqi women couldn't go to the mosque or were segregated within it. Forget about making decisions; that was left to the men in the extended family. Kathreyn and I hoped to have more children; for Iraqi families the government considered fewer than five children a national security threat. The birth of a boy resulted in a big celebration, while a girl's birth was patently ignored. I thought of our little Elizabeth. As a father, I was so proud of our beautiful daughter, and wasn't ashamed to admit she had me wrapped around her tender, tiny fingers.

One of the things that made patrols difficult sometimes was the kids. The contrast between the freedom and safety of my children and the tragedy of growing up in a war-torn country was evident every time we drove through Yusifiyah. Most of the time, children genuinely loved it when American soldiers arrived on the scene. They'd wave and clap, then ask us for money, candy, anything that wasn't tied down. We weren't supposed to give them anything, but we couldn't help it. Sometimes we gave them school supplies such as pens and paper. After repeatedly giving away all the cash I was carrying, I learned to leave my wallet back at camp. I tried to learn some more Arabic so I could communicate with them.

I had one little boy who I ran into quite often on patrol. He had terribly dry skin, and I carried a tube of hand cream for him. Every time I ran across him, I'd tell him, "Come here, little buddy," and would squeeze the lotion into his palms. Not all kids were cute or sweet; sometimes they'd scream "Ali Baba" at us, which translated roughly as "thief," but the life they led was nothing I'd ever want for my kids or my family.

Adam carried a pocketful of Lifesavers all the time.

"Have you ever noticed, SGT Harris, that the kids don't come running for candy when something's about to go down?" he asked.

"Good point," I told him. He was absolutely right. Kids were a barometer for us, harbingers of what might happen next.

Matt wanted desperately to be a doctor when he got stateside and was quick to point out that health care for Iraqi civilians didn't exist. The villages in our sector had no sewers or running water. They were given electricity for four or five minutes a night. We met a man one day whose wife was clearly in the last stages of cancer, but there was nothing we could do to help. "Please, sir, please," he begged us. It was hard to answer him. He went from soldier to soldier, asking us to help his wife. We were out in the middle of nowhere; the nearest aid station was miles away, and they had no treatment protocol for cancer victims. Finding that kind of specialized care on the battlefield was just impossible, but it was heartbreaking to turn away from him, especially for Matt.

On a routine patrol we stopped to watch a bunch of kids playing soccer. Barefooted, they tussled with each other in the dirt to get the ball. Up the rise there was a small medical clinic, and the children had set up their game right next to it. One kid got the ball, kicked it out of the raw sewage in the drainage ditch, and headed for the goal. We looked down. The ground was littered with medical waste—syringes, needles. This was wartime soccer for them, and they had no idea how dangerous it was.

●●●

During my first tour in Iraq, we knew that Saddam Hussein's regime had expert bomb makers to reconfigure weapons of mass destruction. He had chemists to develop highly explosive materials; his electrical engineers prepared timers and wiring; his mechanics designed igniters. After he was removed from power, 650,000 tons of Iraqi ordnance was looted, giving insurgents a huge supply of ammo. Ammo was stockpiled as well as scattered in secret locations across Iraq, and the design of IEDs became a specialized function within the insurgency. As the weeks went by, we received frequent reports of IED damage, and the death toll continued to climb.

Vets will tell you there's no such thing as an atheist in a foxhole. In today's war, we'd probably say there's no atheist in a Humvee. If you don't believe you have some protection, some provision for you and your comrades, that's a pretty hopeless posture. Our prayers were short, one-word tomes: "Help," or "Jesus," or sometimes a simple expletive was actually a prayer. I felt for the chaplains in our unit. What could they say from day to day that we hadn't already heard? How did they get you to take what they had to say and internalize it, make it real? As soon as you heard the call of the muezzin, you started reflecting on your own faith, and what it was costing us to protect the Iraqi people. Most of us didn't go to the chaplain; he had to come to us.

When a soldier in our unit was killed, we lived the warrior ethos. There was no way he'd be left behind; there was no way we'd leave evidence of his death for the enemy to gloat over. Our mindset was this: you're willing to risk your life for a fallen comrade, dead or alive. There's a kind of silence between soldiers where everything you want to say and can't can either break you or bond you. For us, it was the latter. Except for one member of my platoon who was like our little brother, we were all on our second or third tours. We were seasoned.

●●●

Ask any soldier and they'll tell you the same thing—the IED is a coward's weapon. War by its very definition means conflict between soldiers. The men who hid in the darkness to build primitive bombs were not soldiers, but they were the enemy nonetheless. Cowards hid in a shed, built the bombs, and buried them in the terrain around us. They didn't have the courage to face us in battle. We had the firepower to annihilate the nation, but that's not what we were there to do. If it was going to be an IED war, we could wipe these folks out in a heartbeat. But that would mean killing thousands of innocent Iraqi civilians. As much as we wanted to wipe out the cowards, we didn't want to wipe out the nation, and our mission, of course, precluded that course of action.

At the time of my second deployment, there were basically two types of incendiary explosives deployed by local insurgents. The worst was the explosively formed penetrator (EFP). It was nasty: concentrated firepower in a metal cylinder filled with high-energy plastic explosives sealed into a concave copper plate. Once ignited, the copper dish turned into a metal slug using the kinetic force of the explosive blast, and it could penetrate layers and layers of steel, destroying everything around it. It produced a vapor trail that melted everything in its wake, creating molten lava out of metal. I don't want to tell you what it does to humans. The Iraqis and trained insurgents used the EFPs by disguising them inside foam statues, and would set them up in a row of eight or nine statues in desert terrain. Camouflaged with sand, they could be made to look like concrete, debris, or trash. When hit, these foam statues would detonate with over four hundred pounds of explosives. Nothing survived.

The second type of IED, the one most commonly used at this juncture in the war, was an IED made using artillery or mortar shells, with varying amounts of explosives. The round would be buried or hidden and could be easily triggered or detonated. In our area of operations, this type of IED was creating a good bit of havoc, and troops were being maimed, injured, or killed nearly every day. We were deployed to an area with suspicious activity off Route Metallica after numerous reports of IEDs in sector.

We established a temporary FOB in a deserted poultry plant. The area was so hot even our EOD got hit. Four walls surrounded the main meat-packing plant, and we posted a truck at each corner of the perimeter wall with a .50 caliber machine gun facing out. For a couple of weeks, we slept in old walk-in freezers, taking turns in two-hour shifts. The place smelled like death, and we all hated it.

Over the course of the next few days, there were numerous IED explosions. One afternoon we looked up in the sky and noticed what looked like black birds soaring overhead. They were actually incoming mortar rounds. With only about forty men in the FOB, everyone pulled their weight, but shifts were long and nerves were frazzled.

One of the platoons left on patrol and barely ten minutes later we spotted smoke piping into the sky two or three blocks away. They'd hit an IED, but early reports indicated no one had been injured. In light of the volatile situation, the FOB could not be sustained, so we moved our platoons back to Camp Stryker.

We continued to pay close attention to any changes in terrain features or local behaviors so we could find and destroy IEDs before they destroyed us, but we could not travel safely in any direction. The military had developed a vehicle known as the Buffalo along with a metal detector called the Husky that looked like a road grader. The Husky senses metal objects and marks the spot with paint, and the Buffalo moves in to diffuse the bomb. The Buffalo has an "Iron Claw" operated by a soldier who watches its movements on camera, then uses the metal claw to carefully dig away whatever is buried. If it's a huge IED, the EOD team moves in to expose and dispose of the bomb. The Buffalo can handle major explosions from IEDs and antitank rounds. But we didn't have those tools on this mission through the Triangle of Death. We had only each other.

Electronic jamming systems mounted on our vehicles to block radio-controlled explosive igniters were effective only when operated in the right frequency range. Most of the spectrum of radio frequencies in Iraq was unmanaged, and the interference from cell phones, appliances, microwaves, and timers on the ground sometimes made those jammers ineffective. Our jammers did not disrupt the radios in the trucks or the handhelds designed to be compatible with the radios in our vehicles. They just jammed the other stuff; at least that was the intent.

The explosion of the next IED was a matter of when, not if. We kept threat data about IEDs to a minimum so the enemy didn't get any feedback. We didn't want their videos showing up on YouTube. They could care less about innocent civilians; in fact, they exploited them to do their dirty work. Their cavalier attitude about human life revealed them to be cowards as well. Every soldier I worked with feared for his or her life every day, but pushed forward because that was our mission. I don't know of a soldier who didn't dread driving down an unknown road. IEDs made everything suspect—Sunni civilians, Shia farmers, families, kids. You could be driving down the road and questions would pop into your head. You had to stay alert.

Why's that car broken down on the side of the road?
Why's that man herding his sheep so close to the intersection?
Why is there an animal carcass dragged next to the roadway?
There's a group of farmers in the irrigation ditch, but why is one of them on his cell phone?
What's that kid we gave the pencils to doing with the paper and radio?
Does it look like that prayer rug is hiding a detonator?

IEDs made everything holy seem unholy. Everything innocent was lost.

17

SCOUTS OUT

When we mounted up before dawn on February 19, 2007, we were ready to conduct what we viewed as critical but routine route clearance. We got everything tucked into our vehicle: weapons, ammo, commo, water. Shawn, the consummate NCO, ran through the checklist verbally, making sure we were in sync. We walked around the Humvee, checking it over. Our driver, SP4 Adam Devine, had just pulled into the convoy, vehicle number three. As an Infantry dismount, Adam wasn't supposed to be driving my truck that day, but with people on leave and various mission requirements, he ended up behind the wheel.

"Infantry's gotta drive for the dang Cavalry again?" he chided us.

My new roommate, SSG Bryan Dunaway, was acting platoon sergeant and manned the truck behind me. Whenever we were on patrol and drove by a dead donkey on the side of the road, he'd scream "Donkey!" and bray. I started calling him Donkey. Once he got his nickname, he was teased about his natural endowment, and the name stuck.

"Let's get this show on the road, Donkey," I called to him and climbed into my truck.

I sat in the front seat, passenger side, pulled my helmet on tight, and adjusted my headset. I scraped away a pile of dust that covered the American flag decal on our windshield. I looked at Adam, Shawn, Adare, and Matt.

"Ready, guys?" I asked them. "I need 200 percent today; 200 percent. Got that?" I knew they did. I could not have been more proud of my crew.

"Scouts out."

As we got outside the wire, we passed by fields of windswept rice grass, dusty with the sand that covered everything with grit. It was still pretty early in the morning, and we came across a group of civilians congregating near a roadway.

"Looks like they're up to no good," Shawn remarked.

"Yeah," I answered. "Who needs to dig a hole first thing in the morning?"

We stopped a couple of them in order to swab their fingers. The swab would tell us what kinds of explosives were involved if these two suspicious folks had anything to do with embedding IEDs. While Shawn was swabbing the civilians, a report came in from XRAY, the command and control center at our FOB, Camp Stryker. A civilian had called in an IED with two possible locations on either end of Route Metallica. Metallica ran north and south. The IED was reported to be on either the eastern boundary, Route Harley, or the western boundary, Route AC/DC. We needed to take off. The results of the swab didn't confirm the presence of explosives so we loaded up and headed to the next mission.

● ● ●

It would take us a couple of hours to run the route to Metallica. I hated it when the truck was quiet, and egged Matt on when he started to pick on Adam.

"Hey, Adam, how's that water taste?" he asked.

"Shut up," Adam told him. Adam would never live it down. On an earlier mission, he had used a water bottle to catch his tobacco spit. The cap of a water bottle fits perfectly in the opening designed to hold a weapon just above the driver's seat.

The night before, Adare had pulled a long shift as gunner, so long he had to pee in a water bottle. When he got out of the truck, he'd stuck it in that spot above the driver's seat. When Adam tried to use that spit bottle the next day, he'd cried out, "Sweet Jesus, this stinks!"

He continued to spit in the bottle before he finally gave it up. Adare couldn't hold his laughter any longer anyway. He told Adam he'd peed in the spit bottle. There was no way a truckload of Cav scouts were going to let an Infantry soldier forget that rookie move.

The convoy continued to navigate through sector. We were vigilant, watching either side of the road. On one side of the roadway old overgrown fields with scrappy vegetation lay barren, devoid of any activity in the still vapor of late morning. We kept watch, looking for any movement or activity that was out of the ordinary.

Adare sat on the leather belt in the back, his head exposed as he held on to the machine gun mount. "See anything?" I asked him.

"Not yet," he answered.

"Stay low," I told him.

Adare had just returned from R&R. "Hey, how's your mom and your sister?" I asked him. "I wouldn't mind a trip to Alaska right about now."

"Me, either," he answered.

The truck got quiet. No one liked being on this route.

"I feel like some Burger King for lunch today," I told Shawn.

We were going to be close to Liberty Village when we finished our mission, and they didn't have any restrictions against using pork lard in the fryer. It was the right place for fried food.

Shawn agreed, "I could go for some French fries," and Adam added, "I'll fly if you buy."

We were all in agreement. Lunch was settled.

The road was filled with craters the size of small cars, evidence of a lot of IED activity. No one liked the looks of things. I asked Shawn, "When you going on leave?"

Shawn had given up his return home on R&R so another soldier in the unit could get back to the States in time to meet his newborn child. Not many men would have done that.

"Just a couple weeks," he told me. "I'm ready."

We continued to travel down AC/DC, following the lead of the vehicles in front of us. We were two to three hundred meters from Harley when the dismounts came back to the intersection after patrolling that end. We then moved slowly down to AC/DC to continue the search.

"Quiet out here," I told the team. "Too quiet." I adjusted my headset, wiped the sweat off my face with my sleeve. Five guys in a Humvee with a boatload of ammo and equipment on a sweltering day made for pretty cramped quarters. I thought about how proud I was to have this team with me.

Our convoy completed route clearance on the western boundary and turned back onto Metallica. There was no time to send out more dismounts;

we were trying to locate the danger as quickly as possible, and if we located the IED, we were going to detonate or diffuse it before anyone got hurt. I continued to use small talk to settle everyone's nerves.

◆ ◆ ◆

Adam held to the path of the truck in front of us, creating a third row of tracks on top of those left by the vehicles that had preceded us. The road was full of combat scars—ruts and ridges, holes, and craters from previous IED attacks. He kept proper distance from the vehicle in front of us, following every safety measure. Adare was sitting up on the weight belt in the turret, locked and loaded, but he was thirsty, so Adam used his right arm to reach over the seat to get a bottle of water out of the cooler for him.

Adam asked Matt, "Hey, Demiz, you ever gonna finish that joke?"

Matt answered, "I'm getting there, just hold on." Matt was always telling a funny story. After a lack of sleep, no showers, and no decent chow due to back-to-back missions, we were ready for some relief.

In an instant, a loud, high-pitched, god-awful scream began. The air was being sucked out of our Humvee in a tortured wail that seemed to come from the bowels of the earth. Flames shot out of the air vents. There was no boom, no bang, no blast. The vehicle simply erupted. What must have been C-4 explosives implanted in the road detonated beneath the rear wall of the truck, piercing the gas tank and igniting all the ammo stored inside.

Bodies were blown out of the truck in an instant.

Gone.

Tires were blown skyward. The roof, turret, gear, and truck parts dissipated in the black smoke. Canals on either side of the road filled with the debris. The screaming of the IED continued. Adam was blown out of the vehicle and lay on his belly in the sand near where his door used to be.

I fought to get out of the truck as my body continued to char. The AT4 antitank weapon we carried in the truck erupted with a HEAT warhead designed to penetrate nearly two feet of armor. The AT4 was created to destroy a tank, and the explosion that ensued after the IED set off a whole series of huge blasts.

I think I was briefly knocked unconscious, and what was left of the truck was engulfed in flames. I came to and started fighting to get out of the truck, but the ground had imploded beneath us and it was a battle.

Other soldiers from the convoy, Matt Fatherree and Sean Reid, rushed to the vehicle and pulled me away from the inferno. Fatherree was one of our medics. Disoriented, I tried to tell them what to do next. "Pull over, get our men out!" I cried.

Fatherree grabbed me to try to get my body armor off since the fire was melting the material down my leg. The team led me away from the fire to begin emergency aid, and set me down on the ground away from the vehicles. I was frantic to get to my crew.

"Hey, SGT Harris, let's get you fixed up," SP4 Fatherree told me. He'd been an EMT prior to joining the Army. He knew what to do.

SSG Dunaway approached and stood over me. As acting platoon sergeant, he was directing combat lifesaving procedures and assessing the damage. I could see my reflection in his eye protection before he pulled them off and leaned close. What I saw made me recoil. I watched his face as he straddled my body, still on fire.

"Donkey, they got me," I told him.

"You're going to be okay," he told me, his face registering something I didn't recognize at the time. It was the face of fear.

"Where are my soldiers?" I called out. "Where the hell are they?"

Adam was helped to the back of the convoy, blood dripping out of his helmet, his uniform on fire. He had a gaping hole in the middle of his abdomen. He held on to SP4 Diekemper, asking him to help him get his vest off. Diekemper told him, "Eyes forward," and tried to get him to a clear spot. When they removed the blood-soaked vest, more blood dripped from his arms and down the backs of his legs. "Hang on, they're coming to get you out of here," Diekemper told him.

He shielded Adam while they walked to the casualty collection point, protecting him from fire and debris since his vest was gone. Ammo continued to cook off in our vehicle. Missiles from our rocket launchers continued to explode around me. They set Adam down near me.

"Adam, are you all right?" I called to him. "Do you know where the others are?"

He was covered with blood, soot, and debris.

"No, sir," he uttered. "I just wanna go home."

"We'll get you there, I promise," SSG Dunaway answered, before he ran to the second truck for better commo, calling for medevac and air support.

I heard him shouting, "Where's the rest of them?" The dismounts reported what appeared to be what was left of one of my soldiers across the canal, and swam through the murky stench with a body bag.

SSG Dunaway yelled, "Where's Dunkin?"

Shawn had been sitting right behind me in the truck when the vehicle convulsed. I heard Dunaway ask, "What the hell?" as he circled back through the smoke and flames. Ammo from our machine guns continued to cook off. SSG Dunaway called in a report of a second casualty.

The dismounts ran back to a bridge no more than twenty or thirty meters from where our convoy had come to a halt. They located the trigger, an old camera with a flash attachment, the wires running from the bridge down to the explosion site. Next to the trigger sat a pair of rubber shoes. One of the soldiers notified SSG Dunaway that he saw a truck driving north from the site, but they were too far away to fire on.

The platoon located what was left of another body. There are no words to describe how a man places a torso inside a body bag. There is just no way to describe what had to be done.

Dear Jesus.

I could hear the expletives of the dismounts as they tried to render aid.

Together the platoon pushed their vehicles down the road to clear a place for the helicopters to land and began to load up the wounded and the dead.

Medevac soldiers lifted me onto a stretcher and set my body down while cutting burning pieces of clothing and gear away from me. I kept hearing my platoon in the background, and the words kept pouring out of me, "Where are my men? Where are my soldiers?"

On the litter above me in the chopper, Adam called down to me, "I'm right here, SGT Harris."

I looked up. Stacked above me and facedown on his stretcher because of burns on the back of his legs, Adam looked me in the eye. I think it's a look only soldiers recognize. I desperately wanted him to hang on. I called, "Hey, you wanna stop dripping blood on me?"

The Blackhawk rotors sped up, the hot steel squealing with speed as the pilot prepared for takeoff. I blacked out, the battlefield beneath me gone in an instant.

18

FEAR AND TREMBLING

Kathreyn said it was just a normal day. Then she got the call no military spouse wants to receive. She was living in upstate New York, where she'd stayed with our four-year-old daughter, Elizabeth, and my son Josh, when I got deployed. It was about seven in the morning and they were just getting started on the day. Kathreyn was a loan technician for the USDA Farm Service and had just dropped off Elizabeth at her preschool. Josh was on winter break from Indian River High School, sleeping in like any normal teenage boy under a mess of blankets and pillows, unaware that all hell was about to break loose.

Her cell phone rang again, and Kat answered it as she left the preschool parking lot. It was the rear detachment commander, and as soon as she heard his voice, her heart began to pound. She pulled right back into her parking place and listened. He told her there had been an ambush, and she needed to return home. He said there would be a couple of soldiers at her house shortly, and they would give her the details. All she recalled was, "Shilo's been hurt."

Shaken to her core, Kathreyn walked back into the preschool, picked up a confused little Elizabeth, and drove home. Josh was surprised to see Kathreyn back at the house, and she sat down on the edge of his bed.

"There's bad news about Dad."

The three of them waited for the doorbell to ring.

Minutes dragged on as Kathreyn prayed and clung to her faith. Then a chaplain and rear detachment NCO came to the door and entered with news that would change everything she knew. The chaplain told her, "Shilo's been hit by an IED. Burned. They took him to a combat support hospital in the Green Zone in Baghdad, and from there, if they can, they'll medevac him to Germany."

Kathreyn wept into her palms, wiping her face and trying to stay strong for Lizzie and Josh. She gathered them into her arms, feeling them tighten beside her.

"What happened? What happened?" she asked.

"We don't have a lot of the details. We know three of his crewmembers were killed. The driver was injured, as well as Sergeant Harris." The men stood up to leave, telling her, "We'll keep you up to date as soon as we hear any more news. Stay close to your phone. Someone from the family readiness group will be by to check on you as well. If there's anything you need, any questions, just call us."

The Army prepares each military spouse for deployment and death, but the procedures for how to respond to a catastrophic injury hadn't really been covered. The next forty-eight hours were misery for Kathreyn and the kids. She had to notify my two boys in Texas that I was hurt. She had to call my parents. She hardly knew what to say. They all wanted answers, and she didn't have them. Between them, they tried to develop a contingency plan, praying for my survival.

● ● ●

On Thursday morning Kathreyn received another call from the rear detachment commander. "You're going to Landstuhl, Germany, in seven hours. Make arrangements quickly. There's no time to waste." There was an unspoken "if" at the end of that sentence: *if you can get there in time.*

Kathreyn's aunt and grandmother flew in from Coleman to pick up Elizabeth and take her with them back to Texas. From what Kathreyn had been told, if I survived I'd be transferred to Brooke Army Medical Center in San Antonio, and it made sense to have Elizabeth in Texas if that happened. Kathreyn asked for help from friends at Fort Drum so that she could leave Josh in New York. He had lived with us only for the past few months, and she wanted him to stay. Uprooting him to return to Coleman when he was more than halfway through his freshman year in high school made no sense.

She told Josh, "Dad's been hurt, but he's a fighter. You be strong too," and left our children in good hands. She had to pry Elizabeth's fingers from her neck as Lizzie screamed, not knowing where her mother was going but sure in her own way that something was very wrong. Josh was older, but scared nevertheless that he would lose me. Kathreyn raced to Syracuse and boarded the plane to Frankfurt, Germany, with her heart on fire. Life as she knew it was gone.

Worst-case scenario. Does anyone really know what those words mean? Kathreyn was about to find out. There was nobody there to meet her at the gate in Frankfurt, so she made her way through the foreign terminal. In spite of the language barrier, she could make out those three little letters, "USO," with an icon of the American flag on the signage, and located the welcome counter. The NCO in charge of meeting her was not at the scene, and the duty personnel at the USO phoned Landstuhl to find out what had happened to her escort. She was told they were not expecting her until the next day, so the NCO at the USO told her, "Get in," and they rushed up the autobahn to Landstuhl.

The snowy, sunless sky of winter in Germany was all a blur as they made their way to the hospital. The NCO advised Kat that she put her luggage at the Fisher House, which was right next to the hospital, and then she would be escorted to see me. My heart races when I think of how frightened she must have been, not knowing what she would find or if she'd arrive in time. At the Fisher House, she was met by the 10th Mountain Division liaison, SGT Matt Parkman, and he and the chaplain sat with her to describe what she would see when she entered my room.

◆ ◆ ◆

The Army Medical Center at Landstuhl is the only tertiary intensive care unit in the European theatre. If I survived the next few hours, I'd be moved stateside as soon as possible. It was another big "if," and Kathreyn was horrified. She knew from their expressions more than their explanations that nothing they would say could prepare her to see me. My face had been blown off.

I was tubed in every way. My head was swollen to the size of a basketball, and my face was charred and black. My entire body was enlarged, engorged with blood. A gauze bandage was wrapped around my head and under my jaw, and my tongue was swollen and extending from my mouth. Bandages continued from head to foot. I had a thick ventilator hose shoved through a hole in my trachea, and it was taking short, noisy breaths for me. My hands were huge: my palms over four inches thick. I was missing several fingers, and my collarbone was fractured. I was on life support and showed few signs of life. The nurses told Kathreyn to talk to me, to tell me she was there. She spoke, and I swear to God that even without ears I heard her. She took up watch by my side, my sweet girl who'd fought like hell to get to me in time.

By Saturday night, my parents had arrived from Coleman. My mother had never flown on a plane before, much less several of them to reach her overseas destination, but nothing was going to stop her from reaching me. Kathreyn tried to prepare them for what they were going to see. I was experiencing no neurological response, my pupils were not moving, and my C-7 vertebra fracture was serious. The fear of brain damage or brain death was real. I was bandaged over every area except my toes.

The medical team told Kathreyn, "We've got to stop these coma meds to see what's really going on. He's going to be in excruciating pain."

Kathreyn asked the obvious. "Why do it, then?"

"We've got to figure out if he can survive the trip to San Antonio with the trauma team." They warned my family, "The sedation drugs will leave his system in about four hours, and then . . ."

Kathreyn stopped and stared.

"If he survives, he'll experience pain beyond our comprehension."

Four hours later I went into full panic mode. Kathreyn and I came nose to nose and made eye contact for a moment. She saw hell in my eyes. She told me we were in Germany, and then I blacked out, disappearing into a dark abyss that I came to know as hell.

19

DEATH AND DYING

Two percent. If you're drinking milk, it means much of the fat is removed and you've basically got a glass of white water in your hand. Two percent was the number Kathreyn was given that represented my chances for survival, and my milk was a drip of anesthesia that kept my blood vessels narrow, decreasing the pressure and volume of my brain. The whole point of a medically induced coma is to reduce the metabolic rate of brain tissue and cerebral blood flow so you're at a baseline survival point. There is a profound shutdown of brain function. It can be reversed, but once the brain is allowed to return to normal function, it may also swell again and lead to sudden death.

When your brain's impaired, doctors have to stimulate your breathing. The central nervous system shuts down, and your body's involuntary muscles don't do the natural work of breathing for you. Your chest muscles become inactive and this creates a dangerous impairment with no oxygen flow. In order to keep my lungs operational, the medical team kept the ventilator going, and it was keeping me alive. With the severe burns to my face, the tip of my nose missing, and the massive swelling of my tongue and throat, it was difficult to keep my airways clear enough to hold the ventilator in place, and Kathreyn told me later that I seemed to be agitated even in my coma by the breathing apparatus.

As the hours went by, Kathreyn was told that if I could be stabilized, I'd make the difficult trip stateside for further treatment at Brooke Army Medical Center (BAMC) in San Antonio, Texas. The level of critical treatment and care I'd need could be continued only at BAMC. The medical team continued to observe and assess my injuries, replacing vital bodily fluids as rapidly as my body would allow. Dehydration is a huge issue at the onset, with all fluids evaporating rapidly in response to the burn.

When the medical team decided it was time, they assigned me to a CCATT, a three-person critical care ambulance transport team comprised of a physician, nurse, and respiratory technician. While I was still in treatment in the Green Zone, the Army's team from the Institute of Surgical Research (ISR) had been communicating with BAMC. The CCATT team was dispatched to Landstuhl to prepare me for my return to the USA. This "flying ICU" would be home for the next twenty hours as they put Kathreyn and me on the same C-17 cargo plane from Ramstein Air Base to San Antonio. I was further sedated for the trip, and I imagine Kathreyn was wishing for the same relief.

As I was unable to respond evenly to the ventilator, the attending doctor bagged me for over two hours on approach, his compressions giving me the only oxygen they could get into my lungs and to move blood through my heart to resuscitate me until we got to the hospital. We were moved from the air ambulance to the land ambulance and rushed to BAMC. Kathreyn crammed her suitcases on her lap in the crowded hold of the front seat of the ambulance, holding on for dear life as the driver raced toward BAMC.

When they took me out of the ambulance, I was crashing, but the team from BAMC wasn't about to lose me again at this point. They rushed me into the ICU and sent Kathreyn to the waiting room. She sat outside the burn unit on the fourth floor of the hospital all by herself for several hours, not knowing if I was alive or not. She'd traveled 7,500 miles in the span of four days, and little did we both know we had miles and miles and miles to go.

She tried to sleep in the place that would become home for her for hundreds of days ahead: BAMC. Run by the ISR, the intensive care unit of the burn center is the place where the lessons of the past meet the hope of the future. Medical professionals with thousands of hours of experience and collective wisdom treat burn victims, both military and civilian, and if any hope existed in the world, we were going to find it here.

For the family of the critically wounded, it is all about waiting. Waiting for the all-clear to travel, waiting for the debarking, reloading, and transport. Waiting for a sign, a word, a look, anything that would give some clue about my survival. Kathreyn told me she was oddly at peace, clinging to that 2 percent but somehow trusting that this mustard seed of faith in my recovery was enough. She knows what it means to pray without ceasing. I know now what I didn't know then: Someone was listening.

●●●

One of the results of burn trauma is continuous renal failure; your kidneys give out. The burn unit was equipped to handle that, but they nearly lost me twice to renal failure. Combat casualties are complicated; more than one system is involved. If my kidneys were recovering then my pulmonary system would fail. All the debris and dirt off the road in Iraq had to continuously come out of my burned skin or it would increase my risk for infection. Burn victims typically don't succumb to burns at the point of death; it's the infection that kills you. Your body gets septic, your blood gets poisoned, and you get worse before you get better. For days the team at BAMC worked on cleaning out my wounds, repeating anesthetic procedures each time; I could only take so much.

The ICU was hot; I was naked on my bed with arms stretched out perpendicular to my body and both legs separated. A towel covered my private parts. No one could come near me without donning full protective gear, as bacteria and viruses were a huge enemy at this point. Over time more areas of my body were treated and bandages applied. Swelling and edema from burn treatments require splinting, and I was stretched out on my bed as if I were on a cross. My arms perpendicular to my torso, the splints were moved and rearranged to try to prevent loss of mobility in my joints. Despite my injuries, the team of ISR therapists was already at work on physical therapy, moving and manipulating my body during my coma to optimize my chances of recovery.

I knew Kathreyn was nearby. She lived at the hospital, between the BAMC Fisher House and my room. I heard her voice and many others. Yet I was helpless to communicate with anyone. My coma placed me in a netherworld, neither conscious nor unconscious. I felt my mother's hands on my feet, rubbing and massaging them, but as hard as I tried to cry out to her, I was powerless to acknowledge her. I heard my wife in the room and was oblivious to understand why she didn't answer me. I thought I was verbal, but my utterances were mere groans, guttural cries for help that no one could translate or understand. I knew that I wanted to get out of that room, but as hard as I tried, I couldn't speak, I couldn't rise, I couldn't ask for help.

20

GEHENNA

I disappeared during those forty-eight days in a coma so deep and painful that I can hardly describe it. I wish I could tell you that it was a peaceful place. I wish I could tell you that in my coma I was in Coleman, fishing on the lake, with a bucket full of beer and a long string of bass. In my coma, I traversed the timeline of my life and was left for dead at the end of it. I wouldn't wish my coma on my worst enemy. It was as close to hell as I ever care to be. I didn't go to heaven for ninety minutes. I didn't travel "toward the light." I didn't have any conversations with God. I was in a dark place. I was in an abyss. I wasn't asleep.

In my coma, I died over and over again.

I lived in an alternate reality. Every image was dark and distorted. It was as if I had taken up residence in the worst nightmare or horror film you could imagine. I had no impression that I was dreaming. It was as real to me as the paper in front of me is now. It was full of pain and torment. At times I saw myself from outside my body, while at other times I was experiencing hell firsthand.

It wasn't hot, as you might expect when you read a description of hell. Everything hurt, and I had a feeling of utter helplessness. I started in a vast valley or canyon that was not of this world. Everything around me was crumbling. As I traveled through the darkness, the shadowy landscape would change from rural to urban. If I was in the wilderness, rocks were crashing and crumbling around me. If I was in the city, buildings were melting and crumbling next to me, covering me with debris. As I ran past these crumbling walls and buildings, I could feel sand and dirt on my skin, gravel and grit in my teeth.

The landscape was full of scary figures, silhouettes with red eyes that glinted in the dark. I remember having the conscious thought, *This has got to be hell. What did I do to get here?*

I had a level of consciousness that surprises me to this day. I was not alone. Other people were with me. I remember a woman with a large Afro running next to me, and another dark man wearing a gas mask. They were pulling me along as we ran together through a house of fiberglass. The fiberglass looked like long shards of crystal and pierced me through like a thousand swords. I had terrible headaches, and because I felt the rocks in my mouth, I couldn't bite or clear my mouth to scream. I tried to cry out but could make no sound. I wanted the pain to end but it would not.

In one sequence, I felt I was in a place similar to Colorado, with rocky mountains and cliffs. Everything around me was dark and crowded with people. We were in a house similar to a resort, and there was a swimming pool with a jet ski. I felt like an orb, floating above the people in the scene. The pool turned into a raging river of fire, and people cried for help, floating away from me as I hovered on the edge. The water was black, and my head hurt so badly as I watched the river race past me. My body changed from an orb to a shadow, and I tried to reach for people who were drowning. I wanted to reach them, to help them, to pull them out of the river, but I could not reach. I thought if I could save everybody then I could save myself. I looked at the water and knew that if I could just get in that river, I could save us all. But every time I reached for someone, their fingers would slip through my grasp and they would disappear in the burning river.

In another sequence, oddly enough, I was at a golf tournament. The grass was dark but the sky seemed lighter, and I could tell that it was gently raining. I was so thirsty. A large ship entered the scene, and I became trapped on the boat. I could hear my mother but I couldn't reach her. I was in intense pain but was helpless to find a way off the boat. As I spun in pain, I thought it was raining pink lemonade, and that it was gathering in some kind of cistern over my head. I think it's possible that my medication for the coma was decreasing, and perhaps what I was imagining was actually an IV bag by my bed. But in my mind, I saw pink lemonade dripping off the sides of this ship, and all I wanted to do was drink it.

In another sequence, a large, ugly nurse stood over me. I hurt so bad that I wanted to throw up. I begged her for help. She was distorted and shadowed, but I could tell she was a heavy smoker. She had yellow teeth, yellow skin, scraggly hair. I kept trying to call out, "Hurt . . . hurt," but she would twist a clamp on my hand and snarl at me for complaining. She twisted my arm until I felt the pain down into my groin. The image of that nurse wakes me from a dead sleep to this day.

All of the coma sequences were unique and strange. In one scene I was in a large palace, and everything was made from food. The furniture resembled stacks of donuts. I was in an inner tube, and I was circling around and around the palace, trying to reach the tables and chairs made out of food. I had lost nearly sixty pounds at this point, so it's reasonable to think that even in my coma I was truly hungry.

Over and over during my coma, I felt I was being slaughtered, that my skin was being ripped off one shredded layer at a time. At other moments, I pictured my head over a trash can, and a large cleaver was slicing through the back of my skull. The pain was excruciating, but the visions were worse. I have never known such darkness. I have never known such evil. I wanted out. Many times I felt as if I were in a boat, lost at sea, and I would never make it back to shore. If it meant I had to die to get away from the darkness, I was willing to do it.

●●●

I don't remember any relief from the suffering. It was intense. There was no passivity. I was actively fighting to get out of that place. If someone asked me today what hell is like, I would say it is a place of intense torment and suffering that has no endpoint.

Some people have asked me if I have trouble sleeping since the explosion. Memories of the blast do not wake me up at night, but my memories of the coma do. Continuous torment, relentless pain and suffering, and images of darkness and decay from another world haunt my dreams. The Greek word for hell as it's used in the Bible is *Gehenna*. It translates roughly as "a place for the burning of garbage." I believe I went to that dump, and I know that it's real.

Our world has many variations on heaven and hell. Some people believe there is no heaven and there is no hell, that they don't exist. Others believe in a kind of universal experience with versions of heaven or hell on this earth. In my visions and dreams during my coma, I experienced hell and I know that it's real. While I have complete assurance that heaven is ahead of me, it is very hard to put that hellish experience behind me.

In talking with my doctors and nurses over time about the surgeries and procedures conducted during my coma period, I realize that many of the feelings I experienced could well be related to what was being done to me at any given time. A medically induced coma involves a tricky balance of sedation and wakefulness, so that the body can recover and heal. One of the early procedures burn patients must endure is called debriding. Within the confines of my own comatose mind, I could not put what was happening to me in context.

● ● ●

According to Kathreyn, as early as my treatment in the Green Zone at Baghdad, I was placed on a steel gurney and rolled into a shower room heated to 90 degrees while surgeons removed skin, tissue, bone, rocks, dirt, and debris from the blast. The initial debriding is vital because all of the debris left on your body may burn for hours after the initial blast, and the sooner it's removed, the better. Fire lingers in shrapnel, in pieces of your uniform, in remnants of armor, in the fragments of equipment embedded in your skin. It has to be washed out in a warm shower. Additionally, there are strains of bacteria in the dirt from Iraq that can kill you, and the debriding was designed to protect me from further contamination. But the process as I interpreted it was torture. In my coma, I was in a convertible, and as I raced down the freeway showers of jagged glass hit me. It felt like my flesh was being pierced with thousands of razor-sharp needles. There was no turning back or turning around, and it was one of the scariest parts of my experience.

We take respiration for granted every day, but after being in the center of an explosion, my lungs had filled with so much debris that a bronchoscopy trying to get a look at the inside of my lungs revealed a picture similar to what you'd see after someone smoked hundreds of packs of cigarettes in minutes. The fiber-optic scope threaded into my ventilator tube showed lungs full of tar-like soot, not unlike what a chimney sweep would uncover in a clogged smokestack.

Burns sap every ounce of liquid or moisture out of your body, and I was given bag after bag of vital fluids, trying to replenish what I'd lost. The medical team fought the evaporation, and as they did, my edema increased. Because of the swelling, they had to fillet me—slitting my right arm from the shoulder to my wrist to let the fluid seep out of my gaping flesh. The images I had in my coma of being sliced open were real.

In the black of night or day throughout these procedures, I could not rise from within. I was down, buried alive inside a deep hole. Perhaps this is something that all people who draw so near to death realize. Death is a place. It's either heaven or hell. For me, I was in an inferno that I thought I could not escape.

As the medical team began to decrease my sedation, there were times when I thought I could see the light of Kathreyn's face. I knew she was there. I tried to reach for her, but she was just beyond my grasp. I would call for her without words, hoping she'd hear me. My body wrestled internally, trying to move voluntarily, but I was suspended in pain. I knew she never left me, but I was extremely frustrated that I couldn't take her hand. My ears were blown off, but I could hear her voice. My eyes had swollen shut, but I could see her beside me. I couldn't lift my hands to hold her, but I tried to reach her with every muscle in me. The first thing I did when I came out of my coma was to reach for her.

21

AWAKE, ALIVE

After I spent forty-eight days in a coma, the staff at BAMC was ready to wean me from the meds that were keeping me comatose to see if I could survive on my own. My coma meds had been in flux throughout the past couple of months, bringing me in and out of focus, depending upon my pain tolerance. It was a delicate dance, finding the right balance of anesthesia to allow me to function just at the wakeful point. They knew what to do, but Kathreyn didn't. Agreeing to a procedure that could extinguish that 2 percent was hardly something she could do, yet withholding consent would mean I could not recover at all. This is where the rubber met the road, when she used all the trust she had in her to let go and let God.

Stirring. It comes in waves. It's as if blood begins to surge in your cerebral cortex and you have some proof of life. On some cognitive level you realize you have toes. You realize you're weighed down, covered, bound. And you have the memory of skin, fingers, ears. You know your body is a debris field of injury. You have pain that is specific rather than general. You have some clarity of vision. The room comes in and out of focus, and you have connective thoughts. You're disoriented, but you have a realization about the disorientation. You're aware that you have a heartbeat, a pulse. You have a sense that you're suffering; you're confused and you know you're hurt. You think you're alive but you want to ask dumb questions like, "Am I alive?"

I knew I wasn't alone; in fact I had the idea that it got quite crowded at times. In and out of my room would troop surgeons, nurses, pulmonary specialists, more nurses, anesthesiologists, dieticians, psychologists, and again nurses, chaplains, case managers, attending physicians, fellows, residents, and numerous clinical research personnel, and . . . did I mention nurses? All were focused on keeping me alive.

When you get blown up, there are pending questions that life or death may never allow you to ask. There is a lot of noise in a hospital room. Internal noise, even when your eardrums have been destroyed. You hear noise with your head and your heart, even if no one else can. My noise filled up with questions and answers that sometimes lifted me up and other times left me ready to say goodbye once and for all to this earth, this life, this hell. More than a few sets of hands touched my body with surgical tools and bandages and chemicals and gloved fingers. Every touch was foreign and surreal. I had traveled to the bottom of the Glasgow Coma Scale, a place no soldier wants to be.

●●●

As I came out of my coma, I really only cared about one thing: my girl. I had seen her often in my coma. I saw her myopically, telescopically, and at other times I had a bird's-eye view of her sitting by my bed. Sometimes a small part of her was magnified—a palm, a shoulder, a cheek. Pieces of her were within my point of view for forty-eight days. I heard her voice and clung to it. I tried to put sounds into words, words into phrases.

I asked, "Are you here?"

She smiled and leaned in close.

"I'm here," she whispered. "I'm right here."

She told me later that I was never alone; the only time someone who loved me left the room was when a difficult procedure or surgery was taking place and the trauma team ordered her out of the room.

She had divided her time between sleeping at the Fisher House and my room. Zachary Fisher was an honorary veteran and patriotic American who worked tirelessly on behalf of all men and women in the US Armed Forces and funded houses around the world for families just like ours. I don't know what we would have done without the Fisher House. It gave Kathreyn a soft place to land at the end of each horrific day. I asked her, "Where's Josh? Where's Lizzie?"

She told me, "Josh is still in New York, and Lizzie's with my family. Josh is going to finish up the school year and then he'll be here. Lizzie's going to come see you soon."

I faded in and out of wakefulness, listening to her reassurances. "Your mom and dad have been here. We've all been praying for you."

"Where's my mom?" I asked.

"She's been here all along. The folks at Owl Drugs where she works set up a fund to help pay for her travel expenses. She and Solitaire have been coming back and forth from Coleman."

"What about Nicolas and Albert?" I asked her. "Are they okay?"

"They're fine," she told me. "Worried about you, but they're fine."

I knew they were all too young to handle what was happening to me. The only one who could handle the details was Josh, and like most teenage boys, he would not want to come to terms with my mortality. Kathreyn tried to keep things upbeat but realistic. It was a difficult balancing act. I don't know what soldiers with children do without a spouse like Kathryn. As a squad leader, I had heard horror stories of spouses who would visit BAMC or Walter Reed, only to find their loved ones so devastated by injury that all they could do was turn and walk away. Kathreyn had that choice, but it was not in her to even consider such a thing. If you ever want to meet a hero, you need to meet my wife.

I wanted to take her hand, but I couldn't lift my arms. Would I be able to hold her again? Would she want me to? Would she want to stay with a man who was different in ways I had yet to comprehend? I did not know what I did not know . . . that I would never have to ask her these things. Because her hands were mine, had always been mine. Her eyes were mine, had always been mine. Her heart was mine, would always be mine.

◆ ◆ ◆

I had a lot to think about as I came out of my coma.

But as I woke, there was something that slipped into my life, into my heart, and I knew what I knew. From the corner of my eye above my swollen cheekbones, I'd see a nurse come into the room, and I'd know that those were the hands that had cared for me, day after day, doing the hard jobs that no one else wanted to do. A doctor would remove my splints and reposition them, and when I'd see his eyes, I'd recognize them from another time and place. An orderly would come in to take care of cleaning me, and I'd realize he'd been doing it all along. A therapist would enter and give me breathing treatments, and on some level I knew we'd met before. The nurse would try to get me to eat, and as he reattached bags of nutrients, I'd understand that he'd fed me before, through a tube directed to my stomach. When I'd aspirated, he'd saved me. A voice would stir me awake, and I would know that I'd heard that accent before, as another nurse changed my IV bags or a lab technician pulled another syringe full of blood from my veins.

Words would woo me in and out of consciousness:

I'm here.

Hang in there.

I love you.

Come on back, buddy.

Shilo. Shilo.

We're right here with you.

Let's go fishing; come on.

I didn't know what to call it, and I couldn't have uttered the words if I tried, but God was showing me his grace, in every moment. He was leading me to the new unknown.

22

SHARED SORROW

To this day I can't walk by an American flag without wanting to salute. I've watched it hanging peacefully, lifting with the breeze. I've folded it with the color guard at dusk, pressing it into tight folds to make a solid triangle with the sound of Taps at day's end. I've yanked it up the flagpole at our base camp and set it on its standard in the sand. I've watched it wave over the White House, the governor's mansion, my own home. That flag was emblazoned on my uniform and my vehicle. But my eyes, my brain, and my heart will never grow accustomed to the sight of the red, white, and blue draped over a coffin, blanketing a fallen comrade.

I am riding down a dusty trail in Babylon, my four warrior brothers at my side, and in my mind's eye I see the American flag on the windshield of my Humvee over and over again. I'm in the passenger seat; Adam's driving. I wanted to see my crew. I wanted to know they were okay.

● ● ●

One day Kat told me I had a visitor. "There's somebody here who wants to see you."

I didn't know who it was. Over the past few weeks I'd had plenty of visitors, from family and friends to chaplains and other clinical staff. I'd been focused on recovery, and had a few setbacks as I tried to get stronger. Every once in a while a general or high ranking officer would be in the

127

hospital visiting troops and we'd get word that we had a special guest, so I really didn't know who was going to walk in the door.

My driver, SP4 Adam Devine, walked in. Just like he did when we served side by side, he had poise and military bearing, and he saluted me. "Hey, Sergeant Harris." Those three words alone made me happy, made me feel whole. I looked at him with extreme pride, just like I did when we were all still Team Hellcat. He leaned over my hospital bed and we hugged it out. I felt like I was holding a brother.

Adam and I had known each other for only a couple of months before the explosion, but there's a special kind of mathematics in combat. Two months might as well have been two decades. You share a vehicle, meals, downtime, mission requirements; just about everything that happens in a twenty-four-hour period makes a unit a family, a brotherhood. I was ecstatic that he had come. My crew was so much a part of me, and I understood my healing would never fully commence until I knew how they were all doing.

But as soon as I looked him in the eyes, I could tell that he was sad and guilt-ridden.

"What's wrong, buddy? What's wrong?"

He started crying and crying. "I didn't mean for this to happen. I should have done something different. I shouldn't have run over the rim of that road."

I tried to stop him. "It wasn't your fault, man. It wasn't your fault," I told him. Through thick lips and over my swollen tongue, I tried to tell him, "I was the truck commander, I was the one in charge of that vehicle, if anyone's at fault it's me."

He said, "I was so scared," and I agreed.

"It was bad. We were the third truck in the convoy, remember? You were alert. We were all watching for the bad stuff. It wasn't your fault. It was war, man."

I tried to reassure him. "One of these days we'll all get together and talk about what happened."

At that moment, I noticed that something changed. There was an uncomfortable silence that hung in the air between us. He looked at Kat, and they both looked at me.

I asked him, "What were your injuries?"

"I got a hole in my abdomen, and a compound fracture of my arm, some burns on my legs and hip, but I'm okay. Somebody pulled me out of the vehicle pretty quick."

The day of the explosion came back crystal clear. I remembered trying to fight my way out of my seat so I could help him, but there was so much smoke and so much fire, I just couldn't do it. There was a lot to say, and so much that would remain unspoken. It's hard to find the vocabulary for casualties. Survivor guilt is a huge problem for a soldier, and I knew we were both susceptible.

"We knew the risks, we were all just doing our jobs," I told him.

He nodded and looked me up and down, keeping a steady but pained look on his face. He was so young and had been through so much. I hated that he'd been injured, but it looked like he was going to be all right.

I told him, "Well, I'm glad you're doing okay."

"You're my hero, SGT Harris. My wounds are nothing like yours. But you're going to be okay too."

I was touched that he was trying to encourage me, and I felt overjoyed that he was going to fully recover. Emotions were running high between us, but the visit had taken a toll on me. He soon got up to leave. "I'm gonna go. I'll come back to see you."

"You do that. But I'll be out of here before you know it." He was so vulnerable. I didn't want him to leave with any guilt. "Hey, Adam," I called to him. "Thanks for coming. It means a lot, man. More than you know."

He and Kathreyn hugged and walked out the door together, and I looked around the empty room. Something didn't feel right. Kat came back inside a few minutes later and closed the door. I looked her in the eye.

"Okay, how bad is it?" I asked her. "Somebody didn't make it."

She walked back to my bedside and put her hand on my arm. "You and Adam were the only two," she told me, tears streaming down her face. "You were the only two left. No one else made it out."

The world stopped in that moment. I thought I was going to pass out. I began to cry, and I couldn't stop.

The news made my chest cave in.

The guilt and anguish I felt over losing the finest soldiers I knew crushed me.

I cried for three days.

I was inconsolable. I wouldn't let Kathreyn leave at night. "I can't stay here by myself. Don't leave," I said.

All I did was cry. I ran through that day over and over again in my head. I questioned everything I'd done; I questioned who I was; I questioned my ability to lead; I questioned everything about that terrible day. It broke me.

Kathreyn tried to comfort me. "You can't go on like this," she said gently.

The tears and dry heaves would not stop. I could not stop shuddering. The pain waged its war inside me all over again. I saw my men with my mind's eye. I saw the road, the dust, and the dirt. I heard the explosion all over; felt the adrenaline as I tried to get away from the ammo as it cooked off in our vehicle; saw the soldiers who sheltered me against the fire. It all came back. It all came crashing down. In the darkest hour of the night, my tears would not subside. I kept rethinking the whole day, replaying the route down Metallica, rehearsing a different outcome with a long list of "what-ifs." It was pure torture, and I could not fight my way out of my head.

"Oh, God," I cried, needing comfort that was not of this world. I called his name over and over. I groaned his name without words. I railed at him. And finally I got quiet. I prayed that my guys made it to heaven. I asked God, "Please take care of them, God. Please."

I thought about each man I'd lost, trying to recover every memory of the time we had together. I thought about all they'd told me about their families and I wept. I prayed for their families. I prayed for everything, and finally I prayed for peace in my heart. I prayed for peace for all of us.

❖ ❖ ❖

God met me at my point of need. And I learned something about him. No matter how helpless I felt, he planted in my heart a longing for him. I don't know how other soldiers sort it out without faith. It just can't be done. The chaplain came by my room and shared some news with me. "Like a deer pants for water, our souls long for God, Shilo. It doesn't matter how low we go, how far we fall, how much pain you're in, he'll still call for you."

I knew he was telling me the truth. As hard as I might run from God, or away from what happened, I would not be able to survive without the peace that he provides. Besides the actual day of the explosion, the day I found out my crew was killed was the worst day of my life. In the roar of that explosion, God took some of us home and left some of us here on this earth, but I recognized in that period of mourning that this is a temporary home.

My adversaries might have taunted me, crushing my bones, but I understood where my hope came from and I thought of that as often as I could in the weeks following Adam's visit. Buried beneath the rubble of grief that was still bound up inside me, I had to let go of the turmoil and give it to God before it consumed me. I had to live.

There are things a soldier cannot say to you; there are sentences a soldier cannot utter. Men and women who've survived combat know what I am saying. There are no words. The families of the men who died that day deserve to know that their sons, husbands, brothers, uncles, nephews, cousins, and beloved ones died in the line of duty, a duty they treated as a privilege, but I will not tell you more. I am keeping their memory safe and sacred within me, and I will honor their ultimate sacrifice until the day I leave this earth.

23

BABY STEPS

Ten steps. That's all they asked of me. With all the bravado I could muster, I said to myself, *Piece of cake, I'm going to own this hospital in about three steps. I can ruck twenty-five miles with a hundred pounds on my back.*

By the third step, I was wiped out. I could make it no further. I begged Kathreyn and my mom to help me escape. I wanted water, I wanted fresh air, I wanted out. But I was helpless to do any of that for myself. The physician's assistant, Peter Yen, came by and gave me some words of encouragement. Told me if I could stand up I could step down.

I asked him what he meant. "If you get out of ICU and make it to the step-down unit, it means you're on your way to going home," he said. For the next seventeen days, I did nothing but step it up in order to step down. There were plenty of moments of sheer frustration.

My doctor told me, "Burn trauma is one of the most difficult obstacles you'll ever overcome. It's demanding, painful, and every day is a fight. But we're here to see you succeed, and we won't give up."

I heard what he said but thought it would be different for me. I was a warrior in my mind, even though my body wasn't cooperating. I spent every available ounce of energy in physical therapy and focused on my recovery. I wanted to go home.

● ● ●

There was no therapy lab for the work that still had to happen on the inside. I carried a huge burden of guilt over my survival. I struggled with what had happened to my crew, and the chaos of their deaths plagued my thoughts and dreams. I started to visit with an Army chaplain named COL Alfredo Montalvo. He became a regular part of my day. When I felt discouraged at my lack of progress or speed in recovery, he told me, "Shilo, God's spared your life for a reason. Give yourself time."

I told him, "I don't think you understand. I lost three of my best friends in that truck. I am not sure I can go on without them. Why did I live?"

I explained, "God should have saved one of the other men; I did not deserve to survive."

COL Montalvo told me, "You can't live with 'what if.' You have to live with 'what now?'"

As he kept me company while I tried to regain my strength, we talked a lot about the men and women who were in recovery rooms nearby. He'd point out a room where a triple amputee was trying to recover from burn wounds enough to get fitted for three prosthetics. He'd tell me about walking past a soldier trying to handle the latest of fifteen or sixteen skin grafts.

"Live for them," he told me. "Make it for them."

When it came time for COL Montalvo to deploy to Iraq, I felt fearful for his safety. I wanted to go in his place. I wasn't done serving in this war. He said, "You recover. Recover for God. Recover for your family. They need you."

It was hard to say goodbye, but there was much work to be done; I had to have faith in COL Montalvo's faith. I had to believe what he believed: that God would see me through.

⬢ ⬢ ⬢

There were other things I needed to see outside the spiritual realm, like my own face. I'd been avoiding that moment. I could track my recovery by the expressions on my family's faces when they came to see me. But it was time to see for myself what I looked like. In my mind's eye, I was still just Shilo. Kathreyn broke it to me slowly. She used her phone to take my picture, and held it up so I could see myself. Lucky for me it was not high-resolution, but nevertheless, it wasn't easy. Whoa. This was not the face I remembered having. No ears. Half my nose gone. Lips bigger than Angelina Jolie, sort of. Skin scarred and stretched. Who was this guy? I was silent for a few seconds.

But I knew crying wasn't going to give me my face back. The same hazel eyes I've always had were looking back at me, but if you looked real close, they were eyes that had made a record of a lot more trauma than most of us experience in a lifetime. Kathreyn told me: "Same beautiful eyes," and I felt better. Alive and grateful. I remembered the day I begged Kathreyn for those Oakley's, and the grief I caught from my dad over how much they cost. Had she not sent me those expensive sunglasses on my first deployment, I'd have lost both eyes in the blast.

I reminded my dad when he came to visit of how he wanted me to get my shades at Dollar General. He told me, "I'll never tell you how to spend your money again," and we had a good laugh over the irony of that argument. I didn't dwell on my appearance. I cared more about function, and each therapy session or surgical procedure brought me closer to the goal of regaining mobility and utility.

Adam had returned from convalescent leave and began to visit me, giving Kathreyn some relief and taking part in my therapy. He massaged my cheeks to stimulate blood flow so the grafted skin wouldn't die. He'd had skin grafts of his own so he knew the drill. I had my arms extended in casts twenty-four hours a day, and I wasn't sure how much more I could take. Adam kept my morale up through his companionship. I was able to get up and take a few steps across the floor, trying to build some stamina.

As I began to walk further distances, I found out that going outside was pure agony. The sun bore down and shade was essential. The medical staff warned me, "Your body temperature can't be regulated anymore; you're going to have to limit your time outdoors, and forget about spending any time in the sun." I knew as a Texan that was going to be hard. Texas in mid-summer is an oven, but for a burn patient it's on broil.

I was told that if I could make it out of the step-down unit, I'd be given thirty days of convalescent leave at home. This meant I wouldn't have to report for duty to a hospital or unit. I was told to be ready after thirty days to resume my nonstop therapy sessions, but for the next month my job would be to enjoy my life at home. I got the warning: turn into a vegetable on the couch and you're going to have a much tougher time in therapy, so I was determined to come back stronger than ever.

Kathreyn began to shadow my nurses. If our goal was to go home, she was going to be the nurse in charge of my care, and she took on that role with a vengeance. She learned all she could about wound care, following me through each procedure from sunup till after dark. As it turns out, it was a lot more than changing a bandage. Wound care took more than six hours each and every day. I couldn't feed myself. I couldn't touch my nose. I couldn't take care of myself, period. As much as I tried, I wasn't much help.

You may not think of it this way, but our skin is our largest organ. It regulates our body temperature and protects our innards. It gathers information about pain and pressure. Over a third of this organ was gone, first burned and then debrided and grafted. I was still very much a patient, but I was far from patient about going home. If Kathreyn hadn't chosen to take on the role of nurse, I'd probably still be sitting at BAMC today, a shadow of a man. We'd heard the horror stories of spouses who arrived at the hospital, saw what their future looked like, and turned around in their tracks. On the one hand, you couldn't blame them, as that's not what they signed up for. Yet every married couple makes that promise, "for better or worse," not knowing how bad it can really get. I thanked God every single day for my wife.

Our worst day was our worst day. I wanted to check out once and for all. Forget about going home. I was ready to go Home. I was stuck to the bed. My stomach, chest, and back were all exposed. All the donor sites for my skin grafts were exposed. I stuck to the sheets. To get the pillow away from my head and shoulders, we had to peel it off. I felt like I was being skinned alive. I'd been medicated for pain, but could feel every procedure nevertheless. I still have nightmares about that level of pain. Tears in my eyes, I asked Kathreyn, "Can we do this?"

She didn't waver. "We can and we will."

The new chaplain came by to check on me every day, and his face became familiar. I had some questions for him and told him to get ready. He gave me a knowing look. He'd been in the hot seat before.

Time's a funny thing in the hospital. The hands on a clock, the pages on a calendar—they lose all meaning. You track time through how your meds are reduced, how many specialists see you on an hourly or daily basis, what your vitals are saying, how the faces on your visitors appear. If they give you that tragic look, the day gets pretty long.

We finally got the all-clear. "You've been in the hospital for five months. Let's try this at home, see how you do . . ." and my heart skipped a beat. I was so ready to go home.

24

REUNITED

There were no words for the team at BAMC as I left. How do you thank people for saving you? What words match those emotions? They'd seen me through battle, fighting for me when I was helpless, then helping me learn that I wasn't powerless at all. I knew I'd be back, and often, from the prognosis I'd been given, but the first time I left, there were just no words. I watched as Kat loaded our belongings into the car: months of cards, letters, photos, and small objects of affection.

Kathreyn carried a small dispensary into our home: meds, dressings, supplies. I walked around the house, touching everything familiar to me. It felt like a miracle but just crossing the room left me exhausted. She helped me into the bathtub, and we began the daily ritual of soaking my bandages off. She'd fill the tub with tepid water, and I'd lower myself into the water, unable to gauge the temperature by myself. Layer by layer, she'd remove the gauze, cleaning and disinfecting as she went. I'd soak, wolfing down air to keep the pain at bay. She'd reapply the bandages as I dried. We started the pain meds about a half hour before the procedure so they'd still be working by the time we finished, but day after day, that became a close call. By the time we were done, I'd be in agony and so would she. Kat told me, "I have to separate myself from your pain. I can't take it."

I really can't fathom how Kathreyn did it. I couldn't do much by myself, and at least at the hospital there was a team of nurses, specialists, doctors, and trauma teams nearby in case of an emergency. Kathreyn became my nurse, my specialist, my doctor, and more than anything else, my trauma team as I learned to come face-to-face with a face I could hardly recognize.

● ● ●

As I healed, I felt like I could handle having Elizabeth return home, and I wanted so much for some semblance of family life to return. But I didn't realize what an increased burden that would place on Kathreyn to nurse me back to some unknown stage of health as well as take care of the kids. After hours of caregiving, there was little time left in the day for Kathreyn to be a mom. We agreed Lizzie would come to visit, and I could hardly wait to hold her again.

She hid. The first time I saw my little Elizabeth, she hid from me. She used Kathreyn's body as a shield and stayed behind her mother. I was so scary, so foreign to her. Kathreyn was wise and gave Elizabeth a job. She told her, "Daddy needs a helper to hold his drinks."

She took that on like the Secret Service, standing by my side with cold water, ready to help me or protect me at a moment's notice. When we saw how important and needed this made Elizabeth feel, Kathreyn and I had an epiphany. We were able to recognize that for so much of this journey, we had not been communicating enough with our children. We had Josh living with his mother again during my recovery, my two youngest boys with their mother in west Texas, and Elizabeth with her grandparents. It was time to get the whole family involved in my recovery. We had to start sharing more about the path to recovery, as they would be with me every step.

I was exhausted, and so was Kathreyn, but I was also free as a bird. When the kids came to visit we played Xbox until my weak muscles failed. After a full day of gaming, I couldn't move any of my seven fingers the next day, and my thumbs were raw. We had a good laugh as we realized why I was so sore. We were couch potatoes. The healing was going on inside and out, for each one of us. Reality set in too. We were all aware of the new normal, not sure of all the ramifications but very sure that life was going to be lived differently in the Harris household. Gone was the dad who could wrestle them to the ground, give them the people's elbow, or flip them onto his shoulders like little hitchhikers. As I looked at each of my children, as much as I was grateful to be with them, I also had to accept that their lives were going to be as different as mine. I was going to have physical limitations that would be hard for all of us to accept. Change. It was all around us.

After acting like a lazy bum for a few days, I started to use every opportunity to stretch, bend, and work my muscles. Before I drank a jug of milk, I'd do curls as many times as I could before the jug was empty. We went through a lot of milk. If I had to walk, I'd take the long way. If I had to bend over, I'd make it harder than it needed to be in hopes that I'd heal that much sooner. I wanted rehab, and I wanted it bad. I stretched my arms so much that I didn't realize I'd torn the new skin they'd grafted onto my arms. You can't feel scar tissue, it has no nerve endings. You could stick a needle into it and I couldn't feel it. But I was bleeding up and down my arms, and reluctantly got into the car to go back to BAMC.

When we arrived, the doctor said, "All right, let's see where you are." He asked me to demonstrate my range of motion. I lifted my arm and the doctor said, "Holy crap, you've gained fifteen degrees."

I said, "Take that, sucker." I whipped my arm up in the air and tore it again.

He told me, "Take it easy," when he saw my skin tearing. "Your recovery's going to take a lot longer if you keep that up. Just do some gradual work."

I was tired of gradual, but I heard what he was saying and promised to slow it down. I knew that the only way I could learn how to live was to be as independent as possible. I didn't realize that it would be eight months before I could actually feed myself again.

●●●

One day, after the kids had all left, Kathreyn and I were sitting at the kitchen table and I got nasty. She told me I needed to stay positive. It turned me inside out. "How the hell do I stay positive when I've been blown to bits? You try staying positive! You try walking around like a freak show!"

I was cranky and hateful, and she didn't deserve that. I just couldn't seem to get out of my funk. I was having my own little pity party and didn't want any guests who wouldn't buy into giving me sympathy. Kathreyn had had enough. She got up from the table, leaving my glass and lunch just out of my reach.

I knew I'd hurt her, and there was no excuse for that. I was in a foul mood. I can't quite recall how long she let me stew in my own juices. I couldn't feed myself. I couldn't reach my drink on the table. I stared around the kitchen, everything out of my grasp but within my point of view. Lizzie's art on the refrigerator. The kids' photos on magnets on the fridge. Breakfast dishes still sitting by the sink. Blue sky outside the window. What a fool I'd been. I realized I was my own worst enemy.

I asked, "Kat, come back." It was a turning point for me. My depression, my disfigurement, my guilt over surviving, my loss . . . it was all about me. Yet my wife, my children, my family had the greatest love and respect for what I was going through, and they were absolutely going through it with me.

Kathreyn told me, "Get it out, Shilo. Get it out in the open."

I understood what she was asking. I needed to talk. And there were plenty of people willing to listen, if I would let down my walls. Kathreyn told me, "This is how you heal; you talk to those who care about you, those who love you."

I talked, and then I listened.

I've tried to share Kathreyn's wisdom and what we learned as a family with other soldiers. So much of the military persona is about being Army strong, but there's a different kind of strength we can draw on that doesn't require anything of us except surrender. We had to reinvent healing as a family.

One day a squad leader called about not making formation. During my recovery, I'd been assigned to a warrior transition command, and the unit was set up to operate like a typical military organization while making allowances for the medical needs of the soldiers assigned to it. Kathreyn talked to the squad leader on the phone, as she got chewed out about the matter.

I had to rely on Kathreyn to get me to my appointments and surgeries, and to communicate for me—I had no ears to hear what this platoon sergeant wanted to say over the phone that day, but I had a mouth that was fixing to communicate quite well with her. I asked Kathreyn to take me to the unit and went into the platoon area, ready to find the squad leader.

As soon as she saw me and I introduced myself, she started apologizing.

I said, "Stop. Now you know me. If you need me, talk to my wife. I can't talk on the phone because of my hearing loss. I have many doctor appointments, and we're usually not done until late in the day, and I'm exhausted. I'm wrapped head to toe in bandages, and I have a full plate."

I admonished her, "Get to know your soldiers. Know what you're dealing with before you jump down anyone's throat."

● ● ●

I tried to resume my roles as provider, protector, and handyman in our home, and tried to pitch in as the family got settled in the post quarters we'd been given near BAMC. I felt pretty useless. I sat there pouting for a while, and Kat suggested, "You're the one who wants everything level, go hang something."

I had to use a hammer, which is no small feat with seven fingers, weak ones covered with skin grafts at that. With the first swing, I hit my finger with the hammer and I bled like a stuck pig. Lizzie came to my rescue to doctor me up. She got out ointment and bandages, and patched me up pretty well. I tried to finish the job but got so frustrated I left a small hole in the wall where a picture belonged. "Let's go look at clouds, Daddy," she said, and convinced me to share our favorite routine.

We walked outside in the night air to the trampoline. I couldn't bounce, but she and I liked to lay on our backs on the top of the trampoline and star gaze. Pride wounded, picture hung, we looked up at the clouds together. Elizabeth asked me, "Daddy, do you want to pray?

Little one. Do I want to pray? Do I tell her that every breath I take is a prayer? Do I tell her about my moments of doubt, anger, rage, frustration, fear? I chickened out, and simply said, "Yes."

"Do you want me to pray for you?"

"Why don't you do that, Elizabeth?"

She didn't even blink; she just looked at me with those beautiful blue eyes and then bowed her head. "Dear God, I pray for my mommy and my daddy and his burns. I pray for Joshua and Albert and Nicolas. I pray for my grandmas and my grandpas. I pray for all the nurses and doctors who helped my daddy . . ."

Elizabeth prayed her way around the world. "And thank you, God, for helping my daddy hang that pretty picture on the wall. Amen."

I asked her, "Lizzie, is there anything you want to share with me? Tell me how you are feeling."

She said, "Daddy, when I was in Coleman I was so scared. I didn't know what was going to happen to you."

140

"I'm sorry you were so scared, sweetheart. Daddy didn't mean to have you hurt like that." She cried in my arms, letting all the pressure of these last few months pour out. She didn't roll over on the trampoline to see the tears streaming down my cheeks, across the bandages that still covered the places where my ears should be, across the tracks on my face that were still scorched and peeling.

We held hands and stayed in the night air, deep in the heart of Texas, and I wrapped my arms around my little girl. I could still do that. I still had my arms to wrap around my little girl.

● ● ●

The road to recovery for a wounded warrior and his family is paved with pain. Spiritual agony. Physical suffering. Mental anguish. Emotional exhaustion. There are questions you have for God. Hard, hard questions you can barely utter aloud, yet you're screaming for answers.

Where is Jesus when your clothing melts into your flesh?

Where is he when your pain makes you want to trade places with him?

Where is God, you ask. *Where are you? Where were you? Where did you go?*

How can my family endure?

And the answers don't come easy. But in the simple faith of my daughter, she shared some good news. In her sweet little girl voice, she assured me in song.

"Jesus loves you, this I know, for the Bible tells me so. Little ones to him belong; they are weak, but he is strong."

I didn't tell Elizabeth what she was too young to understand: I was the little one.

25

STARTING OVER

At the end of my thirty days, it was time to return to therapy. Right next to BAMC sits a state-of-the-art healing spot: The Center for the Intrepid (CFI). Built by private funds donated by over six hundred thousand folks who used their money to show their gratitude to war veterans, the center had just opened in 2007. I began a string of sessions to strengthen what I had and started occupational therapy to learn how to work with what was left.

I'd been involved in scores of occupational and physical therapy sessions on 4E at BAMC, so I knew what I was in for. But at this point I was an outpatient, and a lot of the motivation for scheduling and maintaining my progress was resting squarely on my shoulders. Thanks to the CFI, I had everything I needed in terms of tools for physical therapy. I knew my competitive spirit would come in handy. I tried using weights to sit up. I used the indoor pool, the track, the climbing wall, and the lab where they fabricated prosthetics for returning soldiers. I had a couple of different peer groups there of people like me, "Too Hot to Handle" and "Some Assembly Required." Guys from 4E with severe burns as well as amputees were always in the CFI, and we egged each other on in our recovery. A little healthy competition goes a long way.

One of the peers I met was a guy most folks have heard of by now, J.R. Martinez. J.R. was treated at BAMC after his injuries, and my occupational therapist, Kim, wanted me to meet him. She gave me an earful. "He travels all over the country telling people to have heart, and you're going to love him."

When Kim finally introduced us, I was kind of surprised. I thought I was meeting Batman, but he was just a regular guy. We had a lot in common: IED blast while traveling in a Humvee in southwest Iraq, drug-induced coma to Landstuhl, critical care transport to BAMC, over 30 percent of our bodies burned, skin grafts and surgeries. Like me, he had a mom who had no doubt he could cope. He told me something I've never forgotten: you survived for a reason.

I saw what Kim saw. J.R. has an indomitable spirit, and he shared his enthusiasm about his recovery as well as some of the tough realities. He took the time to sit and talk with me. I was on a lot of pain medication, but nevertheless, his message hit me hard. His presence alone was enough to inspire me. I studied his face and arms. I watched the range of motion in his movements. I watched the stars in his eyes as he encouraged me, not just in terms of recovery but in terms of having a better life than I could ever imagine.

As I studied him, I was also looking at myself. My hands were still so hurt I could not bend my fingers on my own. Most of my body was still in bandages. I could not stand up straight. My arms were usually at a thirty to forty degree angle from my lower body. I was still missing my nose and ears, and at that point I was still susceptible to frequent infections. I hated waking up in the morning. But I loved going to the hospital, as long as I was an outpatient. I never knew who I would see, who would give me the inspiration, the guts, to make it through another day.

◆ ◆ ◆

When I met J.R., I had just come off a bad infection in my hand; in fact, it's a wonder I still have it. Any time the doctors would say I might have to return to the hospital as an inpatient, it was like they pressed a button that sent me into panic mode. Getting in was the easy part; it was getting out that was hard. I'm not really comparing it to incarceration, but I did not want to get stuck in the hospital. But my hand was getting worse, infection was destroying tissue, and something had to happen fast or I was going to lose it altogether.

I was admitted and had been there for a few days of treatment. I was getting angry because I needed a new IV every four to six hours. The antibiotics were so strong that they irritated the veins and skin around it and the IV had to be frequently moved. But I had only so many good veins. My right arm was completely covered in scar tissue, so it could not be used for the IV; the tissue was like leather. After making over a dozen holes in my left arm, the nurses ran out of good veins and started using my left wrist. Then they moved to my left and right ankles. The pain was excruciating. Over the course of four days I'd become a pincushion with dozens of holes in my arms, wrists, and ankles. To add insult to injury, it was training week at the hospital. Every other nurse was a trainee and missed the first stick over and over. They'd fish for veins with IV needles like toothpicks. It got to the point I was so miserable that I got nasty. I told the nurse, "You've got to promise to get it the first time, because if you miss, we're done."

Sure enough, he missed. He started getting out another needle and I asked, "What are you doing?"

"I'm going to insert your IV," he told me. "I gotta get another one into your arm."

I said, "No, we had an agreement. You're done."

He got the head nurse. She came in and said, "You've got no choice. No IV, no hand."

I was extremely upset. I had spent enough hours in the hospital that people knew I was a cooperative patient. But I'd reached my breaking point. I stood my ground. "You're not going to keep firing holes into me," I told her.

She said, "Comply."

But I had to make sure she knew I was fed up with relaxed care and trainees. I said, "One more try, and if it doesn't work, I'm going to exercise my right to refuse treatment."

She volunteered. "I'll do it myself." She nailed it in my left arm near one of the sites that was starting to heal. It was a tender area, but she got it. The next day a patient care representative came to see me to survey me about the level of care and quality of service I was receiving.

I told her, "Everyone here is extremely professional and has treated me with the utmost respect."

Despite the issue with the IVs, I meant every word, and I still do today.

* * *

As the rep and I talked, she told me she wanted to introduce me to her husband. She explained that he was another burn guy, and told me about

The lyrics to the Neil Diamond song "Shilo" inspired my parents to name me Shilo Allen Harris on October 24, 1974, in San Antonio, Texas.

From the bobcat hills of McCamey, Texas, we moved east to Coleman after I finished elementary school. My folks purchased a bait, tackle, and tire shop to reach the many outdoorsmen who passed through the area to hunt or fish.

Patriotism runs deep in my family. My father's and grandfather's military service inspired me to join the military. On the left, my father, US Army SP (Ret) Allen Blaine Harris; on the right, following in my father's footsteps, I'm in full battle rattle in Iraq, 2006.

I married my best friend and dragged her overseas with me to Schweinfurt, Germany. This was the first time either of us had left Texas. We quickly found out: home is where the Army sends you.

Thanksgiving greetings from me and Garrett Pagani in a photo we sent to family and friends during my first deployment to Iraq. Our message: we miss you, but we're okay.

Between deployments, a family reunited.

When you look into the eyes of an Iraqi child, the reason you're involved in this poverty-stricken place begins to make sense. Some kids called us "Ali Baba," but more often they were friendly, hungry, and desperate for attention.

During off-duty hours, we explored the grandeur of Iraq that was withheld from most of its people during the reign of Saddam Hussein.

Finding enemy munitions or contraband was part of our mission; this is a cache of weapons located on one of our early patrols.

On my second deployment and road weary, I finished a shift as dismount on foot patrol looking for IEDs.

Wherever we stopped, children surrounded us. I had to learn to "batten down the hatches" on my vehicle and uniform or I'd end up losing or giving away half my belongings. These kids made us happy yet vigilant. We wanted to protect them and their families, but the mission came first.

Me and Adare Cleveland messing around.

Adare enjoying some downtime before another mission.

Matt Bowe resting during a prolonged search for IEDs.

Shawn Dunkin with Iraqi military during our second deployment.

Shawn took joy in helping Iraqi kids.

Our Humvee before the explosion.

Humvee after disaster.

The ground imploded beneath us and life as I knew it was gone.

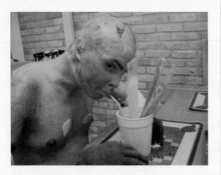

Kathreyn was given a crash course in critical wound treatment and took me home in June 2007.

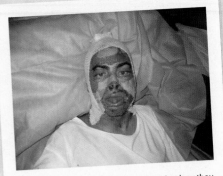

I was not always a cooperative patient, but how they all loved me through my recovery.

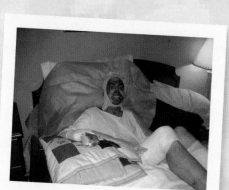

Recovery at home allowed me to pace myself, not knowing there would be another fifty surgeries ahead. Firm through the fiercest parts of the storm, our Lord never failed me.

Meeting my new nephew for the first time, wounds and all.

Following in his sister's and momma's footsteps, Glen gets ready to rope and ride.

This is our trampoline, where Lizzie and I would watch the stars together at night, deep in the heart of Texas.

I did not believe I would fully recover unless I could be outdoors once again. Hunts for Heroes, as well as many other warrior organizations, provide opportunities for vets like me to adjust to our new normal.

My boys Nicolas and Albert and I went hunting together about eleven months after the explosion. They had better luck than me, but it was about being together after spending so much time apart.

This beautiful bear is now a rug, but it means a great deal more to me than that. Purple Heart Hunts was established in honor and in memory of Shane Woods, an American hero. His father, Wayne Woods, continues to single out combat veterans to help them heal and recover some independence in the Alaskan wilderness.

I know what Shane Woods loved about Alaska after his father sponsored my trip to Cordova, Alaska. The salmon were running, and I could finally take a deep breath.

At my retirement ceremony, sandwiched between two heroes: CSM Fred Morris on my right and COL Mark Suich, Commander of 1st Squadron, 89th Cav, 10th Mountain Division, on my left.

After my retirement ceremony, Kathreyn and I renewed our marriage vows with Chaplain Roger VanPelt.

My commander-in-chief, President George W. Bush, and two beautiful first ladies.

COL Alan Sutton and Nancy Hansen fit me for my new magnetic ears.

Nancy continues to assist me with ear replacements. Her friendship has enabled me to adjust to my new normal.

Visiting with wounded warriors at BAMC has built an attitude of gratitude and brotherhood that is a big part of who I am and why I continue to advocate for programs and services that benefit those who serve our country.

The kids and I met Daniel Logan, *Star Wars'* Boba Fett, at a comic convention in San Antonio in 2013. I'm wearing the extra set of ears Nancy made for me: the Spock variety!

Our driver, Adam Devine, nearly lost his life on February 19, 2007, but gratefully recovered and celebrates the sweetness of each day with his wife, Virginia, and son, David.

The Order of St. George medallion is the top award presented to members of the Army's mounted force upon nomination to the US Armor Association of the US Army. St. George was a third-century soldier in the Roman army who was later venerated as a Christian martyr. LTC Mark Aiken nominated and inducted me in an elaborate ceremony at Ft. Lewis, Washington, in 2012. He's joined by LTC Charles Lombardo on his right.

My sister, Solitaire Harris, who is a cancer survivor, and I participated in a Relay for Life event in McCamey, Texas.

With Jamie Foxx at President Obama's Inaugural Party in 2012, Washington, DC.

Talking with students in a public school classroom.

Visiting with Congressman Mike Conaway, serving his fifth term in the US House of Representatives for the 11th District of Texas; he is also an ordained Baptist deacon.

Talking about veterans' issues with the Honorable Eric Shinseki, US Army four-star general (Ret), now serving as Secretary of the US Department of Veterans Affairs.

At Texas A&M University's Entrepreneurship Boot Camp for Veterans (EBV) conducted by Mays Business School. I continue to receive support from this program and am grateful for their interest in the lives of recovering veterans.

Huge supporters of EBV and me: Bob and Robin Starnes.

Speaking on behalf of veterans' issues for VetFran (here, at an International Franchise Association conference), along with owning and operating WIN Home Inspection Services franchise with my son Josh, keeps me pretty busy these days.

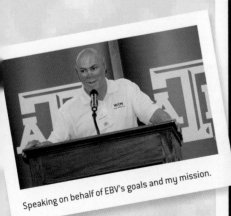

Speaking on behalf of EBV's goals and my mission.

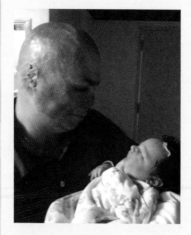
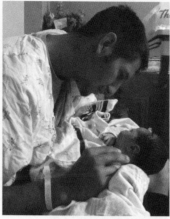

Josh and his wife, Brittany, brought brand-new joy into my life: my granddaughter Kylie Rae.

Getting called "Grandpa" is music to my nubs.

Lizzie's poise and grace were nurtured through the trials of my recovery. She is a remarkable young lady.

These two beauties are cowgirls at heart.

With the lady on my left who started it all, Meredith Iler, founder of Helping a Hero, at the 2013 HAH gala. On the left are Lisa Thomas of Fox News and August Skamenca, a CBS News correspondent.

The house built by ABC's *Extreme Makeover: Home Edition* and Helping a Hero. The hands and feet of our builder, Morgan's Wonderland, with countless volunteers from the Stockdale/Floresville area and veterans' community, all deserve our gratitude and it's impossible to thank them all.

Kat and I were over the moon about our new house and home. We will always be grateful to everyone who had a part in making this dream our reality!

Our motto: Building Bridges to Open Hearts. We put together an extensive list of resources in the back of this book to help warriors and their families find the help they need. As for Kat and me, we will remain committed to serving veterans and their families, and to raising awareness of concerns that impact our communities.

some of his injuries. I could hear a lot of commotion in the hallway and a man's bold voice. She told me her husband was coming down the hall, that we'd had a lot of similar experiences. She explained that he'd been hurt a couple of years earlier than me.

I expected someone to walk into the room that looked more like J.R., but in walked Chris Edwards. He wasn't like J.R., and he wasn't even like me.

He had been crossing a bridge in Iraq when his BFV was hit by a five-hundred-pound IED. He'd been burned over 80 percent of his body and had already survived over thirty-five surgeries. He'd had holes drilled through his lower leg bones, with metal rods inserted to stabilize his gait, and his walk was halted. He had a low range of movement in his joints. He'd had skin grafts over his entire body. I was a bit unprepared to meet him. He was so unexpected. But he had a presence; you knew he was someone you wanted to get to know.

We shook hands, and he said, "I'm Chris. How's your sex life?"

I was thinking, *What did he just say?* In all honesty, that's not a bad question when you've met someone that's been blown to pieces. But it's probably not the first question I'd ask.

Chris laughed and said, "I'm just askin'. I like to get that shock and awe out of people."

I said, "Well, you got it, my friend." We hit it off. We had a lot in common. He'd served in the military with distinction and despite his injuries, he planned to remain on active duty. He made no bones about the difficulty of his current situation. Yet he told me, "Being an NCO is a once in a lifetime thing. I'm not giving it up without a fight."

Chris has an infectious laugh, and said, "Keep 'em laughing. You gotta be humble."

Chris's visit gave my morale just the boost it needed.

I remember telling Kathreyn, "Maybe we ought to think about having another child so we can curb those questions from now on." We got a good laugh out of Chris's point of view. Locker room talk for the war wounded is quite graphic, as well as humorous, and there are a lot of myths that must be dispelled. Every wounded warrior I know has a sex life. Where there's a will, there's a way. It might take some adjustment, and some imagination, but it's worth it. It's something that needs more attention, and having a conversation with your spouse or loved one is a starting place.

As I recovered, Kathreyn and I had difficulty when it came to broaching the subject of intimacy. It was hard to talk about. She had been so good to me, I felt guilty asking for what I wanted. And she had been filling the nursing role for so long, I think it was hard for her to feel lovely and soft around me. I didn't want a mother or a nurse. I wanted the woman I married, and yet I was very insecure about not being the man she'd chosen as her husband. I was really afraid of rejection, but it was wearing me out. I wanted to be seen as the man of the house as well as her husband and lover. Yet because of my injuries, and the months of hospitalization, our roles were all screwed up. We each asked ourselves the same silent question, *Does he want me? Does she want me?*

Sometimes Kathreyn would reach for me, and because of my skin grafts and injuries, I could not feel her touch. I had to explain how these sensations had changed. I remember one night she was being very loving, and rubbed my arm in a tender way. She asked me, "Do you like it when I touch you that way?"

I had to tell her, "I can't feel anything in that area."

It was a matter of relearning our bodies, and relearning how to be intimate with each other. No matter where we were, Kathreyn felt she had to protect me, but I wanted my role of protector back. Fear kept her from relinquishing that role. I tried to convince her that I could take care of her, that she was protected and safe. It took time for us to get some of those thoughts out on the table. Some of those were heated discussions.

Becoming vulnerable and exposed is not something survivors want to do, yet we had to let down our walls if we were going to return to any kind of normal, intimate relationship. She was not aggressive, in an effort to protect me, and yet sometimes I saw her lack of assertion as the absence of desire. We talked and saw a counselor to help us understand what we were each feeling. Our love was strong; that was never in question. But for two people who'd always enjoyed our sexual chemistry, we had some work to do. I can tell you this for sure—we didn't mind our counselor's homework assignments at all.

● ● ●

I continued in physical therapy, Kathreyn returned to work, Elizabeth went to school, and we tried to invent our new normal. But everything was about to change again. Kathreyn woke up one morning, took my hand in hers, and whispered, "I'm pregnant." Those two words were like music to my ears. We were going to have a little boy, and I was ecstatic. I held her in my arms and whispered one word to her: "Hooah."

We just added a few more appointments to the calendar. A day in the life might look like this:

6:30—Elizabeth to daycare

7:00—Kathreyn to work, Shilo to Intrepid

11:00—Pick up Shilo

11:30—Lunch

1:30—Kathreyn to OB

2:30—Shilo to BAMC

3:30—Shilo to Intrepid

4:30—Grocery shopping

5:00—Elizabeth to dentist

5:30—Home to cook dinner

Bath time

Story time

Bedtime

It was a crazy, hectic life. Looking back, I don't know how Kathreyn did it. She took it one step at a time. I had to learn to take those steps one at a time as well.

I was growing impatient with injury, and my impatience led to frustration and anger. As we drove home to Floresville from San Antonio after my latest skin graft surgery, the flat pastures and shallow mesas covered with bluebonnets caught my eye. As spring dried into summer, the number of surgeries had begun to mount and I lost count. When I looked at the earth, I could appreciate the deep soil, rich loam, and what pushed up from the dirt and grew sturdy despite the challenges of a summer that never seemed to end.

Growing up in west Texas, I knew something about the volatility of heat. If a careless cigarette tossed out a car window caught your field on fire in the dead of August, flames would quickly consume what you'd worked all spring to cultivate. If you think about a pasture on fire, at first it's the grass that is whipped by the wind, charred by the heat, then engulfed by the flames. Then the burning surges into a plant's roots, by degrees, so that soon everything beneath the surface is destroyed as well. The pain, temperature, and pressure of fire change every layer.

I had to learn that that's what happens to skin as well. We have layers of skin that we take for granted every day, fatty connective tissue that just rests over blood vessels and nerves. My skin was pretty dark from being in the sun in Iraq, leathered from years of work under the hot Texas sun, but in an instant that pigment layer was gone. Beneath that, oil glands were destroyed, along with the hair follicles and papillae, the nerve fibers, blood and lymph vessels, sweat glands, veins and arteries, and more fatty tissue. Burns create collateral damage. When the outer, middle, and inner layers of skin are gone, fire eats into tendon, bone, ligament, muscle—and every nerve ending is destroyed.

My surgeon, Dr. Evan Renz, told me that in the old days we measured this damage in degrees. With some first aid we can heal from burns to the first or second degree; it's basically equivalent to a sunburn or blister. But hit the third degree and damage is extensive. Infection can easily set in and destroy more skin cells as well as everything in its way. At the fourth degree, bone is destroyed. Few physicians refer to the fifth or sixth degree, as these burn victims are generally examined post-mortem.

Dr. Renz said it was more accurate to describe burns in terms of thickness. I had variable burns over one-third of my body, with full thickness burns in some areas and partial thickness in others. He told me I had to give those layers time to heal. As I met other warriors who entered 4E with burns, I was able to see through their recovery how the healing overlapped, and I could better understand what I'd been through. Early on, even in the Green Zone, doctors had begun to surgically remove the burned skin off parts of my body. I could hardly handle the indescribable pain of debriding, and having Kathreyn witness this process, helpless and hurting in her own way, was an experience we both still strive to forget. For burn patients, pain is the elephant in the room. It's just relentless.

Where is hope when your skin is gone? You try not to think of it that way, but these thoughts creep in like thieves, stealing what glimmers of hope you gather from the words of doctors, nurses, the surgical team. I have a profound respect for the medical teams at Landstuhl and Brooke Army Medical Center; they were my firefighters and I needed them to heal me. I needed Kathreyn with me. I needed all their hope to live. It doesn't escape my notice that God surrounded me with hopeful people. He knew there would be times when I would have so little hope of my own.

I discovered something else about layers; faith builds in the same way. Initially, my faith was fragile and was primarily dependent on Kathreyn's faith. Over time, I found out that God met me at every point of need. When I was in a lot of pain, I needed him so much. My faith increased, layer by layer.

Using skin from areas of my body that weren't burned, the medical team at the ISR cut skin from these donor sites. This means taking healthy skin from my thighs, my chest, my back, my hips. "Taking healthy skin" hardly describes how this is actually done. A tool called a dermatome (think potato peeler) shaves off a uniform layer of smooth skin to serve as a donor to be implanted at the burn site. The thickness of this layer depends on the site needing the graft. When the graft layer is split to partial thickness, you're taking a thicker layer of skin from the donor site. The donor skin is sent through a machine that stretches it and turns it into a kind of human mesh. The graft is attached to the burn site with staples, and the skin drinks plasma, which causes new blood vessels to grow. When you look at someone with burn scars, you might notice a mesh pattern—kind of like bricks on a wall. The cuts create little ditches for drainage, and the graft can be stretched to cover a larger area. The new site of the skin graft is then left open to heal. As the skin heals, it contracts and grows tighter. This hurts. So you've got skin healing at the donor site and skin healing at the graft site, but you've got to believe the healing is happening because it sure doesn't feel like it. It feels like hell.

Surgeons can take deeper cuts of the donor skin to create thicker sheets of skin. These thicker slabs of skin, or autografts, were sent through the machine, creating a mesh that reminded me of graph paper. Because the skin cells were my own, there was a lower risk of rejection. But infection is a big problem nevertheless. Your skin carries a lot of bacteria, and as hard as the trauma team worked to debride and clean the layers of skin, there were still remnants of debris from the initial blast. A virulent strain of bacteria in Iraqi soil creates havoc in the immune system, compromising and contaminating more than just the burn site.

For some burn patients, specialists at the ISR grow a new crop of skin using skin cells from a donor site. Using a Petri dish, burn technicians create a cultured epithelial autograft (CEA) and apply that to a graft site. We didn't use that process, as there was enough skin from donor sites on my body to cover the areas needing healing.

Growing a crop of skin is probably something farmers can understand better than anyone else. The donor skin is like seed, able to grow itself over time with irrigation and climate control. Skin harvested from one area re-grows skin in another, so it's essentially a life cycle. While everything inside me understood this was necessary, after enduring one skin graft after another, I don't think I can tell you in words what pain Kathreyn saw in my face each time I underwent another surgery.

There's a reason why there aren't a lot of mirrors in a burn unit.

26

BUCK FEVER

After needing Kathreyn's support for so long, I received an invitation to go deer hunting up in Kansas. I thought long and hard about accepting the offer. I was still very weak and my stamina was low. I'd lost a lot of weight and had started to regain some of it, but I wasn't strong. Just to make the trip, I'd have to spend sixteen hours in a vehicle, changing my routine, using muscles and skills I'd not used in a long time. But it would be good for me to get some fresh air, and I wanted to see if I was going to be able to handle those things that I used to love to do.

One of my buddies at Intrepid was SSG Brad Gruetzner. He'd lost a hand and arm in an explosion and had also suffered extensive burn injuries. He was further along in his recovery than me and had found that hunting gave him a way to recover on many different levels. Every time he returned from a hunt, he'd share his stories with me, and I was eager to get out and give it a try. I told him, "Keep me in mind next time you hear about a good one, and I'll go with you."

He gave me a call in the fall of 2008, and I was so determined to go I didn't even discuss it with Kathreyn. I was afraid she'd think I wasn't ready, and I felt I was never going to be ready unless I gave it a try. I understood her protective instincts, but I wanted some control over that part of my life.

Brad and I agreed to ride together. We used the long drive to catch up on all the things that had happened to both of us along the way. Sitting in the car wasn't too taxing, and I felt so good about this trip. I had great

151

respect for Brad as a friend and survivor. The drive from Waco, Texas, up to east Kansas took about fourteen hours, giving us plenty of time to cut up and get to know each other better.

We arrived in Lynwood late, but Steven and Kim Johnson and their family welcomed us with open arms. Steven has his own business, All Truck Sales in Kansas City, and outfitted us with boots, hunting clothes, and licenses. Steven had gotten interested in reaching out to wounded warriors through his proximity to the military stationed at Fort Leavenworth, Kansas. His father was a veteran, and he'd passed away shortly before our visit. Steven wanted to honor his father's service and contacted the Patriots and Heroes Outdoors organization, formerly known as Hunts for Heroes, about taking some warriors outdoors and treating them to some Kansas hospitality. Brad and I were the lucky warriors.

As soon as we walked into the house, I spotted a huge white tail shoulder mount on the wall. Surrounding us were many other trophy animals he'd collected in various hunts. We sat in front of a roaring fireplace getting to know each other. Soon Steven got up to leave the room, telling us, "I'll be right back."

He walked back through the door a minute later with a rifle in his hands, presenting me with a brand-new Winchester 300. It was equipped with a beautiful Burress scope and came with a bag of goodies and gear. Brad apparently knew about the surprise in advance, but I didn't. It was a total shock. Brad said his reward was seeing me happy and being treated like a rock star.

Kim fixed a feast for us early the next morning, and we geared up for the hunt. The weather was perfect. Cold, brisk air. Fresh snow. Low wind. I could feel the trophy I was going to get in my bones. I just had a feeling this was the trip when I would finally land "the one." We dropped Brad off at his blind, and as he got out of the vehicle, my new rifle slid out of its case and settled into the doorjamb. Before I could yank it out, my rifle got slammed in the door. My heart sank. I couldn't even hang on to my gun. I knew there was a possibility I was not going to be able to shoot that trophy buck, much less with a damaged or off-sight weapon.

I checked over my rifle as we continued to the ridge where we would set up our blind, and kept hoping the scope was not off. Steven and I got the blind set up, but that's actually giving me too much credit. I was still weak, and I just wanted to see if I could manage any of this at all. I dozed off in the truck until the sun came up, and when I opened my eyes, sure enough, there stood the stag. Three hundred yards away. I could tell he was at least a 150 Boone and Crockett, a solid trophy buck. Steven confirmed range and I set up the rifle. I paid attention to my breathing, then started to squeeze the trigger. I was too excited. I had to shake it off. My buck fever was making me too eager.

I stopped and caught my breath again. Shook my arms and tried to run the routine through my head. Aim, breathe, squeeze. I set up again on the bipod and took aim. Bam! I was so confident about my shot that I looked at Steven with swagger in my grin. Steven smiled and smiled, and then laughed. He said, "That was a great shot. He didn't even move. We'll have no trouble finding him."

We looked at the range and none of the deer had even moved. They continued to graze on tufts of grass poking through the snow, oblivious to what we were doing. I said, "Something's wrong." We used the scope to look around and realized the bullet was so far off we didn't even scare the deer.

Steven asked, "Want to try it again?" I figured, why not? I dropped the reticule down low on the deer's body, looking to basically shoot a Hail Mary after seeing where I thought the last bullet had gone. Same routine and bam! The deer just ducked down a little that time. I didn't faze him. I was closer; I saw the bullet splash in the snow. Steven said, "You know where the bullet hit, so it's up to you."

I went for a third shot. Silly, I know. By now you'd think the deer would have sized me up pretty good. This time, bam! He ran off. It was a sorry shot. I looked at the hillside. No blood. Steven said, "I know you're shooting good; it's got to be the rifle." Steven is an avid hunter and outdoorsman. He had sighted the weapon himself and was confident it was spot on. I was confident in my shooting, as it felt right and I'd always been a pretty good shot.

We decided to drive over to the firing range to figure out what had happened. Once we got there, we realized the knock from the door had indeed done some damage to the rifle. I was not even hitting the target at a hundred yards. Steven gave it a try just to make sure it wasn't my bad arm pulling or flinching with my new 300 Win Mag. After he shot, we had to get a bigger target. Once we found where it was hitting, we figured it was shooting about six to eight feet above the deer at three hundred yards.

We were eventually able to fix the gun, but my ego took a little more work. I was really bummed about not getting my trophy. But here's the thing about hunting: at the end of the day, it's about the friends you meet along the way. Steven and his family are some of the finest folks I've ever met. I also discovered that while I wasn't going to run through the woods after wildlife anymore, it wasn't like I couldn't still do something I'd loved all my life. If I planned my pain meds right, and if I had the opportunity, I could go outdoors and do my thing. I could still hunt. That was something I needed more than any trophy buck. I needed to know I could hang.

Brad and I talked a lot about the future as we drove back to Texas from Kansas. I told him, "We need to do this more often."

While the war had changed many things in both of our lives, it didn't change the fact that we were outdoorsmen, regardless of our injuries. It felt good to enjoy the outdoors. I didn't have the stamina, but the bravado was still part of who I was.

27

YARDSTICKS

I lost my love for the holidays during the early years of treatment and recovery. I can't even remember how we celebrated, to tell you the truth. Those months are still a blur. One day rushed into the next, and the calendar became a foggy trail of appointments, surgeries, and therapies. Kathreyn told me, "You used to love Christmas."

"You're right," I told her. I was ready for 2009 to end. "I kind of forgot how much." We set the wheels in motion to make a trip back home for the holidays. I'd finished another round of skin graft surgeries and was still on a lot of pain medication, but I knew the kids were anxious to see their grandparents and I didn't want to let my family down. It's a long drive from San Antonio to Coleman, but Kat took care of all the details, packing the car, the kids, and the kitchen sink, and we headed west.

We spent Christmas Eve visiting with family and friends in the area. I got to see my mom and sister and visit with my dad. We hadn't seen each other in a while, and everyone was happy to see my progress. I felt the burden of discouragement begin to lift. I also hadn't seen my son Josh in a while, and we got to reconnect as well.

Kathreyn's dad told me the weather was perfect for hunting and asked me if I wanted to go out by the stock tank to see if we could get a deer for Christmas. I wasn't feeling strong enough to do a whole lot, and the pain was only at bay for as long as my meds would last, but I wanted to try to do what I used to love doing in Coleman. As we lay in the grass watching the slope above the pond, we told a few war stories. I thought about how high the wall had been between us. When I asked for Kat's hand in marriage, I pretty much figured my relationship with him could only go uphill. I was grateful for how far we'd come. We didn't end up with a deer that afternoon, but it wasn't really about the deer anyway.

When we got back to Kat's grandparents' house, they'd prepared a huge traditional holiday meal. Kat's Poppa, the patriarch, gathered us all around the table to give thanks. I had everyone I loved around me that day, my family, Kat's family, my children . . . and as I gazed into their faces, life felt perfect. I'd thought I would never feel that way again. I still had a long way to go, but it was the first time I felt like life might actually be worth living again. Everything I cared about and valued was in arm's reach. The harmony around that dinner table filled me with peace.

The kids wrestled over the turkey legs, and we had more than enough to eat. Kat's face just glowed; being with her family meant a lot to her. I looked at everyone gathered around that Christmas table and thought about all they'd been through because of me. They were my heroes.

After we left the table, the gang worked on cleaning up the kitchen and dining area, and I walked out on the back porch by myself. The temperature had dropped a good bit and it was downright chilly. I felt like praying. I told God how grateful I was for the birth of his son, for the birth of my sons and daughter, for the family he'd given me, and the life he'd restored in me. Then I got greedy. I told him the only thing that would make the holiday more perfect would be if he could bring in a little snow. I'd never seen a white Christmas in Texas, and a little powder would just be the icing on the cake.

The next morning I woke up early to a bright glare coming in through the window. I rubbed my eyes and crawled out of bed. I went to the window and looked outside. The ground was white, covered with a blanket of snow. I heard God's Spirit speak to my soul, *This is for you.* Tears rolled down my face. He'd given me an extra gift on Christmas morning.

The kids were ecstatic. They ran outside, just running amuck in the snow. They didn't care about the presents, the things, the objects under the tree. I will always hold that Christmas dear; the value of God's love was evident and all around us. That holiday became a yardstick for me, and I've measured each one since against that feeling I had on Christmas morning in Coleman.

28

FAMILY LEGACY

As I shared my story during my recovery, I came to understand more and more about the relationship between fathers and sons. A father wants to raise his boy to avoid the mistakes he made in his own life. A father wants to teach his boy to protect and defend his family. Fathers are as fiercely protective as mothers are, but I think fewer men have stepped up to the plate. I was raised in a household where the love of country and family was deeply rooted in who we were. There's no mistaking the flaws and mistakes that were made. I have made plenty, and I imagine my sons will make many of their own.

But the men in my life tried to show me how to be a man. I knew my father was a patriot; I knew my grandfathers were patriots. That was their legacy. It was never a burden. I served in the military because I wanted to serve. I knew what I was getting into. The world doesn't owe me a thing because I was injured in the line of duty. I knew the risks before war, I knew them better after war, and I have never been bitter at having been injured. I'm thankful I survived.

I owe this kind of attitude to my father. He went to Vietnam, served as he was told, and returned with his own wounds, shrapnel embedded in his body. He nearly lost his leg, and suffered kidney damage. I wish there had been more open discussion about PTSD back then, because I think my father would have taken advantage of help if it was readily available. I knew from his experience that I needed to recognize the toll the war had taken on me. I also knew from being his kid that I needed to recognize the toll the war had taken on my own family.

● ● ●

Before I deployed to Iraq for the second time, I got a call I didn't expect. It was my son Josh, and he said, "Come get me. I want to be there with you."

I'd never been allowed to have Josh visit, much less live with me, but I think his mother was running into that difficult time that most parents experience with teenage boys, when they're trying to figure out what kind of man they want to become. I remembered those years pretty well. I'd given my parents a run for their money.

I told him, "Josh, I'm packing my bags for my next deployment as we speak. If you think you're coming, you need to be sure, because you can't change your mind. I'll be overseas for the next fifteen months."

"I'm sure," he told me.

I understood what "sure" means to a boy, but as his father, I was going to take whatever I could get. Kathreyn and I had only a couple hundred dollars to spare at that moment, and that included the change in the car. I pulled a four-day pass; we packed up Lizzie and headed from Watertown, New York, to Coleman, Texas. When I got tired behind the wheel, I'd pull over on the side of the road and take a short nap, then keep driving.

When we got to Coleman, I told my family, "I've got two days to get back to my unit." There was only enough time to say, "Hi and bye," and we were back on the road, with Josh and everything he wanted along loaded into the trunk of the car. I'd gotten paid via direct deposit from the military, so at least we could eat. The trip back north was a lot better. Josh was a funny kid; we sang songs and every time we passed a VW we'd play Slug Bug. We stopped at a hotel halfway home and did a lot of talking and laughing as a family. Kathreyn and I worked at getting to know Josh, and vice versa.

The next morning we headed to the restaurant for breakfast and Josh got a cup of coffee. Kathreyn lost her mind. "You are fifteen years old. You will not drink coffee. You are too young!" The two of them looked at me. What I saw were two roads, "Support me, Dad" or "Support me, Husband." I hated being at that intersection.

I told Josh, "Put the coffee in the trash and have something healthy, like a Coke." There's nothing healthy about that, but I needed to support

Kathreyn. She'd be raising this boy for the next year while I was deployed. Josh and I practiced our sound effects and cut up the rest of the drive home, and I was grateful to have some time with my son before going overseas.

When we got back to Watertown that Sunday night, it was late and I had to go to work the next day. We showed Josh his room, and as I was saying good night, he said something I didn't expect. "Wake me up before you leave in the morning, Dad. I wanna see you in your uniform." I didn't realize that was important to him, and I promised I would.

The next morning I was all set and walked into his room to say goodbye. His eyes sparkled when he looked at me, and everything in me understood that I was his hero. We had been apart for so long, and now here we were, father and son.

Over the next few weeks, we had the ups and downs of having a teenager in the house. While I wanted to give Josh things that I hadn't been able to provide for so long, Kathreyn wanted him to earn those privileges. I wanted to spend time bonding with Josh, while Kathreyn wanted to spend time as a whole family before I deployed, a valid desire. We had a hard time finding a happy medium. When Josh was unhappy, he'd tell us he wanted to move back to Texas, and I had to remind him, with orders in hand, that it wasn't going to happen.

"You've started a new high school, you're going to make friends, and this will start to feel like home," I told him. "Hang in there until I get back. We'll make sure we get the time together that we both want so badly."

Six months later life happened. I was injured, and Kathreyn had to make the painful decision to leave Josh in Watertown to finish his freshman year while she rushed to Landstuhl. No one was sure what the future would hold. There were huge question marks in our lives. Josh was left in Watertown not knowing if he'd ever see his father again. Kathreyn kept him updated by phone, but the news wasn't good. Josh kept going to school, living with a family we trusted to watch over him.

As Kathreyn followed me to San Antonio, after spending a good bit of time at the Fisher House, there was a point where she needed a more permanent way of life than living out of a hotel. She was given quarters at Fort Sam Houston, but she made the decision that it was best for Josh to finish his freshman year in New York, and as a high school student he couldn't leave midterm without losing all the credits he'd earned. As soon as Josh completed his final exams, my dad drove up to get him. This time grandfather and grandson made a quiet, painful drive from New York to Texas.

The first time Josh saw me at BAMC, I was covered in bandages and was in a wheelchair. It didn't match the last picture of me that he'd stored in his mind, the 10th Mountain Division Cavalry Scout GI Joe Dad. I could see in his eyes that he was crushed and scared. Not only did he feel like we'd forgotten about him in New York, but he must have been unable to imagine us having any kind of normal life after my injuries. It was a really tough spot for a fifteen-year-old kid. Kathreyn had been given a sketchy prognosis for my recovery, and we knew that it was going to be best for Josh to return home to his mother. As badly as I wanted my son nearby, I was not equipped to take care of him, and Kathreyn had all she could handle. With promises to visit and stay in touch, Josh returned to his mother in Coleman.

Over the next couple of years, we worked at visits that were meaningful and I tried to find a way to reach Josh. I bought an old Jeep and thought we could work on restoring it together over the summer. I didn't have the capacity to do the physical labor, but we could hang out in the garage and I could direct the project, helping out as much as possible. It seemed like a great idea, but the car began to stand for all the tension between us, the gap between what we could have had together and what we were living day by day.

I had a lot of time to think about my son Josh, and the wound that existed in his heart after the wounds that happened in mine. After he finished high school, Josh got married and now has a little girl of his own. I'm still trying to be his dad, and I am working on being the kind of grandfather that his little daughter deserves. Preserving and protecting my family is a full-time job in and of itself. I've had to learn some new skills as a parent, and I want to be a strong grandparent as well.

My own grandfather died right before I went back to Iraq. I was stationed at Fort Knox, Kentucky, when I got the news. I was in an E-6 training course, but I was not promotable yet. It was a huge privilege for me to be there. My assignment to the advanced course was meant to prepare me for war once again, and when I talked to my father about quitting the course and returning home for my grandfather's funeral, he convinced me to stay. It was a selective process to land a spot in the course, and he didn't want me to relinquish it. He said it was what my grandfather would have wanted. It was a tough situation. My grandfather's stories of the battlefield had helped shape my psyche as a warrior. To leave Fort Knox would have left me less prepared for combat; to stay at Fort Knox tore me up inside. I wasn't sure which was worse, but I took my father's advice and stayed at Fort Knox, holding my own kind of memorial for the man who'd had such a profound influence on my life.

One of the first stops I wanted to make when I was able to make the walk on my own accord was my grandfather's grave. The National Cemetery at Fort Sam Houston holds the silent stones of thousands of patriots. Though I call them silent stones, they speak to us. Age calls to age. A few symbols, a cross . . . a name . . . a medal . . . a date, are inscribed in the rock, but that's all. There are rows upon rows, stretching beyond view. I walked to the burial plot with my father by my side. As we strolled, I heard my dog tags jingle back and forth across my father's chest. He was never without them.

We stood at attention, the quiet between us. I pictured my strong grandpa beside the lake, on a stream, in the woods. I heard his bark, his bite, his laugh. I didn't need my ears for that. I could easily have had a plot right here next to my father's father. Bells in the carillon tolled. One after another. And I thought of one after another of my brothers and sisters in arms who'd fallen once and for all. The list was long. There's not a soldier in the military today that doesn't have his own long list. My name could have been on it.

My father and I walked the straight and narrow trail that led back to his car. I had paid my respects to my grandfather, as well as all the men and women who'd served our country and now rested on sacred ground, and I intend to keep doing that. Every day, when I talk to God about my family, I tell him I'm grateful that there is no silent stone with my name.

● ● ●

One of the choices I made as a young man involved bringing two boys into the world without the blessing of growing up with a mother and father bound to one another in sacred vows. When I was working in the oil fields, I fell in love, and Nicolas and Albert were brought into the world long before I had the maturity to parent them. I wanted to give them the kind of family legacy that they deserved, but I have not been able to be a frequent partner in their lives. When they grow up, we will have the kind of conversation that I am not allowed to have with them at this age, and I look forward to that day. I want them to understand what kind of father I wanted to be, more than the father that I was. God's given me mercy and grace to accept the things I cannot change.

When Kathreyn and I decided to have another child, our decision was full of hope and faith. We believed we could be a strong family once again. On the day our son was born, we raced down the highway in San Antonio to get to Wilford Hall Hospital. I was driving, my mom was with us, and we flew to get to the delivery room on time.

Contractions were strong, and our little boy was ready. We had already decided to call him Glen, Kat's father's middle name. As our little guy struggled to arrive, his head got stuck in the birth canal, so Kathreyn had an emergency Caesarean section. I could see what was going on in the reflection off the metal cabinets and mirrors in the operating room, and I nearly passed out. When the doctor handed Glen to me, he cried, I cried, and so did Kathreyn and my mom. I said, "That's not my baby. He's got two ears, ten fingers, ten toes, and a head full of hair. He's not mine!" We all had a good laugh. Kat was so doped up that she called me an idiot and fell fast asleep.

So I've got four sons and a daughter on this earth, and it means I've got to man up for each one of them. I want them to learn from what I did right and from what I did wrong. I want the pieces and parts of our family legacy that make no sense to teach my children the lessons they need to be successful in life. I think they've gotten some pretty powerful lessons in persistence, determination, and keeping the faith. I've taught them how to live through my example and my failures. I've tried to show them what to do and what not to do. But at the end of the day, there is a man with a heart full of love for each one of them. That's my legacy.

29

BIG BAD WOLF

The blast had taken off body parts and left me looking unfinished, like a tortured and abandoned sculpture. I didn't want anyone to see me this way, and yet I could care less about what I looked like if there was any way we could repair or restore my functionality. Along came the big bad Dr. Steven Wolf, who, as it turns out, happens to like pigs. He and his colleagues at UT's Health Science Center and the University of Pittsburgh's McGowan Institute for Regenerative Medicine were working on a long-range experiment to help the war-wounded regrow tissues lost due to direct injuries, with the hope that this would lead to limb replacement at some point. My dad read about their work and brought it to me. "You've gotta try this," he told me.

I agreed, and I convinced my physician's assistant at BAMC, Peter Yen, to call Dr. Wolf and get me involved in the project. Peter was a contract employee at BAMC, and as physician's assistant he had become one of my best friends. He was my advocate, and his eye was always on the prize: recovery. When he contacted Dr. Wolf, they were harvesting pig bladders in a miraculous and experimental procedure called regenerative extracellular matrix. He said scientists had been using a mixture of calcium, minerals, and protein collagen in powder form to create a microscopic scaffold on the surface of body tissue. This matrix of "pixie dust" had the ability to promote tissue growth. I had lost several fingers in the blast, and they wanted to try to regrow what was gone using this stem cell process. Dr. Wolf said the research led them to believe that regrowth was possible, and the risk of infection or failure warranted the trial, especially if I could gain mobility in the finger area.

The first time I met Dr. Wolf, I knew my hands were in good hands. For one thing, he said fingers were commonly injured, and the area he'd be working with to try to regenerate tissue would be relatively small. If the procedures succeeded, I'd have some finger regrowth. On the other hand, if it failed, I was not going to be debilitated by the end results. When Dr. Wolf examined me he said I was the perfect candidate, as well as the first. Although I'd had seven recent surgeries, I was ready to have him pilot his pixie dust on me. He encouraged me, "Keep the positive attitude. That's going to make all the difference."

● ● ●

Stem cells are kind of generic, I found out. They are unspecialized cells that can self-replicate, and when they do, they can decide to become many different kinds of cells. Dr. Wolf said if he could control what kind of cell the stem cell would become, we might be able to grow new nerves and new tissue and repair or regrow bones, organs, or organ parts. I was all in.

In theory, the powder is added to a surgical site where the matrix has been applied, and circulating stem cells see the matrix, differentiate based upon whatever they are near, and regrow. If stem cells are near a bone, they become bone cells. If they're near blood vessels, they become veins, arteries, or capillaries.

Dr. Wolf made a wound at the end of my finger stump by opening up the healed scar tissue through a series of incisions. I had an inkling of what Frankenstein's monster might have felt like. Although my fingers weren't pretty, they'd healed from previous surgeries, but here we were creating new wounds. However, this technique required Dr. Wolf to open the stump. What residual bone was left in that finger had to be exposed. Once the area was open, he packed the extracellular matrix into the wound. My own stem cells were delivered directly into this extracellular matrix surgically implanted on my left hand as well, and the blood flow began to recirculate in normal tissues at the wound site.

Dr. Wolf explained, "Shilo, over time, if the stem cells are attracted to normal tissue, your finger's going to get longer in the right proportions, and this will lead to better functionality overall."

I teased him, "I don't want to play the piano, I'd just like to tie my own shoes."

Once Dr. Wolf incorporated one batch of pixie dust into the wound, he planned to apply additional extracellular matrix, until hopefully the desired results were achieved. After a second surgical implant in October 2008, my index finger had grown nearly half an inch. If you've never lost a finger, you might not realize what a difference half an inch can make. I hoped it would give me enough torque, tension, and sensation to do things I couldn't do with less. I was ecstatic. I knew that I hadn't regrown my fingers, but the seven millimeters of growth of uniform tissue was a step in that direction.

●●●

During the treatment phase, Dr. Wolf changed the dressings frequently and added more pixie dust, but it wasn't long before the wound closed up. Unless I wanted to cut open another finger site, we had achieved the best results we could expect for now.

This is how surgical fatigue commences.

Every wounded warrior draws his or her own line in the sand. When the team at UT started the procedure, they really didn't know if it would work. It hadn't been tried in precisely this manner before. When the wounded finger was cut open, I've got to admit I was not ecstatic to undo the healing that had taken place. But it was worth the pain if in the end I'd have more fingers to work with. My fingers were splinted to keep the new growth from moving too much, which was very painful. Ultimately, Dr. Wolf would have liked to see me grow a new finger. But after the first set of procedures, I was ready to use my hands for normal things to help me determine if I wanted to go further.

The big bad Wolf was like my fairy godmother, giving me hope that maybe I could one day be fitted for a prosthesis. He'd entered uncharted territory with me, and I was glad to be a part of that trip. But the trip was long enough.

I asked Dr. Wolf what was magical about pig bladders, and he explained that, as it turns out, they're a pretty plentiful and generic source of extracellular matrix. UT's Health Science Center had been using pig bladders to actually regrow bladders, so the material was readily available. One of the things this team of researchers plans to study is whether the source of extracellular matrix makes any difference in the regrowth of human cells. They also want to examine whether they can increase the number of stem cells at the site of implantation by taking additional stem cells from bone marrow or fat and placing them in the extracellular matrix. We didn't get a chance to try that, as by the end of the trial I was really ready to move on.

Over time, Dr. Wolf hopes to see more progress with this type of treatment, as the promise of real benefit to wounded patients is evident. I plan to keep track of his progress. If he's able to replant the cells in human subjects for bone growth, his work will provide huge opportunities for helping patients of many kinds, including me. If he's able to use his pixie dust to regrow functional tissue or bone, it will have huge ramifications for wounds of many types.

The wars in Iraq and Afghanistan have provided unique opportunities for health care professionals and medical researchers to dig deep into their repertoires of expertise as well as imagination to find ways to deal with our injuries. For a lot of these scientists, the only barrier is time and money. We know the treatments and cures are out there, but clinical trials and necessary research cost a pretty penny. They're worth every cent if they lead to full recovery for many of us.

30

REST FOR THE WEARY

It's called compassion fatigue. It happens when caregivers who give and give and give get to the bottom of their buckets. The medical and nursing staff who took care of me at Landstuhl as well as at BAMC were required to be strong yet flexible, hard as nails yet resilient, and unshakeable in the face of trauma. They were the face of hope for me. I needed them, but it never occurred to me that they needed me as well. They had a stake in my survival. They were deeply invested. Yet nurses or medics in combat have special requirements and stresses that go unacknowledged for the most part. Their caregiving for every wounded warrior including me took its toll—physically, emotionally, and spiritually. Day in and day out, they had to maintain a high level of empathy and engagement with patients like me who had been ripped open on the battlefield. My caregivers shared my wounds, and in some ways were thus wounded themselves.

Studies on combat injuries and fatalities over the past ten years have shown us that medical breakthroughs make survival possible, but few understand what recovery truly looks like. My nurses at Landstuhl saw injuries that few caregivers ever witness. The signature weapon of this war, the IED, has completely changed the landscape of recovery from battle injuries. Triage on the battlefield enabled many of us to survive injuries that were fatal in previous wars. The military medical teams have borne both the joys and sorrows of survival. We enter their helicopters, their field hospitals, and their trauma centers with horrific injuries. I don't really understand

167

how their brains can process such gut-wrenching situations. I entered their lives without a face; others enter their lives without limbs, with trauma in every system, and they handle it. They handle it all. Optimum sleep, recreation, spiritual renewal, and reasonable work schedules contribute to quick healing for caregivers, but I never met a caregiver who lived in such an optimal world.

Medevac response teams have to deal with not only providing medical treatment but physical safety as well. They land their aircraft on battlefields, at the end of bombed-out city streets or deceptively deserted pastures near remote villages. They live with fear and wear and tear that I can hardly comprehend. They have great responsibility for preserving human life, and yet considered my safety as paramount. I felt a great burden for the folks who took care of me; I felt the need to give thanks, knowing that would only be a cursory word for what I actually felt inside.

One of the hardest injuries caregivers have had to face is assisting soldiers with traumatic brain injury (TBI). We are still counting the cost of this war in terms of TBI. While a medical team can make your brain stop bleeding, they might never be able to stabilize brain function, and such awareness leaks out in telltale ways. Medical experts say we have seen only the tip of the iceberg in terms of diagnosing TBI. In the years ahead, I believe we'll experience a dramatic and traumatic increase in treatment requirements for the unseen injuries of war, the undiagnosed symptoms and syndromes and conditions directly attributable to the frequent, concussive blasts endured by soldiers like me.

But the medical teams take a lickin' and keep on tickin'. Compassion fatigue is actually a term for secondary traumatic stress disorder, or STSD, and it doesn't get talked about nearly as often as PTSD but it's just as real. Compassion creates a stress all its own. Like PTSD, when a caregiver is suffering with STSD there are telltale signs and symptoms. There is the cognitive dissonance—a nurse might appear apathetic or rigid. A caregiver might think incessantly about what trauma will present itself each day and may consider harming himself to get out of harm's way. That harm may look innocuous at first, a few too many drinks, frequent use of sleeping pills or painkillers. There is an emotional connection—ranging from numbness to rage, sometimes in roller-coaster fashion. Someone who suffers from compassion fatigue may act differently, losing sleep, appetite, or motivation. Some begin to direct their anger at God, or they may question his existence.

Those who live with caregivers who are chronically fatigued may see their loved ones as distant or overprotective. Sometimes extreme physical changes will occur—rapid heart rates, impaired immune systems, or even shock. Work may become either drudgery or an obsession. In my recovery years, as I interacted with caregivers directly involved with my treatment, I saw all of these examples of compassion fatigue, and yet I'm not sure I acknowledged what they were going through. Caregivers sacrificed for me, and I will be forever grateful. Most of them served anonymously, but I hope they recognize in these brief words my deepest gratitude.

●●●

I know that over time Kathreyn suffered from compassion fatigue, and my children probably did as well to a certain degree. They were hit with my injuries firsthand and were also continuously exposed to other wounded soldiers in the hospitals where I was treated. They saw beds become empty in the wards around me and had to deal with the precariousness of my survival in the scenarios that surrounded us in intensive and critical care units. Kathreyn met spouses and family members coming and going from the Fisher House, grieving because their loved ones had not survived. Sometimes their stays were very brief, as they arrived only to hear the hard news that it was too late.

I wanted to express my appreciation for the resiliency and perseverance and compassion and dedication of my caregivers. It was time to thank them for all the qualities that make medicine work for wounded warriors.

In January 2011, I made another flight to Landstuhl—this time with the Wounded Warrior Project (WWP). I was traveling with SSG Dan Nevins, US Army (Ret), and Taylor Dawson, and I met up with the WWP's Special Projects VP, Bruce Nitsche. Dan was deployed to Balad, Iraq, in 2004 and was a passenger in a vehicle hit by an IED. He suffered TBI, lost his left leg below the knee, and had significant damage to his right leg that left it virtually useless. He spent years in recovery at Walter Reed Army Medical Center. Dan is a man's man. Never one to draw attention to himself, he'd be the last one to tell you that he received the highest honor bestowed by the Wounded Warrior Project, the George C. Lang Award for Courage.

When Dan's vehicle was hit, he remained conscious but knew he was hurt badly. He realized blood was squirting out of his leg and quickly dug into his wound to try to find the artery and stop the bleeding. When he couldn't find it, he applied pressure to the area around the exposed bone until he passed out. When he woke up, his left leg was gone. Without both legs, you'd think he'd be a pretty slow mover and shaker. Not so much. Today he skis, snowboards, bikes, runs marathons, and works for the welfare of wounded warriors.

Bruce was also disabled in battle, but in an earlier war. He hit a land mine while on patrol in Vietnam with the 101st Airborne Division. This resulted in the loss of his left leg, and his right leg was pretty much shredded. He has spent his life working tirelessly on behalf of wounded warriors through the VA as well as the Wounded Warrior Project. Bruce told us, "It's not about the war, it's about the warrior."

The last time we were in Army hospitals, none of us were given a very promising prognosis. This time, we would walk into the building through the front door, on our own accord. This time, we were on a mission to thank those who had kept us alive and had kept us going.

I wore a kooky hat I'd been given to keep my bald head warm, a sun visor with bleached blonde hair attached. It was January in Germany, cold outside, and I was happy to have the warmth. "You're not really going to wear that hat?" Bruce asked me. I don't think he was too impressed by my hairdo, but I think he warmed up to my sense of humor eventually.

I was both nervous and proud, scared and happy, as we approached the hospital. Even though Dan and I had been through Landstuhl on stretchers during our military days, we had to check in with security and get our badges. I could not specifically remember the setting, the building, the entry point, but it all seemed very familiar nevertheless. I caught myself almost crying a couple of times, just thinking about what I must have looked like or how my family felt as they approached what had been described as my deathbed. My stomach was in knots, but I was excited about the opportunity to say thank you to the professional men and women who helped save my life and take care of my family.

We felt the gravity of what we were about to do. As Dan and I entered the medical center, we stopped by several soldiers' rooms, witnessing their heroic recoveries from gunshot wounds, IEDs, and traumatic brain injuries. It was quiet on the ward, and we were there to provide moral support. Carol Porter with the WWP had arranged for us to meet with a group of young men and women suffering from PTSD. We shared our personal experiences about dealing with our injuries, overcoming depression, and family issues. We also offered some insight about how to watch for PTSD triggers when they returned stateside.

Finally we made our way to the floor where most of our treatment had taken place. I had been in a coma during my last visit, so of course I didn't recognize any faces, names, or locations. But it didn't matter. I knew I was meeting heroes who had saved my life as well as countless others. We didn't need any words. My caregivers could see what their work meant to me when I was able to walk into the intensive care unit on my own two feet.

The day before we left, Dan and I took turns speaking to the staff during an appreciation dinner hosted by the Wounded Warrior Project, Europe. We stood in the serving line and told the caregivers in our midst that it was our turn to serve them. We handed out platters of food and got to know many good people who may not have been at Landstuhl when we were injured but were nevertheless making a difference for the hundreds of soldiers who'd passed through their doors since Dan and I had been injured.

Psychiatrists, doctors, counselors, and chaplains will all tell you that almost all therapy involves telling your story over and over again until it doesn't hurt anymore. It's not that you become desensitized; I think you just gain a greater understanding of your own reality. Talking can leave you drained and depressed, but you have to do it. And the warrior can't be the only one doing the talking. The injured warrior has an injured spouse, injured children, injured family members. For every wounded warrior in our midst, there is a cadre of medical professionals who need to do the talking as well. The wounded warrior has caregivers who need care. Along with Dan and others on that trip, I wanted to show my gratitude as well as listen to the stories around us. War may be necessary but war is hell. Everyone needs healing and help.

31

GOING ON
A BEAR HUNT

O n some level you want to feel normal again, and you don't want
anyone to get in the way of that pursuit. My burns and appearance, my injuries and pain, my doubts and insecurities all made
me wonder if I'd ever be able to do the things I loved again. It bothered
me to think about how diminished my life would be without significant
time outdoors. I'd had several more surgeries since my deer hunting trip
to Kansas. I wasn't sure I could handle being outdoors for any length
of time, or whether or not I had the strength, but I was working on my
recovery every day.

So when the opportunity presented itself to go on a bear hunt, I didn't
hesitate. Wayne Woods invited me to join him in Cordova, Alaska, with
Shane Woods's Purple Heart Hunters. Wayne's son, Shane, was a fellow
cavalry man like me: a tanker. He was stationed with the 1st Battalion,
37th Armor Regiment, 1st Armored Division. But a massive IED explosion near Ar Ramadi in Iraq on August 9, 2006, took Shane's life just six
months prior to the blast that nearly killed me. Shane left behind his mom,
dad, and sister Stephanie, who decided that remembering Shane would
become their mission.

Wayne said that had Shane survived, he would have lived with catastrophic injuries. I spoke that language; I knew what he meant. Wayne

understood that I needed to feel normal again. This would be one of my first big expeditions after my injury. I was told we'd be in a remote location, and the promise of adventure got my adrenaline flowing. I'd always wanted to go into the wild with an outfitter who would show me the ropes. I was exhausted with the recovery process and far from rehabilitated. The opportunity could not have come at a more perfect time. Wayne Woods, Alaska Master Guide #108, was going to take me out of my uncomfortable comfort zone and into his big backyard.

The packing list looked like something I'd seen from one of my deployments. We were told we'd be setting up in a primitive camp and that we should prepare for backpacking into our location. That meant I'd need to carry whatever I brought along. I packed a thermal sleeping bag, along with sturdy hip boots, lots of socks, hunting shirts and jeans, a jacket, a pair of binoculars, rain gear, a visored wool cap, warm gloves, a waterproof duffel bag, knives, rifles, ammunition, and a camera.

I had some fear. I wasn't sure I was going to be able to hang with the other guys around me. It'd been over two long years since I'd borne the weight of that Kevlar vest, ammo pouch, machine gun, and protective uniform. Could I still handle carrying what I needed over long distances? I'd had more than thirty surgeries at this point, and my weight had improved. I was fiercely determined about getting stronger, but I was a long way off. There was one other wounded warrior on the trip, a soldier named SPC Gary Dowd, US Army, who lost an arm along with other injuries in battle, and we were both still in recovery mode. Like me, Gary loved to hunt, and we agreed this trip was a benchmark. We both wanted answers to the same questions. Could we hunt for sport and pleasure? Or would the modifications we had to make ruin it for us?

●●●

The remote village of Cordova sits at the head of Orca Inlet in Prince William Sound on the shorebird-laden coast of Alaska. It's accessible only by boat or aircraft. Cars and trucks can be ferried over, but this little indentation on the map is hidden between glacier-carved mountains and dense wetlands. Winds gust in from the Pacific Ocean, glide over the Chugach Mountains, and dissipate in the dense million acres of forestland. Salmon runs on the Copper River make it the perfect setting for commercial fishing outfits as well as boatloads of fishermen. Surrounded by peaks that rise vertically with elevations greater than parts of the Himalayas, it was definitely the doorway to a world that I wanted to explore.

When we landed in Cordova, I grabbed my gear out of the baggage pile in the tiny terminal and was met by a welcoming and kind-eyed man. We loaded up our bags in the bed of Wayne's old Ford pickup and headed into town from the airfield. The scenery was breathtaking and I was jumping up and down inside. We stopped at a local inn to eat dinner. Over a pile of great food, we shared a few jokes and drank some cold ones as we began to unwind. Wayne, a third-generation Alaskan outdoorsman, said we'd abide by the Boone and Crocket tenets for the hunt—it'd be an ethical, sportsmanlike, lawful pursuit of the largest free-ranging dangerous game animal in North America.

"I've hunted this area all my life," Wayne told us. "Get some rest and we'll pick you up in the morning. We'll get settled and talk about how to spot and stalk."

The following morning we picked up our hunting licenses and then traveled to the airstrip where we packed our gear into a Cessna 206. I didn't think it would ever get off the ground with all the weight, but I was wrong. We flew over the Copper River delta and above thick vegetation filled with the promise of deer, brown or black bears, moose, and mountain goats. Over the noise of the engines, Wayne told us, "Alaska regulations won't allow us to hunt on the same day we fly in, so we'll work on getting the camp settled today."

I told Wayne, "Good enough," knowing that as long as I was in the wilderness, I was good to go. The little prop plane dipped low over the intertidal zone, dropping us off at Gravina Rocks camp, where we'd stay for the next week. This was rustic living. No electricity or running water. No hospital ramp, no physical therapy. No people, partners, pets, or pests. Shelter was temporary and primitive. I thought I'd gone to heaven at last.

I unpacked my gear into a small tent next to the lake and stayed by myself for the first couple of nights. I wanted to feel the elements, hear the wildlife, empty my head. But I'd also heard enough bear stories to know I needed to sleep with my gun.

For the first day or two, I checked my phone for a signal from time to time. I stayed preoccupied with thoughts of home as well as chores I felt I needed to do around camp. It seemed like I just couldn't get my idle speed lowered.

Wayne grabbed hold of me and sat me down. "Shilo, this is your vacation. Relax. Enjoy every minute. An Alaska hunt is almost always wet. Once it stops raining, we're gonna hunt, and you're gonna get a bear."

His words were right on target. Working outdoors built up quite an appetite. That night we ate homemade pizza baked over the campfire and kicked back a beer. These guys knew how to rough it. Life was good. We told our war stories, but these were the tales of the big fish that got away, the deer with eighteen points, the tarpon we wrangled out of the surf. No one talked about combat.

I moved my gear into the cabin and slept like a bear that night, waking up relaxed, refreshed, and ready to breathe. Stress had made me a hunchback, but by the fourth day, I could feel the strain between my shoulders begin to relax. I sat by the lake and stared at my surroundings. There were several groups of hunters who came and went through the camp with various outfitters, so I wasn't alone, but I was feeling like one of the guys for the first time in many, many months. By day five, I could grunt and scratch my butt with the best of them.

From our campsite, we kept bears and wildlife in view using long-range spotting scopes mounted on tripods. From that vantage point, we could see what was happening on the beach a mile away. As soon as we saw action, we'd load into the boat and skip over. I saw quite a few bears, and through my scope they looked like teddy bears that I could bring home to Lizzie; it didn't quite prepare me for seeing them up close and personal. I watched my buddy, Gary, set his sight on a big black bear, and I wondered if he'd be able to take it down with one arm. He was brave, but even from our distance a mile away, we could see that it was just plain huge. As we motored over to the beach, Wayne told him, "Use enough gun."

Wayne slowed the engine as we neared the beach and told Gary to get ready. About a hundred yards from the bear, Gary was ready to take his shot from the bow of the boat. Gary held the rifle butt with his hook and pulled the trigger with his other hand. In a clean one-armed, two-shouldered shot, he'd taken his prize. He downed the bear. It was so massive it took six of us to load it into the boat. We had to get the bear's blood off the beach so we didn't spoil the hunt for anyone else, but it was quite a sight to see all of us loading that massive kill. Our guide slit the bear open in the water, taking out the entrails and letting it bleed out. I have to admit, as happy as I was for my friend, I was a bit jealous. I hadn't been in a position to pull off a good shot yet between the rain and my angle in the rough, and I wanted a bear.

● ● ●

As we sat around the fire that night, I thought about Shane and the life he'd led in Alaska. He'd lived in Palmer throughout his childhood, working in the family guiding business as a young boy. He loved climbing and hiking in the mountains near his home, but his dad told me Shane always wanted to be a soldier. He lived the warrior ethos, putting duty, honor, and country above himself. Shane was also a strong Christian, celebrating the creation that was his home. I could feel Shane's heartbeat around me when I ventured out in the trees or down to the water. Wayne and I walked into the woods together one afternoon, and Wayne asked, "Shilo, can we pray?"

"Sure, let's do that," I told him. The wind rustled the leaves on the ground around us, stirring the air. We said what we wanted to say and sat quiet. Wayne was a good dad, and I understood the grief that he carried with him no matter where he went.

On my last day in Gravina Rocks, I lay beside the Copper River, exhausted. Rain had erased my last chance to get a bear, but still I was satisfied. It would have been nice to carry home a story like the one Gary had, but I had an experience I'd never forget, just watching him take that monster down. I knew for sure that I wasn't ready to go back to cell phones, land lines, or the internet. The only web I saw involved spinning spiders. Alaska had given me exactly what I needed. In the profound silence of the wilderness, prayer had become wordless. I could be still and hear nothing. In the rhythm of the river, in the glancing of an eagle against the sky, in the chill of the wind, I could be still and know.

Wayne would not let me leave unless I promised to return for my bear. I don't know why he wanted it for me so badly. I guess he felt like it hadn't been a successful hunt for me unless I landed a trophy. I'd been raised with men who had that strong hunter instinct. We weren't going to eat that bear, but we were going to shoot one nevertheless. It had something to do with being powerful instead of powerless. I gave Wayne a big hug as I left. "Thank you, sir," I told him, leaving the rest unsaid.

I got back home and shared my cooler of salmon with the whole neighborhood. Everyone was so impressed by how much I'd caught, and I kept explaining how the rain had kept me from landing my prize. After just a few short hours of gloating and tall tales, it was back to the rat race of rehab.

*   *   *

When Wayne sent me a plane ticket to return to Cordova a few months later, I took the bait. He was busy guiding a family at another camp, so it was just my guide, Shawn Schock, an extreme outdoorsman, and me. As we flew in that puddle jumper over the rugged denning areas on the coast, I watched the Childs glacier dump an iceberg into the river and took a deep breath. The weather was much better, and I was hopeful the rain wouldn't interrupt us as often as it had on our last trip. I rested my forehead against the cold window of the Cessna, the vibrations stirring up the excitement in me. I could definitely get used to this.

Shawn told me a little about what we were looking for in the next few days. "We're gonna get you a bear this time, Shilo!"

I was stoked. This time I stowed my gear in the cabin, and we sat and talked once our chores were done.

As we set out on our first morning, I grabbed a handful of berries off a tree. "Bear food?" I wondered aloud. Shawn explained that bears found everything they needed around us . . . sedge, horsetails, all sorts of roots and undergrowth, but with only a few months to store up fat they'd take in ground squirrels as well as small moose or caribou. With their long straight claws, they'd kill their prey at night for the most part, then bury their carrion in the sand in order to return to the spot to finish the meal.

Shawn said, "If you see a bear standing upright, he's probably just getting a closer look or testing the wind; he's not necessarily going to charge."

That was reassuring.

"A black bear can see as well as we can, but he trusts his nose first," he added.

We looked at the area across from the beach, trying to decide where to set up our lookout point. Shawn said, "This hunt is going to be a little different. Instead of taking the boat over, we'll hike over to the river on the inlet and shoot from the beach."

"I noticed last time we had to hunt downwind," I said. "They've got a great sense of smell." I rubbed what was left of my nose, feeling kind of envious. The air up here was great, much easier for me to breathe with the cooler temperatures and the moisture.

Shawn agreed, "They're going to smell us long before they see us, so let's lay up here on this rocky knoll." We set our rifles down on a bed of fish bones, settling in to watch the action on the beach along the water.

I caught sight of a large black bear coming out of the wood line with two cubs next to her. She stood tall on her back legs. Shawn whispered, "She's testing the wind, taking care of her cubs. She's smelling what's up."

I watched the huge bear drop back down on four legs and scoot her cubs back onto a path that cut through the trees. I told Shawn, "I didn't realize bears used trails and roads pretty much like we do."

He pointed out an area of the beach farther along the inlet. "See that? Keep an eye on it. That's a bear trail."

Shawn told me, "Bears like their personal space just like us, and they're always hungry." I could relate.

"Ever come up on one by surprise?" I asked him.

"The funny thing is, a bear would just as soon do the right thing if you give him a wide berth and leave him alone."

By that point I figured I must have been a bear in another life.

With no bear that day, we hiked back to camp and threw a couple of steaks on the grill. The salmon had been going crazy as we returned home, and I was anxious to fish the river. I told Shawn, "Tomorrow I'm bringing my fishing poles along," and he agreed we'd do some fishing as well.

The next day the salmon were thick, swimming up the river as the tide went out. We used our binoculars to study a black bear from our lookout point. Shawn murmured, "Take a good look at that pelt. No sense shooting a bear with an ugly hide."

The bear stood at the water's edge, ready to swipe at a fish with its paw. "I'm pretty sure you'll find a nice one. Let's see if this guy comes our way." I remembered what Wayne had said on our previous hunt: "A well-placed shot should blow the stuffings out of it."

Shawn told me, "You may get lots of movement, or you might need to shoot from close range. Use enough gun."

I held on to my .300 Win Mag with .338 heavy, large-caliber bullets, able to break big bones or penetrate forty-eight inches or more into the bear. Wayne had warned me early on, "Those bullets will give you enough snort to take a bear, but don't count on a second shot."

The bear caught his fish and took it off into the woods before I could get my shot in. As the day went on, we continued to use the water as our focal point, watching for bears that we knew would eventually come in to feed on salmon running upstream. I told Shawn, "I confess, when given the choice between staring at those woods for a bear or catching some fish, I want some salmon."

I set my rifle down and started fishing. I figured the bears weren't going to be the only wild beasts looking for salmon.

Shawn joined me at the river and the two of us wrestled twin salmon, cheering each other on in the process. Rain threatened to drown out the bear movement once again, and we continued to fish. Then thunder and lightning chased us home, and I holed up in the cabin the next day, sleeping until noon, waiting for the rain to let up. Shawn and I drank some coffee, cleaned our guns, and made some killer scrambled eggs for lunch.

When the weather finally cooperated the next day, we struck out early. We found our spot on the pile of fish bones above the stream, watching the incoming bear as well as our backs, so they couldn't sneak up behind us. I saw a midsize coastal black bear, maybe four hundred pounds, feeding on some roots in the tree line before it headed down toward where we were lying near the beach. I could tell it was a male, with a prominent jaw and wide berth between the ears, and he was going to stand at nearly four or five feet if we had to meet face-to-face. As he approached, I searched his hide with my binoculars, and it was a nice pelt. He had a strong, round body and was quite a sight. I felt my heart start to race as I prepared to take him.

I set my .300 rifle on my shoulder, but wasn't sure if I should shoot yet. I didn't feel like I was in any immediate danger as the bear approached, but he was a big boy and I was not sure of his next move. Seeing him up close was extremely exciting. I whispered to Shawn as the bear continued to approach. "You want me to shoot him?"

"Hell, yeah!" he told me. I took aim, and could hear the bear snorting and breathing. I fired when he was close enough for me to jump on his back.

Shawn and I watched the bear for a moment, then he walked over to where the big beast lay on the sand. After taking my shot, I felt so exhilarated I had to stop and catch my breath. I knew he was dead and he was mine. He was nowhere near the size of the bear Gary had shot on our first hunt, but he was a beauty. Shawn picked up the bear and hefted him over his shoulder, then told me, "Let's lighten the load."

He carried the bear over to the inlet, took out his knife, and skinned him in the river. There was no use keeping the meat; it wasn't going to be eaten.

While Shawn gutted the bear, I kept watch for other bears who might want to attack us and take the carcass. A young black bear came out of the woods, but I hollered and waved my arms at him and he ran back into the brush. Shawn told me, "Let's get out of here," and we loaded up the head and pelt to carry it back to camp. When we returned to our site, we began to work on the hide, prepping it for safekeeping with salt.

◈ ◈ ◈

That night I got it. I understood why Wayne hadn't wanted me to have this experience without finding my bear. It was completely empowering to do it. If I could shoot that bear, there was no telling what else I could do in the wild. So what if parts of my hands were missing. So what if I had burns and injuries and pain. That bear didn't care. It was him or me.

The next morning we figured we had about ten salmon left to fill our quota for the week, so we took our rods and reels and went back to the river. I caught three or four after fighting with each of them for fifteen or twenty minutes, and my arms felt like spaghetti. I was exhausted. I had about a hundred pounds of salmon on ice to take home, and I'd accomplished everything I wanted to do.

Shawn egged me on, "Come on, now, let's get your money's worth," trying to get me to get up and put my line in the water one more time as the salmon rushed upstream. When the tide came in, the fish would run the stream to get into the lake, and try again when the tide was leaving. It was the perfect time to fish and a sight to see, hundreds of fish working against the flow to spawn as nature intended.

But I had nothing left in me. I laid my head down and said something I thought I'd never say: "Please don't make me catch another fish!" When we got back to Gravina Rocks, it was time to pack up and push for home. I shook Shawn's hand. "Thanks, man, I can't thank you enough. This was an awesome experience."

"We'll come back and get the big brown someday," he answered.

"It's a date," I told him, and we laughed. "When you hear from Wayne, how about telling him to send me a bigger pelt so I can brag a little more?"

"Will do," Shawn answered, and gave me a short salute as I flew back to Cordova.

Every time I look at my bearskin rug, I think of Wayne and his son. I think of the sacrifices that this family continues to make for soldiers like me. In his kindness and generosity, Wayne allowed me to see a side of Alaska that many folks never experience. He gave me a chance to remember what it felt like to be whole. And while I wasn't going to last as long as I once could, I could enjoy the experience nonetheless. I could hunt. I could fish. That part of normal made me feel great.

As I returned home, I understood that real life is not Alaska. Real life is waking up in a double-wide trailer south of San Antonio and trying to figure out how you're going to support your family now that your military career has ended. Real life is having occupational therapists and physical therapists and doctors help you outline realistic goals in light of and in spite of your impairments. Real life is needing a paycheck and a path when you lost the one you were on. Real life makes demands on you, but so does the wild. I understood that I had it in me. The temptation and fantasy of running off to Alaska stays with me still. I'll always be grateful to Wayne and his family, and to Shane.

32

IN OR OUT?

Acceptance is a word that peppers conversations in recovery, but it can be quite a bitter pill. My most difficult hurdle, once the physical healing was underway, was vocational. I loved the Army. At age three I wanted to be a soldier; at age thirty-six I still wanted to be a soldier. When I was young and innocent and fit, I wanted to be a soldier. When I was a staff sergeant, wounded and recovering, I wanted to remain in the service. The military fit me like a glove, even if the glove had been blown off. I wanted to remain on active duty, but I had a lot of health problems that were going to determine what kinds of jobs I could do in the military, and that bothered me. I thought I could find a way to contribute nonetheless.

But my family had other plans for me. The idea that I would stay on active duty meant that our lives would be in a continuous state of flux. We would move often. I'd be gone for long hours of the day, the month, the year. Despite my injuries, the possibility of another combat deployment to Iraq or Afghanistan was imminent. They ganged up on me and said no. Kathreyn wanted me home, nearby. Elizabeth wanted me safe, nearby. Joshua wanted my companionship, nearby. Nicolas and Albert wanted my security, nearby. And our newest little baby, Glen, who could hardly voice his vote, made me want to stay nearby.

I joined the military for all the right reasons. After 9/11, I simply wanted to protect my family, our country, and our way of life. I had a good job and could have stayed home, but joining the military was a simple decision, born from pure intention. It was the right thing to do. I've overcome adversity all my life. I've endured life-changing and traumatic moments due to decisions I've made as well as circumstances around me. I had to overcome a certain amount of adversity just to get into the military. I'd learned the hard way that I had to be willing to put in the work to accomplish my goals.

I prayed to the Lord that he'd let me join the Army, and he answered that prayer. It changed my life. Even when I thought the challenges were too heavy. Even when I thought hope was gone. I'd found a reason to make it to the next day. Now it was time to pray for his guidance about leaving active duty, and I had to believe he'd see me through this decision as well.

The decision to retire is difficult for every soldier, but perhaps it is most difficult for soldiers when there's a war still going on. Everything in you wants to be part of the fight, because you want your comrades home, you want your country safe. The decision to submit my retirement packet was one of the hardest steps in my recovery. But God did some career counseling with me. He showed me that I had a role and a calling to reach out to other soldiers who'd been wounded in battle.

●●●

The first year I was in the hospital, I had a visit from a man named Ron Kocian. I was bandaged up like a mummy at that point, and I didn't know who he was or why he was at BAMC, but he stopped by to say hello. When he introduced himself, he told me he was founder and president of an organization called Warrior's Weekend. He said, "You might not believe it now, but we're going to get you out fishing before too long." At that time I couldn't even feed myself. I really didn't believe he was telling the truth, but I appreciated his kindness and said goodbye.

What I didn't realize is that Ron is a true patriot. He meant what he said. He called me off and on that first year to remind me of the goal he'd set for me—that we'd be fishing together one day. I reminded him that I could hardly use my hands, that I had a long road ahead. He said, "We'll figure it out, Shilo. We're going to catch some fish. You just keep getting better."

During my second year of recovery, Ron called me again. He invited me to bring the family to southeast Texas that summer to attend Warrior's Weekend. I decided it was a good idea to spend some time together as a family, away from the hospital, the therapy sessions, the medical community.

Kat, the kids, and I drove into Victoria. The road leading into town was lined with American flags, with crowds of people welcoming us at a special flag ceremony. The flags didn't stop at Victoria. They continued to welcome us all the way into Port O'Connor.

Veterans from all over the country met together in a huge tent. There were over eight hundred of us—warriors and their families with varying degrees of injury or disability. I was still in bandages and couldn't use my hands much, but I was up and walking.

I'd decided before we traveled that I needed to be able to spot my family in a crowd, so I'd insisted we all wear Texas A&M University jerseys. I had Lizzie, Nick, Albert, Kat, and my dad along, and we called ourselves Team Harris. As we sat in the big barbecue tent, a man across the way made a beeline for our table. He began to embrace me like one friend to another. "I'm Bob Starnes," he told me. "One Aggie to another, thank you for your service."

I told him I didn't go to A&M, but he assured me, "We're Aggies," nonetheless. Bob said, "I want you on my boat tomorrow. In fact I want you all to be my guests, and I want you to launch from my house." We were extremely grateful for his hospitality and agreed to meet him the next day.

When we got to Bob Starnes's dock the next day, there were too many of us to fit on one boat. Bob's neighbors, William Vaseliades and his wife, Rosemary, came over and said, "No problem, let's use ours." So we divided up into two groups to go fishing. William had a little girl about Lizzie's age, and the two girls hit it off right away. The water was a little choppy, but it felt great to be outdoors, and we sped out into the Gulf of Mexico. I'd done all of my fishing in lakes, ponds, or rivers to this point, and saltwater fishing was new to me. The rods were heavier, and the chop on the water made it hard to spot the fish. I just wanted my family to have a good time. William's son, Peter, would not let me bait my hook. He took care of me the whole time. I kept trying to fix my bait, but Peter wouldn't let me. That little guy taught me how to saltwater fish.

When we got back to town, Bob talked to me about a program at Texas A&M called the Enterpreneurship Boot Camp for Veterans (EBV). He said, "Shilo, we've got a program to teach veterans like you how to plan a new future." I was still on the fence about retirement at the time, and what he was offering just did not fit with what I hoped would be my career path.

I told him, "Bob, I'm hoping the military still needs me." I was hoping to remain on active duty. He asked me to keep the program in mind in case I changed plans, and I promised I would.

Ron checked on Team Harris when we got back to Port O'Connor that afternoon. He wanted to know if Warrior's Weekend had lived up to what he had promised. We'd caught some fish, met some great friends, and been honored by everyone we met. He asked us if we'd come back the following year, and that's just what we did.

The next year I met another Aggie, Dr. Dick Lester, who was working with the EBV program along with Bob Starnes. He said, "Shilo, this is the program for you. You can build your future." By then I'd made the decision to retire and agreed to participate. I needed a career plan, and the past twelve months had been not only hectic but marked with a lot of confusion and indecision.

It started rather subtly; someone would be visiting BAMC and the center would ask me to speak on my recovery process. The story flowed out of me. There were times when I couldn't stop telling that story. There were so many heroes in it, so many moments when grace grabbed hold and took over. I wanted to share my story with as many soldiers as possible. I wanted them to come to know the hope that had become so much a part of me.

As I recovered, my calendar was still filled with medical appointments but there were also many appointments with the press. The Public Affairs Office at BAMC gave me some homework; they asked if I would speak to the press about care for wounded veterans, and the opportunities just grew. One minute I'd get an invitation to speak to a veterans' group, a high school, or a business franchise, and they'd treat me like a celebrity. The next I'd hear from a politician or salesperson who wanted to get behind the warrior community. I enjoyed the speaking; it was cathartic for me.

But it wasn't real life. Real life is getting ready for surgery number thirty-two. Real life is having to choose between two hours of pain relief or two hours of watching your son in a ballgame played outdoors in 105 degree heat. Real life is infection, dead ends, denial, and anger. Real life is marital stress mixed with marital bliss. Real life is years of rehab and recovery. I wanted to share that real life with soldiers and caregivers as often as I could, as often as my health would allow.

After talking to one of our local groups, I was introduced to the Wounded Warrior Project. A representative for the project had gotten to know me as I recovered, and he advised me to apply for a job with the organization. I agreed to give it some thought. We met a couple of times, and he told me more about his duties and what a job with the project would entail. I felt like it was a good match. I'd be doing many of the same things I was currently doing as a volunteer, and if that could supply a paycheck for me and my family after retirement, I thought it might be just the right fit for us.

I decided to turn in my retirement packet, then submitted my résumé on the project's website. It was processed through headquarters in Jacksonville, Florida. I spoke with the CEO over the phone and then flew to Florida to meet face-to-face. I had great admiration for the mission and scope of the WWP, and the interview went well. I was offered a job and felt a huge sense of relief. Maybe retirement was going to make sense after all. I'd get to stay in the midst of soldiers, my compatriots, and would hopefully be able to offer some hope and help. I was proud to be a part of such a visible organization, working on behalf of veterans like myself.

I became very active and involved in the mission, and my duties began to multiply. It seemed like there was no end to the number of contacts we needed to make through the project. Because of that growth, more men and women were hired to expand the project, and over the next few months we were quickly becoming acclimated to life on the road and in the field. It wasn't unusual to be in separate parts of the country on the same day, working on behalf of wounded warriors.

One of my duties included delivering backpacks to inpatient warriors at BAMC. The backpacks were stocked with items to help provide wounded warriors with things that might not be available in the hospital. We included underwear, socks, shirts, and shorts, as well as a CD player with headphones, snacks, and so forth. When Under Armor agreed to marry up with the project, the backpacks included UA brand gear among other things. But the backpacks actually just gave us a foot in the door to start conversations that eventually would lead to healing. By offering a wounded warrior a pack of necessities, we could start talking about their healing, their progress, and their challenges.

I worked on coordinating events at the Center for the Intrepid and took care of some visitors who wanted to learn more about outreach for the wounded. In order for us to track and maintain contact with the warriors, we'd ask them to sign up with the Wounded Warrior Project as an alumnus. This would enable us to include them in future events, as well as cycle them into programs and services to help with their recovery. I got phone calls all the time from people wanting the WWP to be recognized or to bring some swag to a special event or fund-raising opportunity. It was twenty miles from the office to the hospital, and it wasn't unusual for me to make that trip several times a day.

The calls kept pouring in, and I spoke all over the country for the WWP as well as on personal speaking engagements. There was a lot of pressure to speak on behalf of the wounded, both inside the project and in the private sector. I was assigned as a peer mentor for wounded soldiers at BAMC and the Center for the Intrepid, and it became increasingly hard for me to balance all the demands on my time and energy.

While I'd been building my stamina in the workplace, there were plenty of opportunities for flashbacks, fatigue, and guilt to catch me off guard, and I was unprepared to deal with a whole range of emotions. I'd sometimes be talking to a wounded warrior and giving him advice that I needed myself, and yet I wasn't following that advice.

I began to work nights and weekends to make up for all the travel time, but that was difficult as well. It became overwhelming. If you've ever felt panic racing through your bloodstream like a freight train, you can probably relate to what I was feeling. There was never enough time in the day, never enough of me to go around, never enough air to breathe. When my phone rang, my blood pressure would rise, my pulse would race, and I would begin to hyperventilate. I wasn't doing very well.

Sometimes I'd sit in the office until way past midnight, trying to get it all done. While I felt proud of being a part of such an important mission, I could not get a grip on my time. I asked for help from my coworkers and supervisor, but we were all dealing with our own issues. I've since discovered it's not uncommon for caregivers to be terrible at caring for themselves.

Life at home began to deteriorate. Between the long months I'd spent in the hospital, then in therapy, and now on the road, I was not a popular guy with my wife or children. I made an appointment to see a counselor, hoping I'd get some help with filtering the stressors in my life. As we talked, he asked me to visit his wounded warrior group meeting. I didn't mind the idea but I was really focused on trying to get some help for the group of one sitting in front of him. I needed help, and I needed it quickly. I tried to say, "I'm tired, I'm hurt, I'm done," but my words seemed to dissipate in the conversation.

One morning before heading into the office in San Antonio, I overslept. When I finally awoke, the house was silent. I could not recall anyone telling me good morning, or goodbye, or have a good day. My mind was blank. When I checked my phone, it was full of texts and voice mails from people who were concerned about me. I could not return any calls or type any texts. I was in a bad place.

I went into the bathroom and grabbed my pistol from the top shelf. I cocked the gun and put the cold steel barrel in my mouth. I stared in the mirror and saw a man who was not me. I asked myself, *Who are you? Who's that looking at me?* I began to cry and broke down on the floor, cradling my head in my hands. After finally managing to pull myself up off the floor, I grabbed the gun again. This time, I put it away.

I realized I could not go on this way. While the Wounded Warrior Project had given me a focus and a mission for months, it also gave me no relief from the heartache and heartbreak of injury and recovery. I spent more time with a new counselor. I knew God had saved me from that explosion for a reason. Now I needed his help one more time.

"Jesus," I asked him, "help me learn how to live."

33

MY NEW REALITY

I missed my ears. My hearing aids were not working right, and I was getting tired of all the attention being given my aerodynamic abilities—my sleek head uninterrupted by those appendages. I wanted to walk around amongst the living without the stares as people tried to figure out what had happened to my head. It was important to my kids as well. Close to Halloween we took a family trip to Sea World in San Antonio, and some of the pranksters in the crowd told me, "Hey, that's a great costume."

Elizabeth, seven years old, had had enough. She yelled out, "That's not a costume, my dad was injured in Iraq!"

I wanted to reassure her that I didn't care about the comments, but I attached high value to the fact that she cared a great deal. "Quit staring at my dad!" she told them.

The Defense Department had a maxillofacial prosthetics program, and once again, I volunteered to be a guinea pig. I didn't look forward to more hospitalization, but I wanted the end results more than anything. We contacted the team at Wilford Hall Medical Center in San Antonio, and COL (Dr.) Alan Sutton did a 360° image of my skull and planned the implant surgery. Dental magnets were then inserted in my skull, but the surgery had to be repeated because of my burn scars. After a year of preparation, I was finally ready for my ears. I met with anaplastologist Nancy Hansen, who was an expert at ensuring my new ears were going to fit properly as well as look natural on my head. They would also enable me to be fitted with better hearing aids. Nancy took me shopping in the ear gallery at the clinic, trying to help me decide which model was wearing ears I thought would look right on my head. Who knew there'd be so many choices? Long lobe or short? Round or oblong? Flappers or flat? Earrings?

The first thing Nancy did was make a wax impression of the sides of my head, so they knew what they had to work with as far as the base of the prosthetic. Dr. Sutton's team then created a plastic set of ears that we glued on as a temporary fit; I was supposed to test them for comfort, form, and function. Could I wear my Oakley's? Is that where I wanted to wear a hat? Did they stick out too far? The next step would be creating the ears out of silicone, matching my skin tone. Three dental magnets would be embedded in the ears so they could attach to my implants magnetically, making it easy to wear them and remove them for cleaning as needed. The finishing touches would be done by hand, to include veins and blood vessels.

I said, "Hey Doc, while you're at it, can I get a set of Mr. Spock ears?" and he obliged.

I'd gone three years without ears. The first time I saw them, it felt like getting a cherry on top of my sundae, I was so happy. Finally, I was getting a feel for the new normal.

As I started to recover, I really wanted a new Stetson. My old one no longer matched the shape of my new head, and it sure didn't fit now that I had my new ears. Stetsons have an illustrious history in the old West—they started off as hats that could double as feed buckets or water troughs for weary horses. For Cavalry soldiers, the Stetson is a sign of prestige and brotherhood. The black Stetson with a gold cord meant I was a Cavalry soldier, and in my heart, whether I was active duty or retired, I would always be Cav. If I was asked to attend a ceremonial military event, wedding, or other function in my dress blues, I wanted a Stetson that would fit right.

We made our way back to McCamey to visit family, and drove into Midland to get fitted for a cowboy hat once again. The gal who worked at the western store crossed the wooden floor with a couple of samples that she thought I'd like, and we kind of guessed at the size. She tried the first one on; it was so small it did not go past the crown of my head. If you've ever tried on a cowboy hat, you know that fit is everything. If it doesn't feel right, you're not going to wear it. I told her that one didn't quite work, and she tried the next one. She was so confident it would fit that she set it on my head and patted the top of my head to seat it well. As she did, my ears fell off.

The two prosthetics just snapped off the magnetic implants holding them in place and bounced onto the floor. She didn't seem to realize what had happened and started to reach for one of them before she realized it was an ear. I scrambled around to grab my ears; they cost a fortune. When I looked up, I had to laugh, as my helper was making a fast exit to the back of the store. I hollered after her, "If you broke 'em, you're gonna have to buy 'em!" She didn't think that was too funny. I think I scared her half to death, and it took a while for our laughter to die down. I was also a little embarrassed and chose not to buy a new hat that day. My new ears were just a little too tall for the brim. We could have worked on a few more sizes, but I decided I didn't want to give the little lady another heart attack.

34

A FUTURE
AND A HOPE

After leaving the Wounded Warrior Project, I continued to meet my speaking obligations, but I was getting concerned about what to do to support my family. Retirement and disability checks together would hardly pay the bills for a family our size, and Kathreyn was already working long hours. I wanted to work. Bob Starnes called to give me my dates for EBV, and I was excited about finally starting this new chapter.

As the course began, I quickly began to learn a lot about myself. Sponsored by Mays Business School at TAMU, the program was designed for guys like me who'd always nurtured an entrepreneurial spirit. I shared my calendar with business leaders and mentors, and they could see that once I got going, it was hard to rein me in. My mentor, LTC(Ret) Stacy Overby, told me, "Your story is powerful. Why don't you use your speaking ability to reach others, to offer them a future and a hope?"

Every time I spoke, it seemed as if I started a conversation that would not stop. Again and again I heard from people close to me, as well as perfect strangers, that something about my story touched a nerve, touched a chord, touched a heart. I knew that for recovery to be real, people around me needed to learn more about my reality. My words were like a pebble skipped across a pond—the ripple effect allowed many others to open up and to share their wounds or their recovery.

The folks at TAMU showed me how I had created a way to make a living without even realizing that was what I was doing. To be successful, I just needed to formalize the process, which would involve some strategic business decisions. I needed to formulate a plan, and with their support, that's exactly what I set out to accomplish.

● ● ●

The opportunities kept cropping up in my life. I know that these were not coincidences. I knew that I was being led in a purposeful manner. One of the groups I met through EBV was the International Franchising Association (IFA), and they asked me to do some motivational speaking for them. I was interested in one subgroup particularly, VetFran, because through my networking they'd demonstrated that the business world was full of patriots wanting to support servicemen and women returning from Iraq and Afghanistan. I learned about their program, "Operation Enduring Opportunity," which was designed to address the 11 percent unemployment rate amongst returning war vets. Their goal was to recruit and hire thousands of veterans and their spouses as franchise owners.

I learned about many government programs that were falling into place to assist veterans in making the transition back to civilian life. Our Congress enacted the Vow to Hire Heroes Act in 2011, which would give employers a tax credit of $2,400 if they hired a veteran who'd been unemployed for over a month. If the vet had gone without work for six months, the tax incentive jumped to $5,600. If that same business hired a veteran who'd been disabled in a combat zone and had gone without work for more than six months, the tax incentive nearly doubled to $9,600. I wondered whether or not most employers knew about these incentives when a veteran walked in the door, or would I need to educate them? I was hoping that being a veteran would give every applicant a leg up, whether he or she had one or not.

Over time, I learned about more incentives to put veterans back to work. The Help Veterans Own Franchises (HVOF) Act of 2011 established another tax credit for honorably discharged veterans to own their own businesses by offering up to a 25 percent return on franchise fees. The temptation to own a business intrigued me, but I knew that I still had surgeries and recovery in my future as well. I was having a difficult time with my skin, and more grafts were going to be necessary. Further correction of my nose as well as my hands were scheduled, so it was difficult to understand what kind of commitment I could make in terms of owning my own business. As I spoke to various groups of veterans, I learned there were plenty of veterans taking advantage of the opportunity, with one out of every seven franchise businesses purchased by veterans.

The VetFran group continued to pursue me about becoming a franchise owner. I was told I was a great candidate to own a small business. As a soldier, I'd already received plenty of leadership training and had learned to be a team player. Soldiers operate with a set of core values, and that was a strong asset to add to my résumé. I was accustomed to completing the mission, which could mean seating three hundred people an hour in a restaurant instead of covering three hundred miles a day in a Humvee. I enjoyed speaking with the IFA, and explored the options available to me while at the same time sharing my story with their franchisees.

I continued to respond to speaking requests, traveling all over the state as well as the United States to spread the message that adversity is not our enemy, it is our most powerful teacher. And people responded. I heard from people like SGT Jerry Karman Jr. His words reminded me that this was what my new life was all about. Hearing his words helped me attach new meaning to what I was doing. His voice was just one of many, but what he had to say resonated with me.

Dear Shilo,

I heard about your story while listening to an NPR report on the radio while on the way to work one morning. It particularly caught my attention because I heard you were an Armored Cavalry Scout, which was also my military occupation from 1980–1986. I was inspired by your bravery, your sacrifice, and mostly by your attitude while discussing the injury and healing process. It really affected me.

It was hard driving west on the 91 freeway with tears literally pouring out of my eyes (this is the first time I admitted that). I trained for six years driving armored personnel carriers [and] Jeeps, reading maps, and practicing calling for fire on imaginary targets.

Then I realized how fortunate I was, never having been activated or called out to do what I so rigorously trained for. I had a sense of what you were and what you are, an American hero who put your life on the line so we (myself included) can enjoy the freedoms that we have.

You are included in my prayers and my constant thoughts of appreciation and recognition.

> *Jerry Karman Jr.*
> *SGT, E-5 (19 Delta)*
> *2/107th Armored Cav*
> *Echo Company*

● ● ●

While I was in therapy at the Center for the Intrepid in San Antonio one day, I ran into my friend Paul Koch, who had suffered severe damage to his leg when we were deployed to Iraq, and we started to catch up. His father, Danny Koch, was living in Houston, and Paul and his parents were involved in growing support for wounded veterans in their community. We had stayed in touch during those early days of rehab, and our friendship grew. A couple of years later, Danny had moved back to his hometown of Lubbock and one day he gave me a call.

"Hey, Shilo, I want you to come to Lubbock to speak to my Rotary Club and introduce General Freakley." He was the commander of the 10th Mountain Division when Paul and I served in Iraq.

I told Danny, "I'd be honored." The Rotary Club was gracious to me, and I was introduced to an amazing local musician, Russ Murphy. He listened to my story and asked me to return to Lubbock to be a guest speaker at his church, Southcrest Baptist in Lubbock, Texas.

I was introduced to the congregation and began to share my testimony. Over and over again I tried to regroup during a standing ovation from the enthusiastic crowd. I wanted this group of Americans to know how Kathreyn and I felt: "Thank you for allowing me the opportunity to speak with you today," I told the crowd. "It seems to me that at the point of injury, it was your prayers that kept me safe. Your prayers allowed me to be here today."

I handed the microphone to Russ, and through tears he thanked us for speaking. Then he did something that meant a great deal to me. He recognized my mother. During our many speaking opportunities, that had not happened before. It meant a great deal to us. My mom had been so faithful and devoted to us throughout my recovery. She deserved that recognition. Next he thanked my wife and children for their service. I have never seen my family so proud.

After the concert, Russ said, "That was awesome, Shilo, let's get together again."

For the next several months, he'd call me to join him at a concert, and afterward he'd give me some pointers about public speaking. He had an elegant way of just bringing up sound advice. "You're doing good, Shilo," he would say, "but let's make it better."

I loved working with him. Not only did he coach me in my speaking, he helped me grow in my faith. He has the gift of encouragement. Not just through our one-on-one time but with his music as well. He could always tell when I was upset or down and would help me focus on what was important.

Not long after one of the concerts I did with Russ, Kathreyn and I were invited to attend the Inspirational Country Music (ICM) Awards presentation in Nashville. Russ's song, "Cowboys Love Jesus, Too," had been nominated for 2010's ICM Song of the Year. I was backstage in the dressing room getting ready to present the award for Song of the Year. I didn't know who the winner would be, but I was saying a big prayer for Russ. He popped in the room and we hugged. He didn't know we were in Nashville and was surprised to see me. I got called on stage, and it was the first time I'd been in front of such a large audience. I was scared to death. Looking at that group in front of me made me so grateful for the road we'd traveled, and I tried to share my gratitude with the crowd. I was just happy to be alive.

When I tore open that envelope, I got to say some pretty astounding words, "The 2010 Inspirational Country Music Award Song of the Year goes to my friend, Russ Murphy." My grin was huge, and Russ leaped up the steps in front of thousands of guests. It was a true honor.

After I had worked with Russ for a little over a year, he came to me and said, "You and Kathreyn inspired me to write a song, 'That's What Freedom Costs.'"

"How'd we do that?"

"You remember that concert we did at BAMC?"

"I remember." I thought of Russ's performance and how people loved his voice and his message.

"Well, before the concert started, I was walking through the hospital, and I saw some things that changed me. I saw a young boy feeding his dad supper because his father had lost both hands in battle. And I looked at a teenage girl reading the newspaper to her dad who'd been blinded in combat. During the concert, I looked out at the crowd, and I saw amputees, and soldiers in wheelchairs, and I saw you, my friend, struggling to recover from your burns, and I turned to my singing partner, David Spears, and I whispered to him, 'Take a look; that's what freedom costs.'"

"A few hours later, we started writing that song. It's been nominated for the 2011 Inspirational Country Music Song of the Year. The last verse was inspired by you."

I told Russ, "I had no idea. I am really honored."

"It goes: A man and wife in Flagstaff, look at photographs of their wedding day. He was such a handsome man and now there's burns and scars on this warrior's face. He turns to her, 'Now tell me what you see?' She says, 'Soldier, you're still beautiful to me.'"

I got choked up and said, "Thank you, Russ. That means a lot."

When I first heard the song I cried like a baby. Russ was selected as Inspirational Country Music Song Writer of the Year for 2011 and asked me to attend the award ceremonies with him in Nashville. It was a great honor to share his moment in the limelight once again.

Russ and I continued to work together when our schedules would permit. He'd provide music and inspiration, and I'd share my story and journey of faith. One time we were speaking to a group of high schoolers in New Mexico. I love talking to kids because they're usually so forward with their questions. A young lady asked me if I was religious. She wanted to know where God was when this happened to me.

I don't mind that question. People all over this earth endure incredible tragedies, and I didn't hesitate in telling her that he was right there with me. I told her it's not about religion, it's about faith. Religion seems to say that you must find your way to God. Maybe through good works, study, or favor. Faith says that God is with me, in every moment, evident in every circumstance, and there will never be any action on my part that could or would justify his existence. I told her God didn't need me, I needed him. There's a big difference.

● ● ●

On the way home from New Mexico, I was struggling with a lot of personal issues that I couldn't share with many people. Russ pulled the car over on the side of the road and said, "Talk to me; what's wrong, friend?"

"Russ, I don't want to downplay what God's done for me. He saved me. I know that. But sometimes I feel like I'm just beyond wounded. I worry that I'll never really heal."

It was hard to admit that. It ran contrary to what I tried to share with other warriors and contrary to what I thought was the strength of my testimony. But in my heart, I still wanted to be a good-looking man. I still wanted to have a normal body. I appreciated my bionic capabilities, but sometimes I felt like one big medical experiment. I missed running, wrestling, walking without pain. I missed feeling sweat run down the sides of my face, passing a mirror and standing up a little taller. I missed being anonymous, blending in with the crowd.

You didn't have to tell me I had a lot to be grateful for . . . I was spending my days with miracle men and women. But the hurt was still very real.

Russ could get that kind of stuff out of me. He could get me to talk better than most men I know. When I shared my heart, he prayed with me. He's a pastor first and foremost, and he knows what makes a man tick pretty well.

We talked a lot about marriage and how hard it can be. Kathreyn's sacrifices for me were enormous. But sometimes, I just wanted a life without the memory of war. Kathreyn was working full-time with wounded warriors as a contractor with the Army's Wounded Warrior Program; I had worked full-time with the Wounded Warrior Project; my kids were asked to contribute their energy, thoughts, and feelings about the war and their dad, and it just added up to an awful lot of injury. I wasn't trying to have a pity party. Russ just made me keep it real.

He prayed for me as well as with me. He lifted up my family and our needs. He told me to keep my eyes on the goal, on the finish line . . . a life that reflected God's mercy and grace. He was selfless that way, and those highway talks meant a lot to me.

35

TRAUMATIC STRESS

I can tell you about the hard parts of my recovery, but there are parts and pieces of that story you will not like. I became, in my mind, the poster child for the wounded warrior. I had the familiar burned face with a profile that so closely resembles every other burn survivor. I had the grafted skin, the frayed limbs, the palpable signs of severe trauma. You could see my face on television commercials, in fund-raising ads, on *Dancing with the Stars*, in campaign literature. It might not have been me, but it was someone who looked an awful lot like me. It has to do with burn treatment regimens—when doctors and nurses are struggling to save skin, save cartilage, save bone structure. It can seem as if our faces are each painted by the same numbers.

The wounds that I kept inside were harder to heal. There are some folks who feel PTSD is not a real diagnosis—that the problems are mental and emotional and therefore they carry less weight than physical injuries. I know firsthand that it's real. I wish there was a magic potion that could make PTSD go away; I would gladly take a placebo if I thought I could convince myself that it had the power to heal. But there is a healing map I will have to follow for the rest of my life.

Part of that realization left me depressed, unable to lift my head or acknowledge those who'd loved me and fought the fight with me. I'm not proud of those deep, dark holes that I would either fall into or dig for myself. But they were real for me, and when I talked to soldiers and survivors day after day, I knew they were real for all of us.

As I spoke to various veterans' and patriot groups around the country, the subject of PTSD was both relevant and confusing. It's hard to draw the line between mental health and mental anguish. But I understood that the conversation about PTSD had to start and continue if soldiers who returned from the battlefield were ever going to heal. Hundreds of thousands of soldiers have passed through Iraq and Afghanistan over the last dozen years, and each and every one of them carries the scars of battle, physically wounded or not.

If you can imagine rushing down a dirt trail, trying to beat off a ragged pack of dogs that are eating the contents of your comrade's head that has been severed and blown from his body, then you may have some small inkling of why that soldier has trouble getting to sleep at night. If you can imagine washing blood off your armored vehicle, knowing that the blood came from the heart and sinew of someone you loved and served with, you might have the ability to understand why a soldier has lost his train of thought. A moment will trigger a memory; the memory will trigger a horror; the horror will leave you weak at the knees. Every soldier returning from battle, whether an ancient war or a modern one, carries the trauma of that war with him or her every day.

Choosing to self-medicate dominates the discussion when you talk to men and women with PTSD. I've heard a lot of stories of how other soldiers cope with PTSD and they run the gamut—legal and illegal, ethical and unethical, moral and immoral. No one in their right mind would make some of those choices, but when you are in the throes of an episode of PTSD you are not in your right mind.

●●●

Like other veterans I spoke with, sometimes I chose alcohol to deal with my PTSD. It was familiar. I knew firsthand that it absolutely did not work, as I had a childhood full of hard memories that proved it was not going to help. Yet drink I did. Vodka, because it was odorless and easy on the throat.

Kathreyn came home from work one day after I'd finished a particularly grueling week of speaking engagements and appointments, and found me with a half-full bottle of vodka between my knees. The other half was in my gut, and I had no recollection of having taken the first shot. I just knew that I was exhausted, that I wanted relief, and that it was the only solution I could think of grabbing that afternoon.

I'm not proud of that moment, but I want you to understand that such things happen, and they happened to me. I have looked at my reflection and justified yet another drink. I have looked at my profile and justified yet another drink. I have looked at God's grace and felt the shame of taking another drink. In those moments, drink took away the rage, the highs, the lows, the loneliness, the powerlessness, the ugliness. The moment waned, and another drink worked its magic again. You start to spin in a cycle that you want to stop and want to continue in the same swallow. I wish I could tell you I was more powerful than alcohol, but I was not.

Coming off a depressive episode of PTSD, I was able to acknowledge my powerlessness, and I live with the truth of what I am capable and incapable of doing every single day. Every day that I do not drink as a way to self-medicate during a stressful episode brings me one step closer to ending the cycle of abuse that I heap on myself and those who love me.

I met a warrior's father after one of my speaking presentations. He was there representing his son, trying to find help for his boy who returned from combat as a triple amputee. It's hard to feel sorry for yourself when you meet someone in such dire circumstances. No one wants pity. The word starts with a pit and ends with why.

At my weakest point, I doubted myself, I doubted the ability of Kathreyn to love me, and I doubted the motives of people who asked me to speak, to visit, to reach out. I could be asked to speak on a certain date, say February 23, but on February 21 I might fall into that pit and be unable to really give my best on the 23rd. I knew that people were counting on me, and it is in my DNA to try to please others and meet their needs. The expectations were there, the audience was assembled, so I'd put on my happy face, give what I had to give in as real a manner as was possible, and then cave in when the engagement was finished. On stage, I was a dynamic speaker. Off stage, I felt whupped and diminished by my own words. PTSD leaves you unable to define your own identity. If I was speaking in order to be inspirational to others, I felt like a hypocrite at the end of the day. PTSD makes it very hard to maintain your ground; you feel like you are taking one step forward, two steps back.

●●●

I chose cruelty sometimes. I could say cruel things to my wife, not caring whether my words hurt her. On some level, I used cruelty to push her away. I didn't want her to stay with me. I wanted her to go away and start her own life, to leave me alone to make a mess of my own. You might ask how I could think such things, and I don't blame you for the question. It's one I asked myself in those moments. But I need you to understand the reality of PTSD and how it can twist and contort your emotions. You are literally trying to fight or flee, and to hell with anyone who tries to stop you. Divorce seemed like a way to flee at times, as much as it pains me to say that. I adored Kathreyn; I put her on a pedestal. But I also believed that she deserved someone whole and wholly different from me. If I couldn't solve my communication problems with her, the concept of divorce didn't seem like such a tragic idea.

I understood that I could go to counseling. I could find a pastor or mentor to help me, but when you are vulnerable, you are less apt to choose to become even more vulnerable. I will be the first to tell you that the grace of God allowed me to endure the pain and suffering of my injuries. But that same faith in God's grace also led me to confusion. *Why? Why me? Why not? When and how will we heal?* It was confusion regarding my future and my path with my wife that caused a great deal of damage in our marriage. Confusion can shred your faith. This is why it's so important that a community surrounds a wounded warrior with support. Most of us want to tell the truth, but we're not going to volunteer. Ask me no questions, and I'll tell you no lies.

PTSD can sneak up on you—loud noises, crowds, and lack of space can be nearly asphyxiating. The pressure of people and input is tremendous at times. I think this is reminiscent of the concussive blast; your body translates noise and crowds as an explosion of sorts, and you are on sensory overload before people around you are even aware of your circumstances. Again, you respond by either fighting or fleeing. For me, I didn't want to fight so much as I wanted to disappear. My hearing aids have been a blessing and a curse. Sometimes I want to snap them off my head so I don't have to deal with the range of noises and sensations that are broadcast through my eardrums. A crowded mall or restaurant is the worst, yet your family wants you to shop till you drop. The thing is, you're going to drop out of the activity because you simply cannot process what's happening when your brain's a pressure cooker.

●●●

I have chosen rage sometimes as a way to deal with an episode of PTSD. It's probably one of the scariest responses, as it puts you and your family at risk once again for both physical and emotional wounding. I don't want my children or wife to be afraid of me. I know on a molecular level what that feels like because that's how I grew up. I try very hard not to go there, and I'm ashamed and embarrassed when I do. I had plenty of experience with the dangerous mixture of PTSD and rage from my childhood.

I remember one day when my parents were fighting, and my dad used me as a pawn to hurt my mother. As the argument escalated, he grabbed me and told me to get on the bike and we roared out of the driveway, past my elementary school. I looked over his shoulder and read the speedometer: we hit nearly 140 mph as we sped through town. The stoplight turned red, and my father screeched to a halt, burning rubber for nearly the entire length of the block. He revved the engine, did a u-turn, and hauled it once again toward home. When we got into our driveway, he stormed into the house and grabbed his revolver off the kitchen counter. He sent me up to my room, and I flung myself onto my bed, afraid of what he was going to do next.

My father went back into town and shot and killed that red light. A couple of hours later, law enforcement appeared at our door. My father was charged with destruction of property, and it became one of a string of run-ins he'd have with the law. Rage is a destructive symptom of PTSD.

When I traveled to various venues to speak to veterans, I'd inevitably end up talking to service members from Korea, Vietnam, the Gulf wars, or our current wars, having deep and meaningful conversations. There's an understanding between you that you both have seen the underbelly of evil and darkness. You don't talk about it openly, because the warrior mentality says that we can handle whatever we're given. Accomplish the mission. Storm the village. Stand in the breach. We don't cower.

The human psyche develops a mysterious kind of amnesia. But soldiers from each of those wars will tell you that they startle at a loud noise, or the rush of a crowd as you try to attend a football game, or that pool of blood when your son falls off his skateboard. Trauma can trigger a response in you that you either express or quell. You fight or flee. Holding it in is common, but it's not necessarily healthy. I've tried to teach my children to go into a closet and scream, yell, punch a pillow—anything harmless to get it out. It's a lesson I have to reteach myself all the time.

● ● ●

Insomnia is PTSD's most insidious symptom. If I couldn't sleep one night, I couldn't sleep the next, or the next. Once I lost sleep, I couldn't restore my equilibrium. I had trouble concentrating, and anxiety became normative. If I had a speaking engagement, I had difficulty delivering the message I was meant to give, and it took all my attention to focus and deliver. During fits of sleeplessness, my mind would race from one event to another, sometimes with no rhyme or reason. I tried to identify triggers for dreams or nightmares, but it was generally fruitless. That disfigured teenager who hid behind the shed in Samarra when we cleared the village jumps out at me in my dreams when I am overtired. In my dreams, I turn the corner and there he is—a horrid jumble of defective parts. I scream at his family all over again. The horror of how he was mistreated jars me into fits of restlessness.

Sleep deprivation is a very real part of war. We'd go out on missions for weeks at a time, sleeping upright in the back of a Bradley or drifting off in the desert sun. When we finally returned to our forward operating base, I would want desperately to sleep, but getting unwound was a process. Prisoners of war have spoken of sleep deprivation as being one of the most cruel forms of torture. The physical aspect of a lack of rest is hard, but the mental and emotional aspects can be devastating. After several days of poor sleep, you cannot think clearly. You cannot make a decision. You don't want to talk or to listen. You have a short fuse that gets shorter by the minute. Your skin is slack, your pores seem to release toxic waste. Your appetite is gone, your thirst is great.

You look for any remedy. Alcohol disguises the problem, interrupting any hope of achieving a natural rhythm. Over-the-counter sleep remedies seem to worsen the symptoms. Your body pulses for relief. It's a symptom of PTSD that can be fairly easily remedied if you're open and honest with your physician, but very few soldiers want to admit to having a problem that sounds trivial. If you're sitting next to a quadriplegic in the waiting room, you feel pretty stupid telling your doctor you can't sleep. But putting that pride aside can lead to solutions that can help more than the insomniac's cocktail you come up with on your own. Understanding the requirement for qualitative and quantitative rest can greatly reduce PTSD symptoms, and finding a solution with your therapist or medical provider is vitally important to your recovery.

✦ ✦ ✦

PTSD has taken its toll on me, and the more places I'd visit to talk to soldiers, the more I'd hear about soldier suicides. I get it. Suicide has always been on the table as an option, and I wish I could tell you that was not true. There have been many times when I believed that relief could come if I just left this earth. I understand it is selfish, cruel, and murderous to every single soul who loves me, but it stays on the table and at times it seems like a delicious choice. Wouldn't it just be easier if I wasn't here? Wouldn't everyone just be happier if I wasn't miserable? I grow tired of pain and of looking and feeling abnormal. I long to run and not grow weary.

When I talked to families who were struggling with recovery along with their loved ones, I tried to impress upon them the idea that it takes only a minute to consider suicide, and it's a minute you cannot retract. You are dealing with your perception versus your reality, and when you are depressed, your perception becomes your reality. On every level, heart, mind, and soul, I know that self-murder is wrong, but there have been moments, milliseconds actually, when I have been willing to be wrong rather than alive. I am grateful for the grace of God that he has provided a way when there seemed no other way, and I am bereft to understand how I could consider killing myself, but I have to be honest in revealing to you that PTSD makes suicide *seem* viable.

As I spoke, I got asked frequently to help others understand suicide. Over the past twelve years that our soldiers have served in the Middle East, our military has experienced an alarming rate of suicide by soldiers of all branches of service, all ranks, and all occupations. Hundreds take their own lives every year. I need to say that again. Hundreds. Four, five, six hundred soldiers a *year*. I wish I could tell you what you could do to help, but it's not that simple. You've got to reach out. Do the work of contacting and building relationships with the veterans around you. Don't assume they're doing okay. That's probably far from the truth. Just because you see them in church on Sunday morning doesn't mean they don't want to take their own lives on Sunday night.

Living with survivor guilt, shame, injury, chronic pain, and a whole host of impairments can suck the life out of you. Our soldiers have survived injuries that would have killed warriors in earlier battles because our medical treatment and triage on the battlefield has vastly improved. A soldier injured in Tikrit on Monday can be on the operating table in Landstuhl on Tuesday and at Walter Reed Wednesday morning. Recent wars have given us our largest number of triple amputees. Let that idea sink in for a moment.

I met a man whose son returned from Iraq with one arm, a torso, and a head. Medical miracles have allowed this young man to become a triathlete. But he had dark moments, moments when he wished he was dead and wished he'd been left for dead, yet didn't have a hand to self-administer a lethal dose of prescription drugs. IEDs have created a new category of injury for many soldiers—an explosion erupts from underneath a vehicle, and many soldiers have lost their genitals and urinary tract in these incidents. The military has introduced a new type of body armor, bulletproof underwear if you will, to protect soldiers against these types of injuries. But the risk is high nonetheless. Ask any man and he will most likely tell you he would rather be dead than castrated.

◆ ◆ ◆

Denial is a huge part of the PTSD problem. I remember a soldier I met on one of our wounded warrior hunting expeditions. He told me and my buddy that he wanted to resume his civilian career in law enforcement. One night over dinner during our weekend hunt, he kept griping, "The VA's not doing crap for me. Those doctors just send you from one to the other, and no one knows what they're doing."

My buddy and I decided to confront him on the whole VA issue. We had a feeling the guy wasn't telling the whole story, and we wanted to help him. I asked, "Exactly what is the VA not doing for you?"

He said, "I can't get the help I need. No one knows what to do to fix me."

I asked him, "Did you tell them that you're walking around the house for weeks on end, wearing the same clothes?"

"No."

"Did you tell them you were having problems with your wife and kids, and that you were depressed?"

"No."

"Did you tell them you're not sleeping?"

"No."

I knew what he was doing. "You're just telling them what you think they want to hear so you can get back into law enforcement, aren't you?"

He admitted, "That's all I want."

I told him, "You're never going to get better if you don't tell them what's really going on. You have to tell the VA you couldn't get out of bed for two weeks, you couldn't brush your teeth, you couldn't change clothes, you couldn't communicate with your family. You don't want to be the guy on the side of the road holding up a sign asking for food and mumbling to himself, do you?"

A lightbulb seemed to come on. I continued, "Did you ever consider that maybe law enforcement is still going to work, but maybe being in the direct line of fire is not the best option? You can still work in law enforcement, just in a different role."

"I don't want to be labeled a nut case," he answered.

"That's not going to happen if you tell the truth," we told him.

I talked to him a few weeks later and he'd gone back to the VA, discussed the real issues, and got better help. They changed his medication, and he lined up a job in law enforcement. Ten minutes of reality therapy with a couple of warriors who knew what he was going through made all the difference, and from what he told me recently, his career is going well.

I get calls at 2:00 a.m. all the time. They are from soldiers who cannot make it through the night. They need a voice on the other end of the line who understands what they've been through and where they're headed. Many times it's hard to decipher whether they're dealing with PTSD, alcoholism, or substance abuse, but at the end of the call that doesn't really matter so much. What matters is that a veteran, a brother or sister in arms, feels that his life is not worth saving. If you asked him to run into a burning building to save another human being, he'd do it in a heartbeat. Yet he won't rush into his own life to save himself.

I cannot turn away from a cry for help. That doesn't mean I won't beat the crap out of that same friend in order to get him to understand what he's doing to himself and those who love him. But I can listen and take it all in like a sponge if that's what gets that wounded warrior through his darkest night.

This generation of soldiers grew up on video games and TV shows that glamorize violence. We don't speak of pink mist with you; it represents the vapor that once was a whole soldier. Or it might be the remains of the enemy after taking a 25mm high-explosive round to the chest in retribution for trying to hit your Bradley with a rocket-propelled grenade. Either way, a human being becomes annihilated into pink mist.

In battle you discover there is nothing glamorous about violence when you have to set your boots down on what remains of your brother in arms.

As you realize where you stepped, your heart sinks into your toes, you vomit in the ditch, and your need to grieve is enormous. But there is another mission to attend, another road to clear, another battle to fight. There's no pause button, no rewind.

If a soldier speaks of ending his life, take him seriously and get him some help. Intervene, for God's sake.

● ● ●

Sorrow is a very real part of PTSD. There is a grief that you cannot express, a sadness that becomes a deep well, made deeper by news fragments, chance encounters with strangers who need comfort, and trying to come to terms with who you are as well as who you are not. There are stages of grief, and just because we were not killed in action doesn't mean we or our family members don't go through the grief process. Help is out there to navigate the terrain of that journey. It's not a one-way trip. You go back over that geography again and again. I encourage soldiers to cry. It's not a sign of weakness. It's more likely a sign of tears withheld, because the warrior or his family members have tried to be too strong for too long.

One of the symbols you'll find in a military honors burial service is a tripod of sorts—a pair of military combat boots, with a rifle standing tall from between the boots, dog tags, and a helmet resting on the rifle's bayonet. What you don't see is the body of that soldier. It's gone. I think this is analogous with what has transpired. The soldier is gone. For many fatalities in this war, there are no remains. From all appearances, all that is left of a soldier is this set of equipment. But there's a wife grieving the loss of her lover, a child grieving the loss of his daddy. There's a mother who cannot understand why she's outlived her son, a father who can't comprehend losing a daughter in battle. There's a sister who can't fathom not catching a movie with her brother, a brother who can't throw a football without his buddy. There's a unit grieving its gunner, there's a squad grieving its medic, there's a battalion grieving its commander. Our soldiers need time to grieve, and they need to be taught the process of grief-work required to move forward rather than moving on.

Today's soldier didn't fight in Iraq or Afghanistan for a year. He fought for three, or four, or five years, missing almost every key event in the lives of his children and spouse. You have fathers who've never met their newborn children, mothers who've missed their child's first step. Many arrived home to find their homes empty; their spouse could no longer tolerate the strain of single parenting or the loneliness of keeping the home fires burning and found warmth or comfort someplace else.

It is not uncommon to have a wounded warrior return home only to find that his spouse and children are flat gone, along with the furniture, the bank account, and the dog. They came back from battle with little time to reassess, let alone decompress, before they were sent back to war. The term "tour of duty" makes it sound innocuous. In reality, the soldier who was so fresh from battle must surrender to the idea that he's going right back and it's not a one-year tour. It's fifteen months in Afghanistan, followed by a few months at home, and then twelve more months in Iraq, followed by a few months of downtime interrupted by a permanent change of station (PCS) move, followed by another deployment, this time back to Afghanistan.

The standard of keeping a soldier stateside for a year between deployments looks good on paper. It's just not reality. And you are fighting a war at home as surely as you're fighting overseas when PTSD rears its ugly head. Ask any local police department or emergency room how many veterans or family members they see on a regular basis. The numbers will unnerve you.

It's very hard for many military families and spouses to understand that almost to a man or woman, a soldier wants to return to the battlefield because the mission is incomplete. This is a volunteer Army, Navy, Air Force, and Marine Corps. Soldiers and service members answered the call, they weren't called up. Soldiers who fought in Iraq volunteer for duty in Afghanistan because they've seen the threat of Al-Qaeda, the Taliban, terrorism, and oppression, and they believe the mission is just. They've seen poverty, and utter chaos, and tragedies too gruesome to describe. It doesn't leave you just because you return home. In today's Army, soldiers are kept with the same unit, so the unity and brotherhood of this group of likeminded warriors is sometimes more comforting than the strangers you meet in your own home.

Many soldiers will tell you of the adrenaline rush that comes with battle or PTSD, and the need for that "fix" of adrenaline is very real. Soldiers returning from war will typically go out and buy the biggest, baddest, fastest motorcycle or sports car they can find or afford, because their success on the battlefield has convinced them that they're invincible. If they didn't get hit by an IED when the probabilities were so high, then navigating a roadway at 120 mph must be a piece of cake. Visit any military installation, and before you exit the main gate there will be a digital sign that tallies the days between each fatality on the roadways. There's a reason for that sign. It's to remind soldiers as they leave their duty station to slow down enough to recognize their own mortality.

●●●

PTSD is not solitary suffering; there are secondary souls—those who love you—who suffer from PTSD as surely as you do. They are trying to handle what's happening, but most of us don't acquire those helping, healing, or coping skills in our everyday lives. By identifying PTSD as real, we can find a source for healing for the soldier as well as his family. If PTSD is not identified and diagnosed properly, then everyone continues to suffer, adrift in understanding where to go, what to do, or how to help.

Kathreyn had struggles in her college years that were still part of her psyche, and those unresolved issues, compounded with years of caring for our family on her own, not to mention witnessing my wounds up close and personal, made her a perfect candidate for her own struggles with PTSD. I want more Americans to gain a realistic understanding of the sacrifices made by military families and the role a community can play in helping and healing those patriots.

Over time I noticed that my little Lizzie had trouble with injuries as well. If she got a small cut, she was worried she might be hospitalized in the burn unit and need a skin graft. If she spotted a small amount of blood on my skin after I'd gone through another surgery or procedure, she immediately began to worry that I might die. The highs and lows are as real for the children as they are for the warrior. It is hard to find a yardstick for what children can endure or understand when their parents are suffering from catastrophic wounds.

I truly believe that the strongest people are the ones who don't act on dark thoughts and who actively seek help. It is very easy to slip into the dark abyss of hate, burdened with soul-tormenting images and repulsive desires. It is easy to stay there too. But help is out there. I want wounded warriors and their family members to trust me when I say this. PTSD is all about stress and trauma. If we can understand this and then reach out to veterans to ensure they know that there are healthy alternatives for dealing with stress and trauma, we can bring about healing. When we use a Band-Aid on a soldier or family that's hemorrhaging, we are doing that family a disservice.

If you get only one thing from my story, may it be that you take the reality of PTSD seriously, standing in the gap for those who need help.

36

UNCLE SAM'S KIDS

We were in and out of the hospital for several years as I was healing, and we ran into families who were suffering or struggling on a frequent basis. One day we were entering the elevator at BAMC, en route to another appointment. As we entered, there was a soldier with no legs in a wheelchair. He had one arm in a sling, and his wife stood right next to him. On either side stood a young boy, each must have been about seven or eight years old. They couldn't hold their daddy's hands, but they were gripping the armrests of his wheelchair as tightly as they could. Both of the boys reached for the elevator button at the same time as my Lizzie. Here were three kids, each of them trying to take care of their dad. Kathreyn and I exchanged a look. The childhoods of our children were very different from our own.

I don't think the public understands how much this campaign in the Middle East has cost our children. I could see it as I looked at my kids and their pain. Families are ripped apart emotionally during catastrophic injuries or death, as well as by long periods of isolation and deployment. Yet families of wounded warriors live in the same home, carrying on courageously from day to day, and a lot of folks around them don't really understand their journey. There's a lot of heartbreak and heartache, and kids need a voice, they need to be heard. There's a lot of excitement and happiness to share too. Families that aren't affected by the war may not realize how much it costs military kids to carry on with their lives.

Imagine you're three. Your dad is your whole world. He goes to work every day, along with your mom, and when he comes home you know it's play time. You play hide-and-go-seek in the backyard; you go for long walks and family picnics; he reads to you at bedtime. Then he's gone. Your mom says he's gone to Afghanistan. You don't have a clue what that means. All you understand is that he's gone. You see your mom crying sometimes, but you don't understand why. She reads to you at bedtime, but she's exhausted and you have to wait your turn for dinnertime, bath time, and bedtime rituals. When you wake up in the morning, you rush into your parents' room, expecting to find both parents there. But your dad's still gone, and that emptiness goes on for a long time.

When he finally returns home, there's a big celebration. Flags are flapping in the breeze; you're so excited to find your daddy's face in the big crowd. There he is, throwing you up in the air once again. You struggle to get and keep his attention. You see him go to school with your big brother to see why he's getting in trouble. You watch him tuck in your big sister and hug her neck. You whine and cry, wanting and waiting for your turn with him.

You notice that sometimes your mom and dad argue about who's going to the store, what they need to buy, what will happen next. But finally life seems to return to a steady rhythm and you forget how he left, how you felt, how scared you were. Your family settles back into a normal way of life again and your dad hugs your mom a lot. Things feel safe and right again.

One night he comes home from work and you hear him whispering to your mom. You're four now, and you're understanding things a little better. You hear that he might be leaving again, and you start acting out, throwing a fit when he drops you off at daycare. The packing begins, the crying begins, the terrible goodbyes begin. And he's gone. Your mom's holding down the fort. This time you're able to see your dad on the computer sometimes, and you hear his voice. You beat on the monitor to tell him it's time to come back. You want him to come home so badly. You try to be a big kid, just like your brother and sister, but you see that your mom is tired and worried. She watches the news and you see big explosions and fires, and you worry that your dad might be in that picture.

Then he's home, he's home, and the whole family celebrates once again. You pack up the car and everything you own and you move to another Army post. You make new friends and your parents help you get your own room set up. You're six now and you've started first grade. You love to go to school, and your dad walks you up the sidewalk to the big brick building every day. Your teacher hugs you when you come in the door, telling you she can't wait to teach you how to read. You're so excited and race home to tell your dad what you learned in school. But he's packing again. He's going to war. You can't do fractions yet, but some part of you knows that he's been overseas for half your life. Your mom is very upset about the news. She thought he would not have to deploy again, but this unit at the new post is taking him back to Afghanistan.

Your teacher tries to get you excited about school and gives you stickers for every ten pages you read at home. You've had more hugs from your principal than you've had from your dad in the last year. You race home to show your mom your smiley faces, but she's on the phone and she's crying. She tells you that daddy's been hurt. She has to leave. Grandma and Grandpa arrive, and they stay at your house while Mommy flies to someplace called Germany. Daddy's been burned and he's very hurt. You are scared to death. You find out he's coming home, and you are so happy. But you find out he's not coming home-home, he's coming to the hospital-home, and he will be in and out of hospitals for the next two years.

By the time you get to third grade, you're behind in reading and math because your dad's been in the hospital so many times and you've been so frightened. You have to go see the doctor because your tummy hurts and you get headaches all the time. Your big sister gets in trouble for wearing too much makeup to school, and the high school principal sends your big brother home from school for trying to punch a hole in his locker. Your mom looks really tired, and she's trying so hard to make everyone happy.

◈ ◈ ◈

Do I need to go on? Do I need to tell you that this scenario, and many variations on the theme, are repeated in thousands of military homes around the nation and around the world? War takes a toll on families. It always has. Some kids excel, rising to the occasion. Some kids hibernate, waiting for the war to end. Some kids press on, trying to do what is expected of them. Some kids say goodbye so many times that they end up enlisting in the military and serving with their own fathers or mothers in the same war.

Some families don't make it. The kids are parceled out to aunts, uncles, and grandparents while one or both parents go to war.

When a mother and father try to resume family life after combat, there are new stresses on old wounds, new fractures where a marriage foundation has hardly had time to set. For wounded warriors and their families, the divorce rate has been estimated as high as 90 percent and the suicide rate is staggering; the number of walking wounded cannot be counted because so many injuries don't show up in the medical office, they just show up at home.

Too many children have to say these hard goodbyes and never, ever get to say hello again. Their tears and anguish at a parent's departure are justified when they hear the news that their mother or father, grandmother or grandfather, sister or brother, aunt or uncle, cousin or companion, will never, ever return. In the media and in the press they see and hear the arguments about the war and they wonder why their mother or father had to give the ultimate sacrifice when so few people seem to remember or value what triggered the war's onset.

Staring is a problem. It's one thing for kids to do it, but adults who stare just make you mad. They ought to know better. If I could change the conversation parents have with their children, I'd address the importance of helping all children understand disabilities. With thousands upon thousands of soldiers and service members returning with substantial or catastrophic wounds from the battlefield, the public discourse and perception has to change. Have the conversation you need to have now, so that when you're out in public and you encounter a wounded warrior, you or your children don't stare and gawk. It gets really tiresome for my children. They are defensive and sometimes aggressive in their protection of how I'm perceived. You don't need to steer clear of us. Burn injuries aren't contagious. An amputation isn't viral. Get involved enough to know and understand what we need, or look the other way.

I remember Lizzie just biting someone's head off when she thought they were staring at me. It was too much pressure for her. My sons would herd me through a crowd sometimes, trying to protect me from onlookers. I don't want them under that kind of stress, but I don't want to avoid going out in public either. The more the public understands and accepts that there are lots of us out there, the better off all of our families will be. I don't mind if you talk with me about my injuries. I prefer a conversation over the silent stares, and so do my kids. I don't mind it when someone tells my children how brave they are. That means the world to them, and it's a respectful way to acknowledge their sacrifice. The truth is, we'd like to blend in and go about our lives peacefully, just like you. Dignity trumps sympathy every time. I'm not that different from you. I just put my ears on one at a time.

If you have military kids in your schools, neighborhoods, churches, and communities, then you have a solemn obligation as an American citizen to reach out to those children. I believe that with all of my heart. I know firsthand what it means to them. My children will tell you, if you can't take my word for it. Take the kids to a movie; invite a family with a deployed spouse over for dinner; give the spouse a gift certificate for some kind of fun; be the one to step up and listen when you see the edges starting to fray.

The price our kids are paying every day for our recent wars is staggering. We'll pay the price in the courthouse, the medical clinic, or the counseling chair if we don't pay it first in person. There are still eighty-five thousand troops in Afghanistan as of October 2013. We need to step up for their families, and we need to do it often and today.

When I speak to various audiences, I want to tell them: I'll serve in the military for another thirty years without asking you for a dime, except please, please, watch over my family while I'm gone.

37

THANKS LIVING

The endurance courses my father built for me when I was a boy were all about physical strength and stamina, but there was a mental element as well. When the body was ready to give way to the pain inflicted upon it, the mind had to take over and make the next step happen. Staying active in the warrior community helped both Kat and me build and maintain our emotional stamina.

As we continued to represent the wounded warrior population, Kat and I were invited to an event in Los Angeles with First Lady Michelle Obama. I heard J.R. Martinez was invited as well, and hoped we would cross paths again. I'd had quite a bit of work done since the last time we talked—on the inside as well as the exterior. I'd had over forty surgeries for wound repair, and I'd put on some weight. I was lucky enough to find him at this event, and we tried to catch up. But each time we started a conversation, he'd get interrupted to have his photo taken, and people around us would want an interview or another photograph. When it was announced that J.R. would be on *Dancing with the Stars*, I would often get asked for my autograph or if I could show off some dance moves. People thought I was J.R. There were some similarities in our appearance.

One lady would not give it a rest. She was sure I was J.R. Martinez. I told her, "Lady, I'm not J.R. My name is Shilo Harris."

She was relentless, "You are J.R. Martinez, and you better give me an autograph!"

So I did. I figured J.R. didn't need any bad press from a ticked-off fan. The guys I was with asked me what I'd written on the notepad, and I told them I signed J.R.'s name. We had a good laugh.

When Kat and I returned to San Antonio, I attended a veteran's event where J.R. was the guest speaker. After the ceremony, we managed to get a chance to talk, and it was good to see my friend. A fan came up to see J.R. but thought I was him. She told me, "Thank you for your service! I was rooting for you the whole time you were on *Dancing with the Stars*!"

I pointed to J.R. next to me. "That's the guy who was on the show, not me."

I told J.R. what kept happening to me. "We're standing side by side, man, and they still think I'm you." I asked him, "Does anyone ever come up to you at the airport to ask if you're Shilo Harris?"

He laughed. "No, no. Not so much, Shilo. In time, my friend. In time you'll feel my pain."

When I left J.R., I thought about the changes in our lives since we met at the Center for the Intrepid. I don't care about the limelight or giving autographs. I care about victory. J.R. and I share an understanding of what it means to persevere. Endurance is going through fifty surgeries, believing in the idea that the outcome will be worth the pain. Endurance is wondering if your family can handle your injuries and seeing them suffer with you and for you. Endurance is handling the heat of your emotions over time as you wrestle with a lack of control over everything around you. Endurance is hitting the finish line with your strength, dignity, and faith intact.

◈ ◈ ◈

To this day, there are still things I think I can do in my own strength. Trusting God, asking him in faith, means you must accept the fact that God's answer may look very different than your perception. I had to ask for God's protection over my emotions so I might not be tossed about by the wind, unstable and indecisive. There's a kind of balm in sympathy, and it can woo you into spiritual complacency. And the temptations of this world hit you smack in the face, wounded or not. But when you expect God to show up, he will.

I knew I would have to endure continuous procedures to heal my skin. I was going to have another operation on my hand to try to get some mobility back, and I needed laser procedures on my face. I'd been struggling with an infection in my arm for nearly two years. My nose surgeries still didn't give me the breathing capacity I needed. The holes where my ears were would fill with gunk and constantly needed care. Chronic pain had just become a part of life.

Kat and I also had to accept that there is a kind of ongoing grief work that goes hand in hand with catastrophic injury—it involves more than endurance. It requires an attitude of gratitude. Each time I went back into surgery, Kathreyn worried about my survival, and she bore that burden for herself as well as my children. I had to figure out how to balance my emotions through the surgeries and subsequent therapies or treatments. To this day, I may not be able to feel the tears roll down my cheeks because of the scar tissue, but I know they're there. We had to learn to give thanks for each outcome, even when it didn't "fix" the problem. Modern medicine and technology can go only so far. How does a person learn to say, "Thank you, God, for this injury"? How do you say thank you for surgery, surgery, and more surgery?

I can tell you that at the moment of my injury, thanksgiving was not on my lips. Yet through the years of healing, I have discovered that gratitude has to be cultivated. God's Word tells us: in everything give thanks. But does that axiom hold up when your body explodes into flame? I wrestled with these thoughts as we gathered around the dining room table for Thanksgiving in 2012. It was decked out with pumpkins and Indian corn. Turkey. Dressing. Mashed potatoes. The doors were wide open, letting in the sunshine and cool breeze. I looked at the faces of my family around the table. Our lives had changed a good bit since that first Thanksgiving Kat and I shared in Germany "before the war." No more shoebox apartment. I didn't have to fix a plate for Lizzie anymore. She could fix it herself. Decked out in her rodeo shirt, she was helping her mom put food on the table. As I prepared to carve the turkey, I looked at my little boy, Glen, hovering over the goodies in front of him. I realized it had become about more than gratitude . . . it was about teaching my children how to thank God for everything too.

◆ ◆ ◆

As I met wounded warriors with catastrophic wounds returning from Iraq and Afghanistan, when we let down our guard with one another we had to learn to share the doubt, fear, and anger. We also had to learn how to share the gratitude for small steps, pieces of the recovery process. Many of us use humor to mitigate the reality of our circumstances, but when the laughter is gone, it is what it is.

I have spent time with men and women who injured not just eyes or ears, but half the gray matter in between. I have shared therapy sessions with men who'd been castrated by an IED but who could still put balls to the wall. I have tried to mentor men and women who could not keep their minds from panicking but could push their bodies beyond limit. If you ever need to get a grip on gratitude, spend a few hours with a veteran. For Kat and me, talking to other warriors and their families reminded us that we were not alone.

I was proud of serving in the military and thankful for the opportunity. I'm especially thankful for the legion of men and women that are now my peers, mentors, and friends. Am I proud of my injuries? No. But I was proud of being entrusted to serve my country. Can I serve today? I'm trying. By drawing attention to the adversity faced every day by wounded warriors, as well as wounded souls, I hope I can inspire someone to overcome. I also hope I can inspire the public to place their trust in the training and expertise of veterans who are returning to the civilian workforce. We are a force to be reckoned with. If you want to put your money into compassionate aid, put it in research and development for recovery from war wounds and protection from primitive as well as advanced weaponry. The vet who gave skin, arms, legs, eyes, and ears is going to keep on giving. He's not done. Neither is she.

When you face down the enemy, it requires something of you that no amount of tussling on the gridiron or grappling in a think tank can do. Hiring a veteran is the right thing to do. I don't mind coming out of the closet on this issue. If an employer has two individuals standing in front of him or her, and if all things are otherwise equal in terms of training, education, and résumé credentials, I'd hire the vet in a heartbeat. Because guess what? He had my back, and now I've got his.

38

HOME SWEET HOME
ONCE AGAIN

One of the most unexpected gifts that came out of my recovery was an opportunity presented to our family to have a new home. I met Meredith Iler through a program called Helping a Hero. One of their representatives had come to BAMC early on in my recovery and encouraged me to fill out an application for a home from Helping a Hero. Meredith has worked tirelessly with this organization. She knew that Kathreyn and I lived in a double-wide trailer out in Floresville, south of San Antonio. We'd bought the acreage when we made the decision to retire, knowing we'd want to stay close to BAMC and the medical services I was apt to need in the years to come. I was just fine with that trailer; I'll admit it got kind of cozy when all the kids were home, but it worked just fine. Helping a Hero felt differently about that; they wanted us to have a brand new home.

We went through an application process and left it in the Lord's hands. Meredith knew that I was torn about the application, because at that time I was still undecided about remaining on active duty with the military. I had not yet submitted my retirement papers and wrestled with my future based on the extent of my recovery. She kept in touch with our family, and when I decided to retire, she pushed the application process along over the next couple of years.

When former first lady Laura Bush handed Kathreyn and me a key symbolizing the promise of Helping a Hero to furnish us with a new home, we were both elated and humbled. We'd met so many warriors with injuries much more serious and debilitating than mine. It was hard to accept such a huge gift with so many others in need. I tried to turn down the offer of a new house, but at the same time I wanted Kathreyn and the kids to have this gift. Helping a Hero paid off our mortgage on the trailer and land, then auctioned off the trailer and raised $27,000 to give back to the fund to help more returning veterans.

Then we received another bit of unexpected news. It seems Meredith shared our application with the right set of eyes and ears at ABC's *Extreme Makeover: Home Edition*. We were asked if we'd be willing to participate in the application process to receive a home through that organization. Kathreyn and I were stunned. We'd seen a few episodes of the show on ABC, and we knew that the producers and crew could really go over the top in making a family's dreams come true.

There were five families that were being considered for the show; again, we followed through with our application, confident that the Lord was in charge no matter what. A film crew from ABC came out to the house and interviewed us on site. We were told it was "hush-hush" and we couldn't talk to anyone about this exciting possibility in our lives. Then I had to run over to BAMC to do some work one day, and I ran into a buddy at the Center for the Intrepid. He was completely courageous, working hard on his recovery. I started mentally discounting our application, believing that it wasn't right for us to have a new home when this triple amputee was struggling just to make his life work in a chair, much less a home. I really wrestled with this gift, not sure at all that I wanted to accept it if we were eventually selected. What made us the right candidates when someone else was so profoundly injured?

Later we would learn that the money raised during *Extreme Home Makeover* resulted in donations to Helping a Hero of over a million dollars—enough to build ten warrior homes, including one for this triple amputee.

●●●

God's timing is kind of surreal. We let go of the dream and got busy preparing for the holidays. I had a whirlwind schedule of speaking engagements, and Christmas was upon us before we knew it. We had no idea Santa was going to arrive with such a bang. We got a phenomenal phone call right before Christmas. Our family was on a short list of possible home recipients. The folks at ABC warned us we had to act fast. A film crew could be at our house in a matter of days to start work. We tried to ignore the survey crew in our backyard, putting down stakes on our acreage. We couldn't say a word about the production crew working out details with local contractors and community organizations. Our job was to get ready, just in case we were selected.

We were sworn to secrecy through our contract with ABC, which to be honest is just about impossible. How do you not tell the people you love that you may be receiving such a tremendous gift? You want them to be a part of the excitement with you. I quickly learned that the cat was out of the bag, and not because of our loose lips. Someone approached me at the hardware store, telling me they'd heard a certain builder had been selected to build our home for us. Someone else told us when it was going to happen. Another couple told us a few more details about the house. It seemed like everyone knew more about the makeover than we did. Nevertheless, we kept our mouths shut.

ABC told us to get our passports ready; we might be going on a family vacation, and if we did it might involve travel outside the United States. We raced to get the kids' passport photos and applications done and sent the packet in on a rush deal. In the middle of all this, we tried to prepare for Christmas, knowing that the reason for the season was more real than ever. God had something wonderful in store for us as a family.

Then Ty Pennington and his crew showed up in our yard. Using his trademark bullhorn, he hollered for us. We stumbled from our trailer out into the yard, dumbfounded and blown away by the unbelievable news. Suitcases packed, Kathreyn, Glen, Elizabeth, and I flew to Frankfurt, Germany, courtesy of ABC. It was a sleepless flight for me, but the kids were super travelers and we were all excited about going back to Germany. Glen was too young to appreciate the trip, but he was ecstatic nonetheless. When we arrived, we were met by a decked-out USO bus. We were taken in this luxury RV to Heidelberg, Germany, where we'd spend the next four days.

If you've never been to Heidelberg, it's a beautiful mix of old and new. It's the home of the United States Army Europe (USAREUR), so this is a German community that still has strong ties to the American military. On the one hand, you roar off down the autobahn into a modern city, with its mixture of European and American brands. But if you change your direction and make a slight left-hand turn, you're in the heart of a progressive university that's been a think tank for urban dwellers for centuries, home to philosophers, artists, and history and social science gurus. Once you enter the *fussganger*, or pedestrian zone, you wind your way up a well-traveled cobbled road to ancient ruins along the Rhine River. You can stop for soup ladled into copper tureens at Zum Roten Ochsen, buy hot bratwurst from a street vendor, or pick up a sack of freshly baked *brotchen* and chocolates from the corner *backerei*. We posed for photos next to the store with the wooden nutcrackers, made in the same tradition for hundreds of years. The air was clear, chilly, and perfect for a guy like me. Kathreyn, the kids, and I all held hands, taking in the sights and breathing in the brisk mountain air.

We toured the old Heidelberg Castle, taking turns in the jail cells in the dungeon and walking through the gorgeous ballrooms. We were treated to other local sightseeing excursions, enjoying our share of German beer, *wiener schnitzel*, and *pommes frites*, and then hooked up with the USO to return to Landstuhl to thank the caregivers who'd taken such good care of us when I was injured.

I cannot tell you how meaningful it was to all of us to thank these compassionate medical servants for all they'd done for me and continued to do for wounded warriors worldwide. There were a lot of tears that day when those crewmembers who were still at the hospital saw the extent of my recovery. We visited with many wounded warriors at the hospital and shared our story, trying to give them a picture of the future and the hope that God had given us.

While we were in Landstuhl, I received a call from J.R. Martinez. J.R. told me he had a surprise for me and asked if we'd agree to join him in Orlando. He asked my family to meet his crew at Walt Disney Children's Hospital, where he and I would share our stories together with some amazing children that were fighting every day to survive.

Through the magic of ABC, we flew to Orlando and helped J.R. bring cheer to a lot of very important kids. Over and over, we witnessed the generosity of people God had brought into our lives.

● ● ●

Morgan's Wonderland, a builder in our area, partnered with *Extreme Makeover: Home Edition* to build us a home that exceeded our wildest dreams. It's owner, Gordon Harman, was selected due to his involvement in the nonprofit organization he created in San Antonio. He built a twenty-five-acre family fun park for his daughter, Morgan, and other children with special needs, and he was completely committed to building a home that met our unique requirements. He'd created Morgan's Wonderland, and he was ready to create Harris's Wonderland as well.

When we returned to San Antonio, we were taken by limousine to San Antonio's Riverwalk area. Boats decorated for Christmas traveled up the inner-city canal, and we celebrated with ten other patriot families as they were awarded new homes through Helping a Hero. Our friends and well-wishers then followed us out to Floresville to see our new home.

My heart was in my throat as we crossed that dusty gravel road toward the acreage that had once been home to our little trailer. Over 3,400 people had volunteered to help with the construction of our home. The road was lined with people waiting in the cold night air for our arrival. We heard the engine roar of the Patriot Guard, the motorcycle unit that's gained a reputation for fierce allegiance to the cause of liberty throughout the span of this war. They gunned their engines as we approached.

The wind picked up from the north, and we climbed out of the limousine to the shouts and cheers of thousands of people. Kathreyn and I stared at each other in disbelief. Santa was about to make another stop in south Texas. Hollering "Move that bus!" we became a part of television history. With all of our family members, military friends, and Texas neighbors surrounding us, we watched that big bus pull away, and in its place stood a dream.

The first thing I noticed was our flagpole, a huge, sturdy standard that could prevail despite our tough Texas winds. In the front yard, the American flag was displayed again in a mosaic garden of red, white, and blue stones. Kathreyn, Lizzie, Glen, and I just gawked. We were dumbfounded. We walked up to the front door of our Spanish ranch homestead, past a beautiful courtyard with a gentle fountain, plants and trees surrounding the entryway. Next to the courtyard stood a granite bench engraved with my name. I was touched beyond words.

As we entered the front door, to our left and right was a hardwood and Mexican tile breezeway, with picture windows facing the back and front yards. If we went to the left, we'd head toward the master suite and my office. If we went to the right, we'd head toward the family room, kitchen, and kids' bedrooms. Lizzie and Glen pulled us that direction, and we entered the warmest and most inviting family room I'd ever seen. Pictures of us, of Texas, of wildlife, adorned the walls and gave us all a preview of how much work had gone into creating this gift for us.

Lizzie's room was over the top. Designed for her in an Indian princess theme, her platform bed was a round mattress inside a life-size teepee. The bedroom walls were covered with a wide mural of wild horses. Her windows were covered in barn wood shutters with chalkboard interiors. Her closet was almost as large as her bedroom had been in the little trailer. Everywhere you looked, there was evidence that the designers had pulled out all the stops to please my little girl. And they succeeded beyond Lizzie's wildest dreams.

In Glen's room, we entered a railroad depot. On one side of the room stood a caboose, and inside the caboose we found a bed, railroad lantern, and a *Toy Story* theme. In one corner of the bedroom there was a platform for two model railroads, one running atop the other, through terrain scenes straight out of a train buff's wish list. Just about every toy you can imagine was stashed in that room. The kids had their own decked-out bathroom as well.

It wasn't given any airtime on television because of some prickly personal matters between myself and the boys' mother, but Nicolas and Albert had a room too. It was decked out in camo and hunting gear, with an oversized widescreen television on one wall, along with all the latest techno toys. I was allowed to have the boys only once in a while, but when they came to visit, they'd have a place that was all their own. I was especially grateful that ABC made my boys feel like they were part of the makeover, even if they couldn't participate in all the festivities.

Kathreyn and I wandered back to my office. I was given a state-of-the-art executive suite, and I plan on making some big decisions in that room. ABC installed a special air filter for me in the house, and between the set-up in the office as well as throughout the rest of the home, those air handlers were going to make it a lot easier for me to breathe. My burn injuries make temperature regulation an issue (my internal thermostat is broken), and the system keeps a steady temperature of seventy degrees, 24/7.

On one wall of the office hung the photo Kathreyn and I received when we met President George W. Bush and Laura Bush, along with military memorabilia and important family photos. ABC installed a projection screen monitor, along with all the bells and whistles any mogul needs, and I have high hopes and aspirations for what I can accomplish.

Finally we walked into the master suite. Kathreyn and I have never had a lot in terms of fancy furniture and fine linens, but that seems to have changed. Against a wall treatment of raw Texas twigs, we had a huge bed with matching pillows and covers. I didn't see a sippie cup or a Pillow Pet anywhere on our bed, which made me smile from nub to nub. We walked into the master bath, and there sat a massive electronic bathtub that fills, sings, bubbles, and vibrates. The separate steam shower creates a mini rainforest and fills the room with aromatic vapors. The water treatment system was going to give my lungs some welcome relief from the dust and wind outdoors. To tell you the truth, I am still trying to figure out how to turn things on and off.

The kids started dragging us out to the backyard. We had a patio decked out with a fine grill and furniture, and in front of the patio ran a row of beautiful pottery fountains, cascading one into the other in a stream of water that led slightly downhill over a bed of river stones. Apparently Lizzie had asked the producers to make a miniature golf course for us, so sure enough, there it was. Across from the fun stood a small Western village, child-sized for Glen, Lizzie, Nicolas, Albert, and all their friends. It contained a jail, a general store, a parlor, and a hitching post. Each area was stocked with all the props, costumes, and equipment needed for dramatic play. The kids could dress up like cowpokes, buy their vittles in the general store, and ride off into the sunset on their stick horses.

We continued to walk across the property and found one of the most precious parts of the dream. ABC had built Kathreyn a barn with a set of horse stalls. A big carved K was mounted on the side of the building, along with a sign that directed her to let all her cares go. Kathreyn has a palomino and a sorrel mare, and they were standing in the stalls. A tack room held all her gear. Mark LaCroix of MetalTech in LaVernia donated his time and materials to fabricate the metal horse barn, working thirty-one hours straight, followed by a brief rest and another twenty hours of labor, to get the job done in time for the reveal. Kathreyn was so touched that the producers decided to create an area just for her, and the tears streamed down our faces.

The idea that we would receive not only a new home but virtually every gadget, gizmo, and possession you might need to make that home putter along into the twenty-first century was totally unexpected. Throughout the home we found stunning pieces of artwork, signed, numbered, and chosen for our family. There were so many unique projects and gifts of love, service, and loyalty reflected in that home, and we still don't even know who to thank for some of them.

If you ask us to tell you the truth, we'd say it's all totally undeserved. What did we do to deserve such a grandiose gift? I can't answer that, but from the bottom of our hearts, we will always be saying thank you for what we received. Everyone seemed to understand the greater good. This was not about an Extreme Home Makeover; we were in the midst of an Extreme Life Makeover, and with this kind of support surrounding us, we felt blessed beyond measure.

39

MENDING AND
HEALING

A few months after the big reveal from ABC, I received a call from Operation Mend in Los Angeles. The reconstruction of my nose was giving me quite a bit of difficulty. I kept fighting one infection after another, and nothing seemed to help. Operation Mend reaches out to wounded veterans in all branches of service who were injured in Iraq or Afghanistan. They have a team of reconstructive surgeons whose sole mission is to help us establish our new normal. They'd helped over fifty men and women, and they thought perhaps they could help me heal the wounds that made me look and feel separate and apart from the normal population. Did I really want and need a fifty-first surgery?

Some of us hide under our hoodies, our Ray-Bans, and our ball caps because it's easier than getting stared at. Scars and disfigurement have become part of our military uniform. Yet the more you carve us up, the more fatigued we become. One more surgery? I really had to struggle with my decision. Surgical fatigue is real.

I remember eavesdropping on a conversation one time in which the lady insisted that more could be done to reshape her son's face. He could get a more pronounced jaw line, a stronger nose, cheek bones. The part she didn't understand is that her son had probably already had about fifty surgeries in terms of skin grafts and treatment for his other injuries. While she supported his recovery, he was the patient. He was the one going under the knife each time. I could understand his reticence. He was probably completely content with a face for radio.

My doctor at 4E, Dr. Renz, had already told me what I didn't want to know but needed to understand. For burn patients, our injuries last a

229

lifetime. They're different from an extremity fracture. The burn scars are with us for life; the tension, soreness, dryness, temperature sensitivity, inability to sweat and release heat, and other characteristics of the grafts would never go away. The research being done today in the ISR is not going away either; they're committed to improving the quality of our lives over time. They're even experimenting with spray-on skin. This war has produced a huge number of burn injuries, and we don't even know what aging looks or feels like. So as I approached Operation Mend, I tried to keep it real, expectations at a minimum in light of my experience.

Despite my feelings of fatigue, I decided to proceed. I wanted my nose to work better and to quit collapsing, and I wanted to breathe easier. I was told most procedures were outpatient; I'd be greeted at the airport by a representative of Operation Mend who would connect me with a Buddy Family. The Tiverton House at UCLA is set up similar to the Fisher House—it gives wounded warriors and their companions a place to call home during the surgery and recovery phase.

Operation Mend was started in 2006 by Ronald Katz, a philanthropist who enlisted UCLA's reconstructive surgeon, Dr. Tim Miller, a Vietnam vet, to help military like me by connecting us with top-notch diagnosticians and surgeons to see how far we could go in the restoration process. Doctors at UCLA came up with a treatment plan to help me with my nose and breathing issues. Apparently there were some things they thought they could do to restore more function and form to that part of my anatomy.

As I visited with the folks at Operation Mend, I realized once again that I was lucky to have my arms and legs. I might have spinal injuries and I might be missing a few digits, but I can walk unassisted and I'm extremely grateful. It might not be easy, but I can live with my injuries. And I'm not alone. There's a brotherhood amongst the wounded, both military and civilian. You know what you know without saying it aloud. Sometimes your harshest critic is your brother who's lost a leg. Sometimes your most ardent supporter is your sister whose arm ends at her elbow.

●●●

While I was in LA, I was staying up late at my hotel, trying to knock out some emails and get my schedule settled for the week. At about two in the morning, I received a call from a brother, a wounded warrior who was stationed in the Pacific Northwest. We'd been friends through several deployments, and he found that he could talk to me. As soon as I picked up the phone, I knew something was wrong.

"What's going on, buddy?"

His voice was low and weak. "I've done something to myself that I haven't done in a long time."

I got a sick feeling in the pit of my stomach. I was afraid he'd done something to himself that he couldn't fix.

"Man, what did you do?"

"I may or may not have accidentally cut myself," he told me.

"Dwayne, why? What's wrong?"

"I can't take it anymore. I can't take it," he whispered.

"I'm calling 9-1-1."

"Naw, man, don't do that. I just need some help."

"Talk to me," I told him.

He proceeded to fill me in. He had suffered for a long time from gastrointestinal problems and lived with vomiting and diarrhea. I thought a lot of that was related to stress as much as anything else. His nerves were shot; you could tell by the sound of his voice. He had a new baby boy at home and a lovely wife. He'd just gotten married and had a lot to live for, but he wanted to go back downrange. His family was back in Pennsylvania, and he was at Fort Lewis. He wanted to be with his wife and son, but more than that, he wanted to get shipped to Afghanistan. He wanted to be a soldier and do his duty.

"I can't leave combat, Shilo. Our guys are still over there."

"Dwayne, you've done three deployments, man. You've served. It's someone else's turn."

"I'm torn up," he told me.

I knew he was a cutter. In my mind, his cutting represented a deep chasm: wanting to serve, but wanting to meet the goals and expectations he had as a new husband and father. He'd been very ill on his last deployment; he was sick before he left, sick overseas, and sick when they sent him back home. There was no physical explanation for the vomiting and diarrhea. No ulcers, no disease, just stress. Copious amounts of stress.

"What's the trigger?" I quizzed him. "What happened tonight?"

"I don't know, man. I just couldn't save him, man. I couldn't find him."

He told me about the driver of his Humvee, killed by an IED during his last deployment, and he filled me in on all the gory details. He'd witnessed all of it. I knew he'd experienced blackouts and flashbacks. "It haunts me, Shilo. I see him over and over. But I don't see him. He's nothing but mist. Pieces of meat, hair, blood. I can't take it."

"Dear Jesus." The description he'd given me made me sick. I tried to explain, "You're suffering from PTSD, Dwayne. You're not alone. Let's get some help."

"I don't think I can right now. I don't want to disappoint my family."

"You can't be everyone's hero," I told him. "You didn't do anything wrong, Dwayne. You can't dwell in the past. You have to find a foothold, something to hang on to. You've got to live for your son, and for your wife, and for that friend you lost, and every other fallen warrior."

He was silent on the other end of the phone.

"What did you cut, Dwayne?"

"I cut my arm, man. Three deep gashes. The bleeding's about stopped."

My mind was racing. I didn't know his family's phone number, or who else was close enough to get to his side. "Tell me where you are, Dwayne."

"No, man. I'm all right."

Tears streamed down my face. "I can't lose you, buddy. I can't lose another warrior. Let me help you."

"I'm okay," he told me.

"You're not okay," I answered. "You can be okay, but you need some help. Have you told your doctor that you're a cutter?"

Silence.

I knew the answer. If he told his doctor what was really going on, they might discharge him for good. But if he didn't tell his doctor what was really going on, he might cut himself so severely he'd never wake up.

"Dwayne, tell me where you are so I can get you some help."

"Nah, I'm in the barracks, man. I quit bleeding. I'm going to bed."

"Dwayne, Dwayne . . ." I called to him. No answer.

Finally I heard a faint answer. "I'll call you in the morning."

"Promise?" I asked him. "You've got to call me in the morning."

"I will," he told me.

"Dwayne, I know what this is. There's no quick fix. It's PTSD. You've had a significant loss. It's not your fault. Call me tomorrow. We'll get some help."

It took me a long time to fall asleep after that call. My adrenaline was racing. I had another appointment in the morning with Operation Mend, but Dwayne was on my mind, and as soon as I finished at UCLA I was ready to head for the airport to go home, but I still hadn't heard from Dwayne. Finally, I called him.

"You promised to call," I told him.

"What?" he answered.

"You told me you'd call. Last night. After you cut yourself."

"What are you talking about?" he snapped.

I replayed the events of the night before. He didn't remember a thing. I asked him, "Were you drunk?"

"No, man. I swear. I don't remember anything. I don't remember calling you."

"Dwayne. You scared me to death. It must have been a blackout. You've got PTSD, man. Tell your doctor. You've got to have help."

He gave me a half-hearted response, and I had no assurance that he would in fact go for help. "I've had blackouts, Dwayne. I know what it's like. Trust me. Get some help."

◉ ◉ ◉

As I caught my flight back to San Antonio, I remembered one of the blackouts I'd experienced. It was after my first deployment, and we were still living in Schweinfurt. I was playing video games late one night when Kat came in the door. She snapped at me, "Can't you put down that video game and say hi?"

I followed her to bed, took a sleeping pill, and went to sleep.

The next morning, I woke up and Kat was sitting next to me on the bed. She had all of her suitcases packed on our bedroom floor. "Hi, baby. What are you doing?"

"Don't baby me," she cried.

"What are you talking about?" I asked.

"Please, that's enough."

"Kat, I don't know why you're so upset. I took a sleeping pill last night and went to bed."

"No, you did not. You were up all night, ranting and raving, throwing stuff all over the place. You told me things you should never say out loud about what happened to you in Iraq."

233

"Kat, I swear, I have no idea what you're talking about."

"Look," she whispered. "Look around this room."

It looked like a tornado had struck. I had thrown everything around the room, ripped down pictures, dumped out boxes and clothes all over the floor. I could not believe what I had done.

"Shilo, you could have killed us, and you would not remember a thing. I will not live with this kind of chaos."

I flushed the sleeping pills down the toilet and poured what liquor we had in the house down the sink. If I was going to have another blackout, there was not going to be any fuel to add to the fire.

As I reflected on my own blackout, I thought about Dwayne again, and what it was going to take to get him to be honest and open up to the right professionals so he'd get the help he needed. I remembered how hard it was for me to tell the truth. I had Kathreyn, mirror of my moods, but my friend felt he was all alone. If the war had taught me one thing, it was the value of the warrior community. We had to stick together. No more casualties of war.

When I got back to San Antonio, my determination to keep serving was renewed. I realized that the conversation had to change, that I needed to communicate a different truth. I needed to spread the news that the wounded warrior community is not a place . . . it is a framework, a network of friends, family, services, and resources. My job as a soldier was far from over. The battlefield had just been altered and I was going to continue to fight on behalf of friends like Dwayne, who were struggling every day just to make it through the night. The calls, emails, texts, and visits kept coming.

"Shilo, can you talk to our Rotary Club?"

"Shilo, would you visit our high school?"

"Shilo, can you help us dedicate a new home to a wounded warrior?"

"Shilo, would you visit my sister? My son? My uncle?"

Yes, I told them. Yes. Yes. I would say yes to cries for help from friends like Dwayne and many others. As often as I could, I said yes to sharing my journey of healing and hope and restoration.

40

A LOVE STORY

If I told you at the onset that my story would be a love story, you'd probably toss the book against the wall and look for something else to read. Our world is pretty jaded when it comes to love. But you can't separate the explosion that tore our lives apart from the love that bound it back together. I'm talking about my wife, Kathreyn. From the day I joined the military, we came under the supervision and authority of the military. We did what we were told to do. Worked when they told us to work. Moved when they told us to move. Went to school when and where they told us to go to school. Kathreyn supported me 100 percent in joining the military and supported me 100 percent in giving what the military required of all of us. She had no idea that when I enlisted, she was in for a future that neither of us could have imagined or wanted.

Trauma and divorce probably should come from the same root word. Trauma taxes everything you know to be true about your relationship with your spouse. The divorce rate for military couples is much higher than that for the civilian population. For wounded warriors, some estimates rank the divorce rate even higher. That's not unbelievable to me. On any given day, a military family deals with PTSD, TBI, physical injuries, combat fatigue, compassion fatigue, caregiving, family support, deployment, redeployment, financial hardships, pregnancy, loss, suicide, substance abuse, grief, and adultery. It's no wonder that the divorce rate is high. When you spend

235

more time apart than together and stir in some combat, some injury, and some trauma, it's no wonder some military families can't keep it together. War exacts a price.

My life is not more important than Kathreyn's life. But you could not convince her of that. She has been sacrificial and selfless in her devotion to me. She has never looked at me like I was a wounded mess. She looks at me with eyes of acceptance and respect. I have seen pain in her eyes when I have hurt her or we have hurt each other. I have watched her eyes fill with tears too many times. We have logged a lot of miles on the apology turnpike, but we have learned to forgive.

◆ ◆ ◆

Not long ago I arrived home from a speaking engagement, completely unaware that I owed anyone an apology. I'd been on the road speaking at quite a few different events when Kathreyn confronted me with a long list of areas in which I'd let her down, let the kids down, let my friends and extended family down. I was more than irritated to learn that my schedule was not serving the needs of my own family. I'd gotten to the point where I couldn't see the forest for the trees.

I argued, "Kathreyn, this is how I'm supporting our family . . . this is how I'm supporting the warrior community. What's wrong?"

"You have a family that needs your support, and it's not always about other people," she said.

"What is it?" I implored. "What do you need?"

"I need you home," she told me.

I watched as her shoulders shook with sobs, and her eyes were fixed on mine, walls up all around. "You need me home more?" I asked.

I got an emphatic, resounding, and unequivocal, "YES."

Kathreyn's hopes and dreams were getting lost in the shuffle of my hopes and dreams for recovery. Kathreyn had left her job with the Army's Wounded Warrior program in order to focus more on home and family. She'd also been working on completing her master's degree, which was truly important to her. The bulk of her day involved taking care of our preschooler, mentoring and tutoring Lizzie in school and horsemanship, and responding to all the friends and family who are a part of our lives. Not to mention the fact that we now had quite a homestead to manage.

It's a lot easier to keep up with a small mobile home than to maintain the big house, yard, stable, and acreage that were now ours.

From her point of view, I was always saying hello or goodbye, meeting her coming and going with a suitcase in my hand. The front door was a revolving one, and I never quite unpacked. I was always on my way to my next destination. She told me flat out, "This is not working."

I realized that as much as I wanted to speak and work as an advocate for wounded veterans, none of that would ever matter if I could not make my own family work as it should. All the travel was taking a toll on my marriage and family, and I couldn't stand the idea that I was, once again, causing my family pain.

We talked about the opportunity I'd been offered during EBV to start a franchise with WIN Home Inspections. I had been on the fence about what to do. If I went through with the application, it would mean less time for my speaking commitments, but it would mean more time at home, working in our surrounding community. For Kathreyn, it was a no-brainer. After all the heated discussion, we decided to follow through with our application and were awarded a partnership in a new home inspection business. This would allow me to work from home with both Kat and my son Josh without the long days and nights on the road.

Kathreyn agreed with me about my desire to continue to speak on behalf of wounded warriors. We compromised: I'd continue to speak on a selective basis, and those decisions would always be mutual. Kathreyn wanted her voice to be heard, and I needed to listen.

We were invited to join a group of veterans included in President Obama's inaugural festivities, and Kathreyn and I were excited about taking a couples' trip to Washington, DC. We'd be with other veteran friends and spouses, which is always uplifting and encouraging to us. As we participated in various inaugural events, we were both really overwhelmed with the outpouring of support for the warrior community. I shared my decision to limit my speaking engagements with the people around me. There were few dissenting votes; everyone agreed with our choice. If my girl said she needed a husband, then that's where I needed to be, right by her side.

If Kathreyn and I had focused on what we'd done wrong in our recovery, we'd have lost our way. Instead, we've tried to stay focused on the prize, the idea that over time the crown of victory will be ours. We've learned that yesterday's gone; we have today. And we can behave a little better today than we did the day before. Kathreyn believes in what I am capable of doing right. Right now. Sometimes that's a lot of pressure. I'd like to just stew in my own juices and be wrong. But she's not going to let me do that for long, and I don't blame her.

We've had some fierce conversations. We've thrown some shoes against the wall, some barbs at each other, done some cussing and stomping and acting out our frustrations. And we've learned that we're not alone. I remember reading in the book of Deuteronomy: *I have wounded, and I will heal* (32:39).

I try not to forget that. If I hurt the one I love, I have to offer sorrow and regret for the pain I've caused. Because someone suffered for me. God is going to hold me accountable for my actions. I want Kathreyn to trust me not to hurt her. My girl's been through enough.

I wrote her a letter, and I have wrestled with how to present it to her. Throughout our last seven years of injury and recovery, I have stored up quite a few things that I want her to know. I want others to know what I know about her . . . she is the love of my life.

Dear Kathreyn,

I don't remember much of my past before you came into my life. I remember it not being as bright every day. Before you, I see only chaos. From the moment you caught me stealing your beer and trying to work my Don Juan on you, your smile has forever been on my mind.

You have brought so much joy into my life. We have been blessed in so many ways. I know that God is with us and has always had a plan for us.

I wanted to know God more, like you did, and I remember you saying, "If you want to date me, you're going to have to go to church with me to meet my family." I was not too familiar with church and ultimately declined. But you wouldn't take no for an answer. You came looking for me. Maybe you knew I needed you. You called me a diamond in the rough and talked me into going to church with you.

I think it was a setup. I swear your pastor, Brother John, knew I was coming. Your family probably warned him I'd be coming so he'd have a fire extinguisher on hand in case I combusted. The morning I sat next to you I felt like he was talking directly to me. I knew that was exactly where I belonged: right next to you at the First Baptist Church of Coleman, Texas. We've come a long way since then. Today I belong in the same spot—right next to you. There's a quote I read once, "Walk in front of me, I may not follow. Walk behind me, I may not lead. Walk beside me, and be my friend." That's what you've done as my wife. You've stayed by my side.

We set out on many adventures, hand in hand. Sometimes I had to pull a little extra to get you moving, but you were there with me, and chose me over so many others. I warned you it would be a rough road with me. I even gave you the opportunity to change your mind before the wedding, but you accepted me, eyes wide open.

During my military career, you excelled as a military spouse, ultimately representing me and our family in ways that I could not. You volunteered, participated in Army events, and encouraged other spouses to be involved in the community. Your leadership on the home front truly made me proud.

I cannot even begin to imagine how hard it must have been for you to hear the news of my injury. I have heard the story a thousand times and it still gives me a knot in my stomach. Again, you stood up and set the standard as a military spouse.

We have kind of joked around about how we planned for the worst case, such as planning my funeral, but this was something different. We had to learn how to live again, love again. You have sacrificed so much of yourself for me and our family to ensure we all got what we needed. I cannot begin to thank you for all you have done.

I want you to know that I don't think I could have done it without you. I love you so much. This road we have traveled has been long and hard. It has left us in awe at times, and at other times questioning our love, our marriage, and our sanity. But we are still here, together!

Thank you for taking this journey with me. I see many more adventures in our future, and all I can say now is, "Buckle up!"

Your Shilo

41

COURAGE

In my dreams I have a Cavalry saber, and I am cutting my Purple Heart into pieces. I stare at the simple icon that was first awarded as the Badge of Military Merit. I think of its history, going all the way back to 1782 when General George Washington wanted to honor troops who were killed or wounded in action as the result of an act of the enemy.

When I received my medal, I learned the story behind the story; how the badge was forgotten after the Revolutionary War, and how two hundred years after Washington's birth, General Douglas MacArthur revived the award for service members whose meritorious service in combat resulted in severe wounding, death, or death after being wounded. He said it was supposed to inspire the living. It does that for me. There are strict rules about how the medal is awarded, and while politics make it sound complicated at times, it's really pretty simple: Were you wounded and needing medical treatment while fighting a war? Were your injuries a direct result of enemy action? There are some specifics, but these are the basic requirements.

I turn the Purple Heart over in my hands, thinking of the men who died next to me on February 19, 2007, making the ultimate sacrifice for each one of us. I saw firsthand their courage and their bravery. It breaks me to think of them for long. I look at my medal and I want to divide it into pieces, to give a portion to each person who loved me through the battle. I'd give it to the medevac crew, and then the medical staff at Landstuhl, the burn unit at BAMC, the surgical teams that rebuilt my face, my skin, my fingers, my spine. I'd share it with the chaplains and counselors who prayed with us and guided us. I'd want my dad to have a piece of it, for on some level he seemed to know that I would have to have extraordinary strength to fight the battles in my life. I'd want my mom to share it with me for the nights she lost sleep, worrying about my safety, for the tears she wept as I was injured and recovered. I'd want my kids to wear it proudly, for they've borne my injuries as surely as I have. I'd want my sister to share it too. Any service member who wears the Purple Heart over his own heart knows what it really represents: the sacrifices of a family for the veteran it honors.

And I'm not sure they've invented the right medal for the service member's spouse. Kathreyn's sacrificial love was her gift to me. I've often called her my rock. I would have crumbled without her. She never faltered or wavered in her devotion to me, in her belief in my recovery. They'd have to forge her medal out of the hardest steel that can be made.

The thing about tempered steel is that it becomes strong in the cooling process, not in the heat. It is when the temperature is reduced, withdrawn, that the steel begins to harden and temper. And that describes my wife. Once the heat had done its damage, the process of tempering began, and it has been her strength that has led me to recovery. It was her faith that I clung to when I did not have enough of my own. Kathreyn always said I was a diamond in the rough. But neither of us had an inkling of what rough really meant.

I am reading a passage from Luke, and I come across a parable that I see with new eyes and a new heart. I have knocked on a lot of doors at midnight. When I was a young man and times were tough, I was knocking on the wrong doors at midnight. I thought I could meet my own needs. Soldiering put me on the battlefield at midnight time and time again. I have fought under a blanket of stars over Persia and questioned how I would make it through the night. I have seen dark in the middle of the day during a firefight. I have come through black and painful and lonely passages, and I have found what we each must find: a friend at midnight.

I thought I could figure it out. I tried hard to acquire the skill set I needed to do what had to be done. But something happens to us when we need something we do not have. We become beggars or thieves. In the humility of our need, we find a friend at midnight; and when we find that friend, we yearn to know him. In our hunger and thirst, we find the friend who is God, and he reveals his character to us. He does not turn us away.

My story is not so much about the power of God, though I have certainly learned how powerful he is. And it is not so much about what he can do, though I have learned firsthand that he is able to meet every need. My story is about what he will do. I found on earth a father of power; I found in faith a Father of infinite love.

Sometimes the theology of our world would say that God must have permitted the IED blast to bring me to my knees; to bring me to him; that he uses the bad to bring about what he requires of us. When we see him face-to-face, I think we will understand why and how God allows the good, the bad, and the ugly in our lives. He says we live in a fallen world. Combat allowed me to see how fallen a world can be. My journey before, during, and after the explosion has taught me that there are parts of God's character I cannot live without: his mercy and his grace.

The Gospel of Luke says,

> Suppose you have a friend, and you go to him at midnight and say, "Friend, lend me three loaves of bread; a friend of mine on a journey has come to me, and I have no food to offer him." And suppose the one inside answers, "Don't bother me. The door is already locked, and my children and I are in bed. I can't get up and give you anything." I tell you even though he will not get up and give the bread because of friendship, yet because of your shameless audacity, he will surely get up and give you as much as you need.
>
> So I say to you: Ask and it will be given to you; seek and you will find; knock and the door will be opened to you. For everyone who asks receives; the one who seeks finds; and to the one who knocks, the door will be opened.
>
> Which of you fathers, if your son asks for a fish, will give him a snake instead? Or if he asks for an egg, will give him a scorpion? If you then, though you are evil, know how to give good gifts to your children, how much more will your Father in heaven give the Holy Spirit to those who ask him! (11:5–13)

I asked my Father for bread; I asked him again and again for bread. I begged him for bread. He gave me no stone. He gave me no snake. He gave me no scorpion. He gave me bread. He overloaded our baskets and our bushels with his manna, and he does it still today. He gives because it is his nature to meet us at our point of need. It is his character to love us beyond and despite our asking.

I ask God every day to make my life the reason he answered that door; I ask God every day to be my friend at midnight. He answers, 24/7. I ask him. I seek him. I knock. He answers. He always does. He does it for me, and he will do it for you.

NEVER FORGOTTEN

After the flags are folded,
the living fall
into each other's arms.
They've left spaces
trees can't completely fill.

> Yusef Komunyakaa,
> "Missing in Action"

Adare W. Cleveland of Anchorage, Alaska, age 20
Born January 14, 1987, Ontario, Oregon; died February 19, 2007, Al-Farat, Iraq

Adare, from Anchorage, Alaska, attended West High School and was active in Boy Scouts, judo, choir, and band. Always quick to help a friend, Adare loved country music and ranching. Adare joined the Army in July 2005, and attended basic training and advanced individual training (AIT) at Fort Knox, Kentucky. He selected his occupational specialty in the Army's Cavalry, as his great-grandfather and favorite uncle were cavalrymen.

Adare was a gunner and dismount with Team Hellcat on Task Force Vigilant with the 2nd Brigade Combat Team, 10th Mountain Division. Interviewed in Iraq for the 10th Mountain Division Public Affairs Office, Adare told the reporter, "I love my job. I love the little children in Iraq." Adare is survived by his mom, Dianne Cleveland, his father, William Simonds Jr., his stepmother, Esther Wehr, and his sister, Maylyn Cleveland. Adare was laid to rest at Fort Richardson National Cemetery in Alaska.

Shawn Michael Dunkin of Columbia, South Carolina, age 25
Born February 27, 1981, Petersburg, Virginia; died February 19, 2007, Al-Farat, Iraq

Shawn lived in Virginia throughout most of his life. He became a hero for the first time when he was twelve years old. He and his cousin rescued five girls from drowning on a Michigan river and received medals for their bravery. Shawn loved to fish, camp, hunt, and snowboard. He loved sleight of hand tricks, and he practiced his magic on us.

Shawn was my roommate. We were best friends. He completed basic training and AIT at Fort Knox, Kentucky, and planned to make the military his career. He served in Iraq in 2003 and was awarded the Bronze Star, Purple Heart, and the Army Commendation Medal during his first rotation to the Middle East. He is survived by his wife, Ashley, his father, Mike Dunkin and wife Janice, his mother, Darlene Kelly and husband Donovan, his brother, David, his sisters, Erin and Tracie, and his grandmother, Arley Dunkin.

When Shawn was buried in Chattanooga, Tennessee, the parochial school across the street from where his service was held, Our Lady of Perpetual Help, sent their students out to the schoolyard, and the children began to sing the national anthem. Church bells rang out in the city. The Patriot Guard Riders honored his service, along with many friends, family members, and strangers. Shawn had that kind of effect on people.

Shawn loved the military and his family. His mother described him: "He was just a hero." Everyone who knew him understood that Shawn had a higher calling. A scholarship fund was established in his memory.

Matthew C. Bowe of Coraopolis, Pennsylvania, age 19
Born June 17, 1987, Coraopolis, Pennsylvania; died February 19, 2007, Al-Farat, Iraq

Agile and athletic, Matt was a wide receiver for his high school football team. He enlisted in the Army right after graduation from Moon High School, Moon Township, Pennsylvania, in 2005. He attended basic training at Fort Benning, Georgia, and AIT at Fort Sam Houston, Texas. He was a trauma specialist and wanted to be a doctor. Both of Matt's grandfathers were military veterans. He was deployed as an Army medic and was awarded the Purple Heart and the Bronze Star for Valor for his heroism in saving the life of SGT Thomas Hewitt in an IED blast in September 2006. Hewitt lived for a week after the blast, long enough for his family to see him at Landstuhl before he passed away.

A big Steelers fan, Matt loved to sing and write songs as well. He loved to hunt and fish. At nineteen years of age, Matt had already earned a Purple Heart, Bronze Star, Army Good Conduct Medal, National Defense Service Medal, Iraq Campaign Medal, Global War on Terrorism Service Medal, Army Service Ribbon, Overseas Service Ribbon, and the Combat Medical Badge. His high school football stadium has been renamed in his memory, and the jersey he wore so proudly, #8, has been retired from the roster at Moon High School. At 1-89 Cavalry/10th Mountain Division headquarters in Fort Drum, NY, Matt's fellow soldiers renamed their medical bay the Private Matthew C. Bowe Memorial Aid Station. On February 19, 2011, SFC Zul-Tan Jackson and his fellow medics placed a white carnation on the aid station door to recognize what Matt continues to mean to the soldiers of 1-89 Cavalry.

Matt is survived by his parents, John and Lori Bowe, as well as his sisters, Amanda, Megan, and Tiffany, his brother, John Jr., and his grandfather. Matt's mother remains committed to honoring Matt's life through her advocacy for his music as well as the rights of young people who are recruited to enlist in the military.

BUILDING BRIDGES
TO OPEN HEARTS

RECOMMENDED ORGANIZATIONS
AND MINISTRIES

A bridge interrupted the road my convoy traveled on February 19, 2007. On that bridge, a buried detonator led to the charge beneath our vehicle and the subsequent explosion and loss of human life. Unlike the enemy, the American soldier and patriot does not destroy bridges; he or she builds them. In the life Kathreyn and I have been given, our goal is to match warrior veterans and their families with the resources they need for recovery. Through compassionate assistance, hearts will be opened and hearts will be healed.

This is by no means an exhaustive list of resources; it represents the kindness, generosity, and ingenuity of our nation. Help is out there. We are living proof.

Center for the Intrepid, San Antonio, Texas. I spent hundreds of hours at the CFI. Their mission is to provide rehabilitation for service members with amputations, burns, or functional limb loss. The center sponsors education and research across the full spectrum of recovery. It's a high-tech environment, with many labs and therapies to enable every veteran to rehabilitate. Funded by donations from over six hundred thousand private citizens, it is now an integral part of SAMMC, with the Army funding its day-to-day operations. It is a state-of-the art, state-of-the-heart facility. I would not have reached my level of recovery without the CFI. For warriors stationed in other parts of the country, the Military Amputee Training Center in Washington, DC, and the military-medical center at San Diego Medical Center in California offer similar operations, for example.

Brooke Army Medical Center (BAMC)/San Antonio Military Medical Center (SAMMC) at Fort Sam Houston, Texas. BAMC is a University of Texas Health Science Center as well as a teaching hospital and home to the Army Burn Center. It opened in 1879 as a small post dispensary and was named for Army Brigadier General Roger Brooke, who assumed command in 1929. It received an overwhelming number of casualties from the WWII battlefields and has continued to grow since that period. It is a Level I trauma center, and for many months, BAMC was my home. The Burn Center at BAMC is part of the San Antonio Military Medical Center (SAMMC) consolidated tower at Joint Base San Antonio, Fort Sam Houston, which offers medical care through both BAMC and Wilfred Hall Hospital. The burn center at BAMC has been the only Department of Defense burn center for more than fifty years, and is also the regional burn center for south-central Texas. Hundreds of civilian ER patients are served at the burn center every year.

Through teleburn consultation, the center's trauma surgeons can provide consultation to emergency medical technicians anywhere in the world, twenty-four hours a day. The center recently completed a huge expansion of its physical/occupational therapy section to serve inpatients at the ISR. Since 2003, the staff of over three hundred at the center has served over 1,000 military and 2,500 civilian casualties.

The burn center maintains an ongoing relationship with the Armed Forces Institute for Regenerative Medicine, awarding research and development dollars to projects such as Recell, a technique under scrutiny to determine the ability to apply "spray-on skin." Dr. Stephen Wolf, mentioned in chapter 29, continues to pioneer regenerative stem cell research and collaborates with ISR. PEO Soldier works dynamically with the burn center to research, develop, and test protective clothing for soldiers based on injury patterns.

Using advanced telecommunications and technology, surgeons in the ISR can transmit live videos through cameras installed in surgical lighting to monitors in operating rooms, nurses' stations, conference rooms, and educational settings. Using 360-degree design features, each of the forty beds in the burn center's intensive care unit can be rotated to optimize care and quality of life. By sharing resources between BAMC and Wilford Hall, SAMMC is a mega-medical command. The San Antonio area has become home to many wounded warriors due to the expertise and advanced technology found in the SAMMC community.

Fisher House Foundation, Inc., www.fisherhouse.org. By 2011, seventeen thousand families had received the hospitality of the Fisher House, with average stays of ten days apiece. This has been estimated to have provided twenty-five million dollars in savings to military families in lodging costs, meals, and transportation. They offer several programs including scholarships for military children, Hero Miles (a portal to donate frequent flyer miles to injured service members and their families), and Newman's Own, a grant program for military charities. If you want to make a donation of time, talent, or treasure, this is one organization that absolutely makes every dollar stretch to serve the needs of the military. Service members and their families positively derive benefit from your generosity. For individuals who are doing estate planning, I highly recommend this recipient, as there will never be a day when this organization falters in delivering essential services to military families. Contact 111 Rockville Pike, Ste. 420, Rockville, MD 20850, or visit their website.

Wounded Warrior Project, woundedwarriorproject.org. This organization is set up to honor and empower wounded warriors through athletic, employment, and rehabilitation programs. They have a wide assortment of programs, services, and events for injured soldiers of all branches of the service. The WWP offers wounded warriors a platform for outreach, and my story would not be the same without their direct influence on my recovery. You can find out more about how to help through their website, or call 877.TEAM.WWP.

VA Veteran's Administration National Suicide Hotline, 1-800-273-TALK (8255). The hotline is staffed by the VA with mental health professionals ready and able to assist.

Warrior's Weekend, warriorsweekend.org. This foundation grew from the abundant heart and generosity of Ron Kocian, whose desire to honor wounded warriors and their families has resulted in a huge annual fishing event. From the time warriors arrive at Houston's International Airport until they travel through Victoria, Texas, to Port O'Connor, veterans are welcomed with flags and heartfelt appreciation. The entire community contributes to a perfect weekend of fishing, food, and fellowship. This event changes hundreds of lives every year. It changed ours.

Military Child Education Coalition (MCEC), militarychild.org, offers information and assistance to help military families ensure that every military child affected by mobility issues, family separation, and difficult transitions is still going to receive a quality education.

Entrepreneurship Boot Camp for Veterans with Disabilities, www.ebvfoundation.org. This program began under the Small Business Administration and Syracuse University and is offered in consortium through several universities around the country, including Texas A&M University. It's designed to help wounded warriors establish a new or revised career path for themselves, and it did that for me. Donations can be made to the TAMU Foundation, Mays EBV Program, 401 George Bush Dr., College Station, TX 77840; or through their website. Point of contact is Dr. Dick Lester.

Trevor Romain—Comfort Crew for Military Kids, trevorromain.com. This is a kid-centered approach to helping military families through videos, audiotapes, programs, and presentations. The Comfort Crew visits schools with Comfort Kits to facilitate communication for military children and their families. They also offer a "Taking Care of You! Support Kit for Kids of Injured Heroes." It contains a DVD, journal with prompts, calendar, map, activities, an achievement patch, and a comfort mouse named Coco. I talked at length about how important it is for our children to express themselves about their parents' injuries and their family's recovery.

Purple Heart Hunts, Wayne Woods, Alaska Master Guide #108, www.woods-outfitting.com. Fishing expeditions as well as bear and big game hunts are conducted near Cordova, Alaska, in memory of Shane Woods,

Wayne and Mae's son, to help all wounded veterans enjoy hunting and fishing in the great outdoors.

Patriots and Heroes Outdoors (formerly Hunts for Heroes), www.patriots andheroesoutdoors.com, connects wounded warriors and avid hunters, fishermen, and outdoorsmen to promote healing through recreation. Army veteran Billy Hodges founded Hunts for Heroes, which has morphed into Patriots and Heroes Outdoors. Hundreds of sporting enthusiasts support this organization to offer wounded warriors a short respite from treatment and recovery. They sponsor an annual program, MSGT Gonzales Memorial Fishing Event, to offer fishing activities to wounded veterans and their families. Contact PO Drawer 1663, El Campo, TX 77437, or visit their website.

Show of Support Military Hunt, Inc., showofsupport.org. This organization provides outdoor activities for injured service members and their families. Started by Terry Johnson in 2004, the group seeks to honor military service by saying "Thanks" like we do in Texas—deer hunting, camaraderie, and hometown celebrations are the hallmark of an SOS Military Hunt. You can contact them at PO Box 11225, Midland, TX 79702, or visit their website.

When Kathreyn and I went to Midland, we were met by some wonderful flag-waving patriots who welcomed us to the community, then invited us to an outstanding cookout and a fairly relaxing evening. The following day, a ceremony was held with surprise goodies, and I'm not allowed to reveal what actually happens at that event. The next day, warriors went hunting while their partners did "girl stuff" all day. The guys camped out, spent time unwinding with each other, and so forth. There's no such thing as an empty hunt; everyone goes home with a trophy buck. SOS pays for processing and mounting, and my trophy is on my living room wall.

Give an Hour, www.giveanhour.org, is an organization devoted to listening. This is a national network of volunteers capable of responding to acute and chronic difficulties experienced by military members. Mental health professionals who work separate and apart from military channels offer many therapeutic services. You can donate your time to listen to a wounded warrior, relating to the problems he or she is facing, or offer assistance as a volunteer in many other ways. Your job is not to offer solutions, but to offer compassionate relief.

VetFran, www.vetfran.com. The International Franchising Association sponsors a strategic initiative that offers member companies financial incentives, mentoring, and training for veterans who want to own their own business. Started in 1991 by the Dwyer Group, this organization has helped more than 2,100 veterans become franchisees. It was my honor to address this group of patriots on more than one occasion. I became a recipient of a home inspection franchise and am indebted to this organization for the opportunity I've been given to run a successful business.

Tempered Steel: The Story Behind the Scars, www.temperedsteelinc.org. This organization is near and dear to my heart, as it is designed to support wounded veterans through raising public awareness. Started by SGT (Ret) Scott Stephenson and his mother, Luana Schneider, after he was seriously wounded in Iraq in 2006, it was established to educate the public. Their goal is to have at least one soldier in each state who was severely wounded in combat service speak to schools, community groups, and assemblies with the "stories behind the scars." At their website you can learn more about their mission and goals through photography, videography, and storytelling.

USO, www.uso.org. I remember all the times in my life when I heard the initials USO, but it wasn't until we were in the military that I learned what a service organization this really is. With 160 locations in 27 states and 14 countries, USO volunteers make America's troops and our families feel better! It was a volunteer at a USO counter who got Kathreyn to the hospital in Landstuhl before it was too late. If you want a place to volunteer or give donations that result in tangible gains, then support the USO.

Operation Mend, http://operationmend.ucla.edu. This organization assists wounded warriors with follow-up plastic or reconstructive surgery to assist us in returning to the look that represents our "new normal."

Operation Comfort, www.operationcomfort.org. This group makes a direct impact on the lives of wounded warriors and their families as well. They began by remodeling waiting rooms at BAMC and grew from there to raising money for sports equipment like hand cycles, road bikes, recumbents, and tandems. Janis Roznowski, an American Airlines flight attendant who transported soldiers to and from the Middle East, was the spark behind Operation Comfort. They offer financial assistance as well as many rehabilitative therapeutic programs during recovery at BAMC.

Russ Murphy Ministries, www.russmurphyministries.com. Russ is a gifted guitarist and songwriter who travels extensively, sharing the love of Christ through his musical talent. He and his wife, Saralyn, became a part of my life after I was injured. Russ has had ten songs on the Inspirational Country Music charts over the last six years; his prolific songwriting and message of hope and inspiration have blessed thousands of us. His schedule is available at his website.

Coalition to Salute America's Heroes, saluteheroes.org, is a nonprofit organization that provides emergency aid and other support services to our troops who have been severely wounded in Iraq or Afghanistan. An outstanding resource for all patriots who want a role in serving our military through rebuilding lives and restoring hope.

Operation Homefront, www.operationhomefront.net. This group provides emergency financial and other assistance to wounded veterans, to the tune of over $92 million by 2011. Financial assistance is paid directly to mortgage lenders, auto mechanics, contractors, hospitals, doctors, dentists, and so forth. Needs are met within 24 to 72 hours. Their primary clients are in pay grades E-1 through E-6 enlisted ranks, and this organization has earned the highest marks you can get from Charity Navigator, with over 94 cents of every dollar going to people and programs, not personnel.

Racing for Our Heroes, www.rfoh.org. This group supports our recovery through participation in motor racing. Hero Days offer a private opportunity to ride in an actual race car, with full access to the world of professional motor sports. Racing for Our Heroes offers a unique opportunity for wounded veterans and their families.

Veteran Outdoors, http://veteran-outdoors.com. The motto "Giving Back to Those Who Gave" is evident in every expedition planned by Veteran

Outdoors, who provide quality hunting, fishing, and outdoor activities. Their goal is to raise public awareness about the therapeutic value of outdoor activities.

Accessible Racing, www.accessibleracing.com. This organization offers wounded veterans and their families an opportunity to experience the national automotive racing scene by sponsoring targeted events around the country. You can find out more information about these events at their website.

American Legion. At www.legion.org you can learn about many programs, but specifically about "Heroes to Hometowns," which is a transition program for severely injured service members. They sponsor welcome-home celebrations, temporary financial or housing assistance, home and vehicle adaptation, and family support. Every local American Legion Post can give veterans and their families more information about these worthwhile programs.

Disabled American Veterans (DAV), www.dav.org. This is the group that's going to offer you a lot of help with service-connected disabilities. They have eighty-eight offices worldwide to assist with the process of filing and claiming disability benefits, free of charge. There are also programs for vocational rehab and employment. If your military records are incorrect, this group will help you, as well as conducting business regarding other official panels. Disabled veterans are misnamed. A triple amputee can ride a bike, run a corporation, build a house, and volunteer. A burn survivor can swim, swing, hunt, and fish. We're not disabled; we're enabled in new ways. The DAV helps us rethink our vocabulary and respond to service-connected abilities in inspiring ways.

Veterans of Foreign Wars (VFW), www.vfw.org. The VFW has been around since the Spanish-American War to lead the charge to maintain veteran's rights. Without the VFW, there'd be no VA, GI Bill, national cemetery system, or compensation for Agent Orange or Gulf War Syndrome. Sponsors of the Vietnam War, Korean War, World War II, Women in Military Service, and Disabled Veterans for Life memorials, the VFW has 2.1 million members that contribute 11 million volunteer hours a year. The VFW is not a bar or a supper club; it's a service organization that has made a huge difference in our lives as veterans.

Operation Giveback (OGB), operation-giveback.org. This organization facilitates events and opportunities to raise funds and awareness for wounded and disabled veterans. Through its partnerships, OGB assists with homes, jobs, and essential rehabilitative medical care.

Veterans Leadership Forum (VLF) is a Halliburton affinity group comprised of Halliburton employees with the primary objectives of leadership development and increased retention of veterans in the Halliburton organization. Originally started by and for veterans in September 2013, VLF membership is open to all Halliburton employees. Halliburton values leadership, teamwork, and commitment instilled through military service, and believes those traits can translate into successful careers in civilian life. VLF offerings include mentoring opportunities, leadership and professional development training, and quarterly social and service events. Halliburton's launch of the Veterans Leadership Forum to support veterans at the company and to attract servicemen and women to its organization is a remarkable example of how the corporate world can support veterans in the workforce.

Apps to Assist Wounded Warriors. iPhone or Android apps available (as of late 2013).

> **Tactical Breather**—monitors heart rate, emotions, concentration, and provides feedback for behavioral therapy.
>
> **Breathe 2 Relax**—monitors fight/flee response to help stabilize moods and manage stress.
>
> **T-2 Mood Tracker**—tracks emotional experiences over time and provides a tool to share this information with health care providers.
>
> **Life Armor Mobile Application**—DOD mobile app for wounded veteran resources.
>
> **Mild TBI Mobile Application**—pocket guide for treatment options for mild TBI.
>
> **PTSD Coach**—downloadable, interactive ebooks pertaining to PTSD and disabilities.
>
> **PE Coach**—mobile app supports tasks associated with PTSD.

Mobility Assistance for Vets

Segs4Vets.org—Segway assists victims of IED blasts by providing this mode of transportation.

4 Paws for Veterans—4pawsforability.org helps with placing service dogs with select disabled veterans who are experiencing mobility problems. This organization spends 80 percent of its funds on the programs and services it delivers.

Operation Independence—vans4vets.com makes wheelchair-accessible van ownership a reality for veterans. Veteran mobility benefits are available through the VA.

Patriot Paws—patriotpaws.org is a Texas-based service organization involved with training and placing mobility assistance service dogs. Texas Department of Criminal Justice inmates are the primary dog trainers of these dogs placed with disabled veterans.

Giving Assistance

The decision to assist our veterans is absolutely essential. However, giving is a process deserving of study; **charitynavigator.org** is a national service that celebrates and evaluates charities of all types. Accountability and transparency are vital markers in your stewardship decisions.

A FINAL NOTE

The word "hero" gets lobbed about quite frequently in our culture, so much so that I think it has lost a bit of its luster. If I told you that a man was going to walk into the room with a Purple Heart, a long series of medals for valor and soldiering, and a story so devastating and real that you would never view the war in Iraq or Afghanistan the same again, would you not sit up a bit straighter, perhaps even stand when he entered? This is the way I felt when my brother described Shilo. "Wait till you meet him, Rob," Stacy told me. "He's not like anyone you've met before."

My brothers and I know something about soldiers. In Arlington National Cemetery, at Marker 66-3041, you will find the silent stone of our parents and patriots, Lauren and Virginia Overby, buried one above the other, together still. Beneath the spreading oaks we could sit together and tell you the stories our father told us, of young men and women who gave their lives for our freedom. So when Stacy said, "Rob, Dad would have loved him," I had a hint of greatness. I expected someone larger than life. But in walked a man of gentle demeanor, with softly worn blue jeans, roper boots, a fine silver belt buckle, and a great smile. In walked a man with a story to share, a story that began a long time ago, of what it takes to make a man, break a man, and make him once again. It has been my honor to be a part of *Steel Will*.

Robin Overby Cox

RECOMMENDED READING

Books

Anderson, Bryan with David Mack. *No Turning Back*. New York: Berkley, 2011. The story of an Iraq war veteran who lost three limbs in combat.

Bellavia, David with John Bruning. *House to House: An Epic Memoir of War*. New York: Pocket Star, 2008.

Blehm, Eric. *Fearless: The Undaunted Courage and Ultimate Sacrifice of Navy SEAL Team SIX Operator Adam Brown*. Colorado Springs, CO: Waterbrook Press, 2013. The inspirational story of SEAL Team SIX member Adam Brown.

Borch, Fred L. *For Military Merit: Recipients of the Purple Heart*. Annapolis, MD: Naval Institute Press, 2010.

Carroll, Ed Andrew. *Operation Homecoming*. New York: Random House, 2006. A collection of soldiers' and families' stories and eyewitness accounts, journals, and letters from Iraq, Afghanistan, and the home front.

Jadick, Richard with Thomas Hayden. *On Call in Hell: A Doctor's Iraq War Story*. New York: NAL Caliber, 2008.

Kennedy, Kelly. *They Fought For Each Other*. New York: St. Martin's Griffin, 2010.

Martinez, J.R. with Alexandra Rockey Fleming. *Full of Heart*. New York: Hyperion, 2012. The story of J.R. Martinez's injury and entry into television's *Dancing with the Stars*.

Williams, Mary Beth and Soili Poijula. *The PTSD Workbook: Simple, Effective Techniques for Overcoming Traumatic Stress Symptoms*. Oakland, CA: New Harbinger, 2002.

Woodruff, Lee and Bob Woodruff. *In An Instant*. New York: Random House, 2007. ABC news anchor Bob Woodruff was injured in an IED explosion in 2006.

Bible Verses to Give You Comfort

> Praise be to God,
>> who has not rejected my prayer
>> or withheld his love from me!
>>> Psalm 66:20

Now faith is confidence in what we hope for and assurance about what we do not see.

Hebrews 11:1

> The Lord is my helper; I will not be afraid.
>> What can mere mortals do to me?
>>> Hebrews 13:6

Consider it pure joy, my brothers and sisters, whenever you face trials of many kinds, because you know that the testing of your faith produces perseverance. Let perseverance finish its work so that you may be mature and complete, not lacking anything.

James 1:2–4

> Hear my prayer, LORD;
>> let my cry for help come to you.
> Do not hide your face from me
>> when I am in distress.
> Turn your ear to me;
>> when I call, answer me quickly.
> For my days vanish like smoke;
>> my bones burn like glowing embers.
> My heart is blighted and withered like grass;
>> I forget to eat my food. . . .
> But you remain the same,
>> and your years will never end.
> The children of your servants will live in your presence;
>> their descendants will be established before you.
>>> Psalm 102:1–4, 27–28

BIBLIOGRAPHY

"Army Sgt. William S. Kinzer Jr." *Honor the Fallen*. January 1, 2012. http://projects.militarytimes.com/valor/army-sgt-william-s-kinzer-jr/622464.

Bails, Jennifer. "Regenerative Medicine: A Growing Future." *Carnegie Museums*. November 2, 2011. carnegiemuseums.org/cmag/feature.php?id=183.

Bentley, Theresa (Shilo's mom). Series of personal letters. December 30, 2011.

Bowe, Lori (Matt's mom). Telephone interview. December 14, 2012.

Bowling, Brian. "Pitt Stem Cell Procedure Gives Hope for Regrowing Limbs." *Pittsburgh Live*. November 2, 2011.

"Bruce Nitsche." *Wounded Warrior Project*. woundedwarriorproject.org. July 29, 2013.

"Center for the Intrepid." US Army Medical Command. bamc.amedd.army.mil. July 1, 2012.

Christenson, Sig. "Iraq War Spurred Advancements in Military Medicine." *San Antonio Express-News*. March 24, 2013. http://www.mysanantonio.com/news/military/article/Iraq-war-spurred-advancements-in-military-medicine-4381062.php.

"Culture of Iraq." *Countries and Their Cultures*. October 10, 2011. http://www.everyculture.com/Ge-It/Iraq.html.

"Dan Nevins | Bush Center." George W. Bush Presidential Center, 2013. bushcenter.org. July 29, 2013.

Devine, Adam. Telephone interviews. December 14, 2012; January 15, 2014.

Dunaway, SSG Bryan. Telephone interview. December 14, 2012.

Fitzroy, Maggie. "A Wounded Warrior." *The Florida Times Union.* February 14, 2008. http://jacksonville.com/tu-online/stories/021408/met_246691005.shtml.

Gutierrez, Natalie. "Soldiers of Fortitude." *Mission Magazine.* UT Health Science Center, March 2009. http://uthscsa.edu/mission/article.asp?id=549.

Harris, Allen (Shilo's dad). Telephone interview. October 12, 2012.

Hayes, Martha J. *Compassion Fatigue in the Military Caregiver.* Carlisle Barracks, PA: US Army War College. February 3, 2009. http://www.google.com/url?sa=t&rct=j&q=&esrc=s&frm=1&source=web&cd=1&ved=0CCsQFjAA&url=http%3A%2F%2Fhandle.dtic.mil%2F100.2%2FADA498593&ei=Ya7WUuK4IqGGyAGej4GQDw&usg=AFQjCNFWbSnHNH2B2fFUie4M4Ui0MmSL5Q&sig2=A0v6JwPt5KdDtr9cqX_ruQ&bvm=bv.59378465,d.aWc.

"IED Attack: What It Is." Department of Homeland Security. July 6, 2011. https://www.dhs.gov/ied-attack.

"Iraq War Clinician Guide, 2nd Edition." *National Center for PTSD.* US Department of Veterans Affairs. December 20, 2011. http://www.ptsd.va.gov/professional/materials/manuals/iraq-war-clinician-guide.asp.

McCann, Chris. "2nd BCT Soldiers Keep Peace in Al-Furat." *The Mountaineer Online.* Fort Drum IMCOM, November 30, 2006. http://www.drum.army.mil/mountaineer/Article.aspx?ID=3355.

Murphy, Russ. "Russ Murphy Ministries." 2013. russmurphyministries.com. July 29, 2013.

Myers, Christi. "Using 'Pixie Dust' to Help Soldiers Heal." *KTRK-TV.* June 22, 2009. http://abclocal.go.com/ktrk/story?section=news/health&id=6216619.

Oakes, David. "Linwood Exec Helps Wounded Vets Heal." *DeSoto Explorer.* Linwood, KS. December 23, 2008.

"The Purple Heart." *National Purple Heart Hall of Fame.* October 25, 2011. www.amervets.com/phmedl.htm.

Renz, COL Evan. Telephone interview with Shilo Harris. June 20, 2012.

Russell, Steve. *We Got Him: A Memoir of the Hunt and Capture of Saddam Hussein.* New York: Pocket, 2011.

Tan, Michelle. "Wounded Staff Sgt. Finally Getting New Ears." *Army Times.* November 18, 2010. http://www.armytimes.com/article/20101118/NEWS/11180329/Wounded-staff-sgt-finally-getting-new-ears.

Tyrell, Kate (social worker). Personal interview, BAMC. June 20, 2012.

US Army Institute of Surgical Research. US Army Medical Command. usaisr.amedd.army.mil. October 25, 2011.

"What is PTSD?" *Post Traumatic Stress Disorder*. Nebraska Department of Veteran's Affairs. 2007. http://www.ptsd.ne.gov/what-is-ptsd.html.

"Who We Are." *Critical Care Air Transport Team*. January–February 2012. http://www.ccatt.info/index.php/ccatt/ccatt-who-we-are.

Wolf, Dr. Steven. Email interview. UT Southwestern. March 20, 2012.

Woods, Wayne. Email interview. May 3, 2012.

———. "Shane's Purple Heart Hunts." Woods Outfitting. 2011. http://www.woods-outfitting.com/PHH.html.

"Zachary Fisher—Builder, Philanthropist, Patriot." Fisher House Foundation. October 25, 2011. www.fisherhouse.org/about/our-history.

Shilo Harris (SSG, USA, RET) is owner and operator of WIN Home Inspection Services in Floresville, Texas, and speaks to companies and affinity groups across the nation in support of veterans. Shilo is married to Kathreyn Phillips Harris and has five children and one grandchild.

Robin Overby Cox is a career educator and librarian. A graduate of Florida State University and the University of South Florida, she calls College Station, Texas, home. She has five children and six grandchildren.

WITHDRAWN

21.99   9/15/14.

LONGWOOD PUBLIC LIBRARY
800 Middle Country Road
Middle Island, NY 11953
(631) 924-6400
longwoodlibrary.org

LIBRARY HOURS

Monday-Friday	9:30 a.m. - 9:00 p.m.
Saturday	9:30 a.m. - 5:00 p.m.
Sunday (Sept-June)	1:00 p.m. - 5:00 p.m.